Morality, Harm, and the Law

MORALITY, HARM, and the LAW

edited by
GERALD DWORKIN
UNIVERSITY OF ILLINOIS AT CHICAGO

Westview Press
BOULDER • SAN FRANCISCO • OXFORD

Copyright © 1994 by Westview Press, Inc.

Published in 1994 in the United States of America by Westview Press, Inc., 5500 Central Avenue, Boulder, Colorado 80301-2877, and in the United Kingdom by Westview Press, 36 Lonsdale Road, Summertown, Oxford OX2 7EW

Library of Congress Cataloging-in-Publication Data
Dworkin, Gerald.
Morality, harm, and the law / Gerald Dworkin.
    p.   cm.
  ISBN 0-8133-8710-8. — ISBN 0-8133-8711-6 (pbk.)
  1. Law—Philosophy.   2. Law and ethics.   I. Title.
K235.D96   1994
340'.1—dc20   93-38471
                                                                                                              CIP

Printed and bound in the United States of America

The paper used in this publication meets the requirements
of the American National Standard for Permanence of Paper
for Printed Library Materials Z39.48-1984.

10   9   8   7   6   5   4   3   2   1

For Lisa and Julie

Contents

Credits

1 Introduction

In the state of Vermont it is illegal to refuse to aid someone who is in serious danger, if the cost to the rescuer is relatively minor.

In the state of Georgia it is illegal for two men to engage in homosexual sex.

In the state of New Jersey one woman cannot contractually obligate herself to bear a child for another couple.

It is legal in the United States to burn or deface the American flag.

It is legal in the United States to insult people by using racial epithets. However, recently some states have passed statutes providing greater punishment for racially motivated assaults than for other assaults.

Thus speaks the law on certain controversial moral issues. But knowing what the law says does not answer the question of whether the state has a *right* to enforce a standard of morality. The readings in this book are addressed to this issue.

One or another claim about the legitimacy or illegitimacy of the enforcement of morality has attracted much attention in the philosophy of law and political philosophy ever since the publication in 1859 of John Stuart Mill's classical defense of liberalism, *On Liberty*. One finds such statements in the philosophical literature as the following:

> The only purpose for which power can be rightfully exercised over any member of a civilized society against his will is to prevent harm to others.[1]

> It is not the duty of the law to concern itself with immorality as such. It should confine itself to those activities which offend against public order and decency or expose the ordinary citizen to what is offensive or injurious.[2]

> The harm principle is a principle of toleration. The common way of stating its point is to regard it as excluding consideration of private morality from politics. It restrains both individuals and the state from coercing people . . . on the ground that those activities are morally either repugnant or desirable.[3]

> Is the fact that certain conduct is by common standards immoral sufficient to justify making that conduct punishable by law? Is it morally permissible to enforce morality as such? Ought immorality as such be a crime? . . . To this question John Stuart Mill gave an emphatic answer in his essay *On Liberty* one hundred years ago.[4]

Much ink, and perhaps even some blood, has been spilled in debates concerning the views expressed in these propositions. But a clear formulation of the intuitive idea underlying these claims is not easy. As usually stated, either the claims fail to express any precise thesis, or the thesis expressed is so clearly false that it could not plausibly be defended.

To understand in an intuitive way what the controversy is about it is useful to set out specific laws that are favored or opposed by the contending parties. Consider the following legal restrictions that are very likely to be favored by all parties to the debate (category A):

Laws against murder

Laws against theft

Laws against income tax evasion

Laws against public sex

Laws against sexual abuse of children

Laws against perjury

The following are legal restrictions likely to be opposed by all parties to the debate (category B):

Laws forbidding members of racial minorities from living in geographical proximity to racial majorities

Laws regulating the type of music that people can listen to in their homes

Laws restricting the type of religion one may profess

Perhaps the most crucial category is of laws that are often favored by those wishing to enforce morality and rejected by their opponents. Examples include (category C):

Laws against the private consumption of pornography

Laws against consensual homosexual acts between adults

Laws forbidding defacement of the flag

Laws against bigamy

Laws forbidding the sale of bodily organs such as kidneys

Laws forbidding the use of racial or sexual epithets

Over some laws, even within each camp there will be variations of opinion as to their legitimacy. These laws will include various paternalistic laws (laws against suicide), laws where it is not clear if there is harm (laws forbidding brother-sister incest), laws that require forms of positive aid to others (good samaritan laws), and so forth. Even within the category of laws favored by all, or the category of laws that is supposed to define the dispute (category C), there may be variations of opinion produced by something other than the question of the legitimacy of state power. For example, even someone who favors the enforcement of morality may think, like Devlin, that the costs of enforcing, say, laws about the consumption of pornography in the home may make it unwise to have such laws. The difference then could be expressed in terms of why one favors or opposes a given law. Is the objection to a particular law that it is merely unwise or that it violates some principled restriction on the powers of the state? The latter point is the one at issue, and I shall begin by supposing that those who oppose the enforcement of morality are prepared to produce a plausible principle that would justify passing the laws in category A and that would forbid passing the laws in category C.

However, it is not obvious how they will do this. Consider how opponents of the enforcement of morality might try to distinguish between the laws they defend and those they consider illegitimate. Suppose the thesis is stated as follows: The law ought not to enforce moral values. Then, since they believe that the law ought to prohibit murder and theft, they must claim that in doing so the law is not enforcing moral values. But if, say, murder is not forbidden because, at least in part, it is regarded as wrong or unjust or wicked, then what justifies its being made illegal?

One response is to assert that *another* reason can be used to justify such laws; one that does not rely on a moral judgment about the conduct in question. The most prominent candidate for such a reason is that the conduct is harmful to the interests of others. Murder and theft are legitimately made illegal because they are harmful, not because they are wrong.

If, however, one examines the concept of *harm* it is obvious that this notion is itself, directly or indirectly, linked to a judgment about the wrongness of the conduct in question. The most thoughtful and developed notion of harm, that of Joel Feinberg, explicitly distinguishes between a "non-normative sense of 'harm' as set-back to interest, and a normative sense of 'harm' as a *wrong,* that is a violation of a person's rights."[5] (italics orig.) It is only the latter sense of harm that figures in the harm principle as developed and clarified by Feinberg.

It is fairly clear that there is no way to avoid this interjection of normative content into the analysis of harm. For if the idea is that harm is merely a setback to interest, and if interest is purely a descriptive notion, such as that which a person has, or takes, an interest in, then those who propose to prohibit, say, the private consumption of pornography may, correctly, claim that they have an interest in not living in a society that allows such consumption and, hence, that such behavior harms them. For that matter, as Mill pointed out, do not the rejected applicants for a job have an interest that is damaged? The argument against criminalization in these cases must take the form of arguing that the mere setback to interests, or harm in its nonnormative sense, is not something that individuals ought to be protected against.

That individuals do not deserve such protection is a moral judgment, and when we decide the other way—to protect certain interests against invasion—that is equally a moral decision.

There is another line of argument in support of the same conclusion.

Consider laws against theft. Are such laws justified by reference to a nonnormative sense of harm or are values built in here as well?

The concept of theft presupposes a definition of property. Protecting against theft assumes certain views about exclusive rights to ownership. In the absence, for example, of copyright and patent laws one cannot be accused of stealing someone's ideas. Recently, in the *Winans* decision the courts had to decide when a reporter's information could be considered to belong to the newspaper and hence be misappropriated. These definitions and conceptions of ownership are conventions of the society and differ from one society to another. Although they are conventional they are not arbitrary and are defended or opposed in terms of moral and political (as well as economic) arguments. Consider, for example, recent legal discussion about whether living organisms may be patented. Laws against theft, therefore, presuppose prior moral determinations and are another way in which moral values are enforced.

So the nonenforcement thesis cannot be formulated in terms of a simple distinction between laws designed to prevent harm and those used to enforce moral values. Some other way of making the distinction must be found. At the very least one would want to distinguish between the moral judgments involved in making assertions about harm and other moral judgments.

One way to clarify the thesis is to distinguish between that part of morality having to do with rights and that having to do with ideals. This is the tack that Joel Feinberg takes in his book, *Harmless Wrongdoing*. For Feinberg the law should be limited to the protection of *particular* values, namely personal autonomy and respect for persons.

> The harm principle mediated by the *Volenti* maxim protects personal autonomy and the moral value of "respect for persons" that is associated with it. ... But there are other moral principles, other normative judgments, other ideals, other values—some well-founded, some not—that the harm principle does not enforce, since its aim is only to protect personal autonomy and protect human rights, not to vindicate correct evaluative judgments of any and all kinds.[6]

This, in essence, is Feinberg's solution to the definitional problem. Of course the law enforces morality: The interesting question is what parts of morality it ought to enforce. Now we have a substantive claim that needs to be argued. Feinberg's solution is that the law should protect only rights. This contention, however, requires some justification. Why should we protect rights and not ideals? Why should we protect personal and not group autonomy? Why shouldn't a community be able to use the law to defend its moral ideals?

The readings in this book are designed to help us to think about these important questions. They are divided into two parts. Part 1 includes various theoretical reflections, both for and against the legitimacy of the legal enforcement of morality. Mill and Fitzjames Stephen represent the classical division on this issue and I have tried to bring the discussion up to date by including the most recent philosophical contributions to the debate.

Part 2 represents a body of statutory and case materials that illustrate in a concrete fashion the kinds of issues that are at stake and how courts have reasoned about them. In addition, I have included theoretical material that is directly relevant to the cases and controversies. The order in which the readings are presented reflects my philosophical prejudice for going from the general to the particular. You may want to proceed in the opposite direction.

Notes

1. J. S. Mill, *On Liberty* (London: n.p., 1859), Chapter I.

2. Report of the Committee on Homosexual Offenses and Prostitution (CMD 247), 1957 (Wolfenden Report) (New York: Stein and Day, 1963), para. 257.

3. J. Raz, "Autonomy, Toleration, and the Harm Principle," in R. Gavison, *Issues in Contemporary Legal Philosophy* (Oxford: Clarendon Press, 1987), p. 327.

4. H.L.A. Hart, *Law, Liberty and Morality* (Stanford, Calif.: Stanford University Press, 1963), p. 4.

5. J. Feinberg, *Harm to Self* (New York: Oxford University Press, 1986), p. x.

6. J. Feinberg, *Harmless Wrongdoing* (New York: Oxford University Press, 1988), p. 12.

Part One

Principles

2 Classical Theories

JOHN STUART MILL
On Liberty

The object of this Essay is to assert one very simple principle, as entitled to govern absolutely the dealings of society with the individual in the way of compulsion and control, whether the means used be physical force in the form of legal penalties, or the moral coercion of public opinion. That principle is, that the sole end for which mankind are warranted, individually or collectively, in interfering with the liberty of action of any of their number, is self-protection. That the only purpose for which power can be rightfully exercised over any member of a civilized community, against his will, is to prevent harm to others. His own good, either physical or moral, is not a sufficient warrant. He cannot rightfully be compelled to do or forbear because it will be better for him to do so, because it will make him happier, because, in the opinions of others, to do so would be wise, or even right. There are good reasons for remonstrating with him, or reasoning with him, or persuading him, or entreating him, but not for compelling him, or visiting him with any evil, in case he do otherwise. To justify that, the conduct from which it is desired to deter him must be calculated to produce evil to some one else. The only part of the conduct of any one, for which he is amenable to society, is that which concerns others. In the part which merely concerns himself, his independence is, of right, absolute. Over himself, over his own body and mind, the individual is sovereign.

It is, perhaps, hardly necessary to say that this doctrine is meant to apply only to human beings in the maturity of their faculties. We are not speaking of children, or of young persons below the age which the law may fix as that of manhood or womanhood. Those who are still in a state to require being taken care of by others, must be protected against their own actions as well as against external injury. For the same reason, we may leave out of consideration those backward states of society in which the race itself may be considered as in its nonage. The early difficulties in the way of spontaneous progress are so great, that there is seldom any choice of means for overcoming them; and a ruler full of the spirit of improvement is warranted in the use of any expedients that will attain an end, perhaps otherwise unattainable. Despotism is a legitimate mode of government in dealing with barbarians, provided the end be their improvement, and the means justified by actually effecting that end. Liberty, as a principle, has no application to any state of things anterior to the time when mankind have become capable of being improved by free and equal discussion. Until then, there is nothing for them but implicit obedience to an Akbar or a Charlemagne, if they are so fortunate as to find one. But as soon as mankind have attained the capacity of being guided to their own improvement by conviction or persuasion (a period long since reached in all nations with whom we need here concern ourselves), compulsion, either in the direct form or in that of pains and penalties for non-compliance, is no longer admissible as a means to their own good, and justifiable only for the security of others.

It is proper to state that I forego any advantage which could be derived to my argument from the idea of abstract right, as a thing independent of utility. I regard utility as the ultimate appeal on all ethical questions; but it must be utility in the largest sense, grounded on the permanent interests of man as a progressive being. Those interests, I contend, authorize the subjection of individual spontaneity to external control, only in respect to those actions of each, which concern the interest of other people. If any one does an act hurtful to others, there is a *primâ facie* case for punishing him, by law, or, where legal penalties are not safely applicable, by general disapprobation. There are also many positive acts for the benefit of others, which he may rightfully be compelled to perform; such as, to give evidence in a court of justice; to bear his fair share in the common defence, or in any other joint work necessary to the interest of the society of which he enjoys the protection; and to perform certain acts of individual beneficence, such as saving a fellow creature's life, or interposing to protect the defenceless against illusage, things which whenever it is obviously a man's duty to do, he may rightfully be made responsible to society for not doing. A person may cause evil to others not only by his actions but by his inaction, and in either case he is justly accountable to them for the injury. The latter case, it is true, requires a much more cautious exercise of compulsion than the former. To make any one answerable for doing evil to others, is the rule; to make him answerable for not preventing evil, is, comparatively speaking, the exception. Yet there are many cases clear enough and grave enough to justify that exception. In all things which regard the external relations of the individual, he is *de jure* amenable to those whose interests are concerned, and if need be, to society as their protector. There are often good reasons for not holding him to the responsibility; but these reasons must arise from the special expediencies of the case: either because it is a kind of case in which he is on the whole likely to act better, when left to his own discretion, than when controlled in any way in which society have it in their power to control him; or because the attempt to exercise control would produce other evils, greater than those which it would prevent. When such reasons as these preclude the enforcement of responsibility, the conscience of the agent himself should step into the vacant judgment-seat, and protect those interests of others which have no external protection; judging himself all the more rigidly, because the case does not admit of his being made accountable to the judgment of his fellow-creatures.

But there is a sphere of action in which society, as distinguished from the individual, has, if any, only an indirect interest; comprehending all that portion of a person's life and conduct which affects only himself, or, if it also affects others, only with their free, voluntary, and undeceived consent and participation. When I say only himself, I mean directly, and in the first instance: for whatever affects himself, may affect others *through* himself; and the objection which may be grounded on this contingency, will receive consideration in the sequel. This, then, is the appropriate region of human liberty. It comprises, first, the inward domain of consciousness; demanding liberty of conscience, in the most comprehensive sense; liberty of thought and feeling; absolute freedom of opinion and sentiment on all subjects, practical or speculative, scientific, moral, or theological. The liberty of expressing and publishing opinions may seem to fall under a different principle, since it belongs to that part of the conduct of an individual which concerns other people; but, being almost of as much importance as the liberty of thought itself, and resting in great part on the same reasons, is practically inseparable from it. Secondly, the principle requires liberty of tastes and pursuits; of framing the plan of our life to suit our own character; of doing as we like, subject to such consequence as may follow; without impediment from our fellow-creatures, so long as what we do does not harm them, even though they should think our conduct foolish, perverse, or wrong. Thirdly, from this liberty of each individual, follows the liberty, within the same limits, of combination among individuals; freedom to unite, for any purpose not involving harm to others: the persons combining being supposed to be of full age, and not forced or deceived.

No society in which these liberties are not, on the whole, respected, is free, whatever may be its form of government; and none is completely free in which they do not exist absolute and unqualified. The only freedom which deserves the name, is that of pursuing our own good in our own way, so long as we do not attempt to deprive others of theirs, or impede their efforts to obtain it. Each is the proper guardian of his own health, whether bodily, or mental and spiritual. Mankind are greater gainers by suffering each other to live as seems good to themselves, than by compelling each to live as seems good to the rest. . . .

Of the Limits to the Authority
of Society over the Individual

What, then, is the rightful limit to the sovereignty of the individual over himself? Where does the authority of society begin? How much of human life should be assigned to individuality, and how much to society?

Each will receive its proper share, if each has that which more particularly concerns it. To individuality should belong the part of life in which it is chiefly the individual that is interested; to society, the part which chiefly interests society.

Though society is not founded on a contract, and though no good purpose is answered by inventing a contract in order to deduce social obligations from it, every one who receives the protection of society owes a return for the benefit, and the fact of living in society renders it indispensable that each should be bound to observe a certain line of conduct towards the rest. This conduct consists, first, in not injuring the interests of one another; or rather certain interests, which, either by express legal provision or by tacit understanding, ought to be considered as rights; and secondly, in each person's bearing his share (to be fixed on some equitable principle) of the labors and sacrifices incurred for defending the society or its members from injury and molestation. These conditions society is justified in enforcing, at all costs to those who endeavor to withhold fulfillment. Nor is this all that society may do. The acts of an individual may be hurtful to others, or wanting in due consideration for their welfare, without going the length of violating any of their constituted rights. The offender may then be justly punished by opinion, though not by law. As soon as any part of a person's conduct affects prejudicially the interests of others, society has jurisdiction over it, and the question whether the general welfare will or will not be promoted by interfering with it, becomes open to discussion. But there is no room for entertaining any such questions when a person's conduct affects the interests of no person besides himself, or needs not affect them unless they like (all the persons concerned being of full age, and the ordinary amount of understanding). In all such cases there should be perfect freedom, legal and social, to do the action and stand the consequences.

It would be a great misunderstanding of this doctrine, to suppose that it is one of selfish indifference, which pretends that human beings have no business with each other's conduct in life, and that they should not concern themselves about the well-doing or well-being of one another, unless their own interest is involved. Instead of any diminution, there is need of a great increase of disinterested exertion to promote the good of others. But disinterested benevolence can find other instruments to persuade people to their good, than whips and scourges, either of the literal or the metaphorical sort. I am the last person to undervalue the self-regarding virtues; they are only second in importance, if even second, to the social. It is equally the business of education to cultivate both. But even education works by conviction and persuasion as well as by compulsion, and it is by the former only that, when the period of education is past, the self-regarding virtues should be inculcated. Human beings owe to each other help to distinguish the better from the worse, and encouragement to choose the former and avoid the latter. They should be forever stimulating each other to increased exercise of their higher faculties, and increased direction of their feelings and aims towards wise instead of foolish, elevating instead of degrading, objects and contemplations. But neither one person, nor any number of persons, is warranted in saying to another human creature of ripe years, that he shall not do with his life for his own benefit what he chooses to do with it. He is the person most interested in his own well-being: the interest which any other person, except in cases of strong personal attachment, can have in it, is trifling, compared with that which he himself has; the interest which society has in him individually (except as to his conduct to others) is fractional, and altogether indirect: while, with respect to his own feelings and circumstances, the most ordinary man or woman has means of knowledge immeasurably surpassing those that can be possessed by anyone else. The interference of society to overrule his judgment and purposes in what only regards himself, must be grounded on general presumptions; which may be altogether wrong, and even if right, are as likely as not to be misapplied to individual cases, by persons no better acquainted with the circumstances of such cases than those are who look at them merely from without. In this department, therefore, of human affairs, Individuality has its proper field of action. In the conduct of human beings towards one another, it is necessary that general rules should for the most part be observed, in order that people may know what they have to expect; but in each person's own concerns, his individual spontaneity is entitled to free exercise. Considerations to aid his judgment, exhortations to strengthen his will, may be offered to him, even obtruded on him, by others; but he, himself, is the final judge. All errors which he is likely to commit against advice and warning, are far outweighed by the evil of allowing others to constrain him to what they deem his good.

I do not mean that the feelings with which a person is regarded by others, ought not to be in any way affected by his self-regarding qualities or deficiencies. This is neither possible nor desirable. If he is eminent in any of the qualities which conduce to his own good, he is, so far, a proper object of admiration. He is so much the nearer to the ideal perfection of human nature. If he is grossly deficient in those qualities, a sentiment the opposite of admiration will follow. There is a degree of folly, and a degree of what may be called (though the phrase is not unobjectionable) lowness or depravation of taste, which, though it cannot justify doing harm to the person who manifests it, renders him necessarily and properly a subject of distaste, or, in extreme cases, even of contempt: a person would not have the opposite qualities in due strength without entertaining these feelings. Though doing no wrong to anyone, a person may so act as to compel us to judge him, and feel to him, as a fool, or as a being of an inferior order: and since this judgment and feeling are a fact which he would prefer to avoid, it is doing him a service to warn him of it beforehand, as of any other disagreeable consequence to which he exposes himself. It would be well, indeed, if this good office were much more freely rendered than the common notions of politeness at present permit, and if one person could honestly point out to another that he thinks him in fault, without being considered unmannerly or presuming. We have a right, also, in various ways, to act upon our unfavorable opinion of any one, not to the oppression of his individuality, but in the exercise of ours. We are not bound, for example, to seek his society; we have a right to avoid it (though not to parade the avoidance), for we have a right to choose the society most acceptable to us. We have a right, and it may be our duty to caution others against him, if we think his example or conversation likely to have a pernicious effect on those with whom he associates. We may give others a preference over him in optional good offices, except those which tend to his improvement. In these various modes a person may suffer very severe penalties at the hands of others, for faults which directly concern only himself; but he suffers these penalties only in so far as they are the natural, and, as it were, the spontaneous consequences of the faults themselves, not because they are purposely inflicted on him for the sake of punishment. A person who shows rashness, obstinacy, self-conceit—who cannot live within moderate means—who cannot restrain himself from hurtful indulgences—who pursues animal pleasures at the expense of those of feelings and intellect—must expect to be lowered in the opinion of others, and to have a less share of their favorable sentiments, but of this he has no right to complain, unless he has merited their favor by special excellence in his social relations, and has thus established a title to their good offices, which is not affected by his demerits towards himself.

What I contend for is, that the inconveniences which are strictly inseparable from the unfavorable judgment of others, are the only ones to which a person should ever be subjected for that portion of his conduct and character which concerns his own good, but which does not affect the interests of others in their relations with him. Acts injurious to others require a totally different treatment. Encroachment on their rights; infliction on them of any loss or damage not justified by his own rights; falsehood or duplicity in dealing with them; unfair or ungenerous use of advantages over them; even selfish abstinence from defending them against injury—these are fit objects of moral reprobation, and, in grave cases, of moral retribution and punishment. And not only these acts, but the dispositions which lead to them, are properly immoral, and fit subjects of disapprobation which may rise to abhorrence. Cruelty of disposition; malice and ill-nature; that most anti-social and odious of all passions, envy; dissimulation and insincerity; irascibility on insufficient cause, and resentment disproportioned to the provocation; the love of domineering over others; the desire to engross more than one's share of advantages (the πλεονεξία of the Greeks); the pride which derives gratification from the abasement of others; the egotism which thinks self and its concerns more important than everything else, and decides all doubtful questions in his own favor—these are moral vices, and constitute a bad and odious moral character: unlike the self-regarding faults previously mentioned, which are not properly immoralities, and to whatever pitch they may be carried, do not constitute wickedness. They may be proofs of any amount of folly, or want of personal dignity and self-respect; but they are only a subject or moral reprobation when they involve a breach of duty to others, for whose sake the individual is bound to have care for himself. What are called duties to ourselves are not socially obligatory, unless circumstances render them at the same time duties to others. The term duty to oneself, when it means anything more than prudence, means self-respect or self-development; and for none of these is any one accountable to his fellow-creatures, because for none of them is it for the good of mankind that he be held accountable to them.

The distinction between the loss of consideration which a person may rightly incur by defect of prudence or of personal dignity, and the reprobation which is due to him for an offence against the rights of others, is not a merely nominal distinction. It makes a vast difference both in our feelings and in our conduct towards him, whether he displeases us in things in which we think we have a right to control him, or in things in which we know that we have not. If he displeases us, we may express our distaste, and we may stand aloof from a person as well as from a thing that displeases us; but we shall not therefore feel called on to make his life uncomfortable. We shall reflect that he already bears, or will bear, the whole penalty of his error; if he spoils his life by mismanagement, we shall not, for that reason, desire to spoil it still further: instead of wishing to punish him, we shall rather endeavor to alleviate his punishment, by showing him how he may avoid or cure the evils his conduct tends to bring upon him. He may be to us an object of pity, perhaps of dislike, but not of anger or resentment; we shall not treat him like an enemy of society: the worst we shall think ourselves justified in doing is leaving him to himself, if we do not interfere benevolently by showing interest or concern for him. It is far otherwise if he has infringed the rules necessary for the protection of his fellow-creatures, individually or collectively. The evil consequences of his acts do not then fall on himself, but on others; and society, as the protector of all its members, must retaliate on him; must inflict pain on him for the express purpose of punishment, and must take care that it be sufficiently severe. In the one case, he is an offender at our bar, and we are called on not only to sit in judgment on him, but, in one shape or another, to execute our own sentence: in the other case, it is not our part to inflict any suffering on him, except what may incidentally follow from our using the same liberty in the regulation of our own affairs, which we allow to him in his.

The distinction here pointed out between the part of a person's life which concerns only himself, and that which concerns others, many persons will refuse to admit. How (it may be asked) can any part of the conduct of a member of society be a matter of indifference to the other members? No person is an entirely isolated being; it is impossible for a person to do anything seriously or permanently hurtful to himself, without mischief reaching at least to his near connections, and often far beyond them. If he injures his property, he does harm to those who directly or indirectly derived support from it, and usually diminishes, by a greater or less amount, the general resources of the community. If he deteriorates his bodily or mental faculties, he not only brings evil upon all who depended on him for any portion of their happiness, but disqualifies himself for rendering the services which he owes to his fellow-creatures generally; perhaps becomes a burden on their affection or benevolence; and if such conduct were very frequent, hardly any offence that is committed would detract more from the general sum of good. Finally, if by his vices or follies a person does no direct harm to others, he is nevertheless (it may be said) injurious by his example; and ought to be compelled to control himself, for the sake of those whom the sight or knowledge of his conduct might corrupt or mislead.

And even (it will be added) if the consequences of misconduct could be confined to the vicious or thoughtless individual, ought society to abandon to their own guidance those who are manifestly unfit for it? If protection against themselves is confessedly due to children and persons under age, is not society equally bound to afford it to persons of mature years who are equally incapable of self-government? If gambling, or drunkenness, or incontinence, or idleness, or uncleanliness, are as injurious to happiness, and as great a hindrance to improvement, as many or most of the acts prohibited by law, why (it may be asked) should not law, so far as is consistent with practicability and social convenience, endeavor to repress these also? And as a supplement to the unavoidable imperfections of law, ought not opinion at least to organize a powerful police against these vices, and visit rigidly with social penalties those who are known to practise them? There is no question here (it may be said) about restricting individuality, or impeding the trial of new and original experiments in living. The only things it is sought to prevent are things which have been tried and condemned from the beginning of the world until now; things which experience has shown not to be useful or suitable to any person's individuality. There must be some length of time and amount of experience, after which a moral or prudential truth may be regarded as established: and it is merely desired to prevent generation after generation from falling over the same precipice which has been fatal to their predecessors.

I fully admit that the mischief which a person does to himself, may seriously affect, both through their sympathies and their interests, those nearly connected with him, and in a minor degree, society at large. When, by conduct of this sort, a person is led to violate a distinct and assignable obligation to any other person or persons, the case is taken out of the self-regarding class, and becomes amenable to moral disapprobation in the proper sense of the term. If, for example, a man, through intemperance or extravagance, becomes unable to pay his debts, or, having undertaken the moral responsibility of a family, becomes from the same cause incapable of supporting or educating them, he is deservedly reprobated, and might be justly punished; but it is for the breach of duty to his family or creditors, not for the extravagance. If the resources which ought to have been devoted to them, had been diverted from them for the most prudent investment, the moral culpability would have been the same. George Barnwell murdered his uncle to get money for his mistress, but if he had done it to set himself up in business, he would equally have been hanged. Again, in the frequent case of a man who causes grief to his family by addiction to bad habits, he deserves reproach for his unkindness or ingratitude; but so he may for cultivating habits not in themselves vicious, if they are painful to those with whom he passes his life, or who from personal ties are dependent on him for their comfort. Whoever fails in the consideration generally due to the interests and feelings of others, not being compelled by some more imperative duty, or justified by allowable self-preference, is a subject of moral disapprobation for that failure, but not for the cause of it, nor for the errors, merely personal to himself, which may have remotely led to it. In like manner, when a person disables himself, by conduct purely self-regarding, from the performance of some definite duty incumbent on him to the public, he is guilty of a social offence. No person ought to be punished simply for being drunk; but a soldier or a policeman should be punished for being drunk on duty. Whenever, in short, there is a definite damage, or a definite risk of damage, either to an individual or to the public, the case is taken out of the province of liberty, and placed in that of morality or law.

But with regard to the merely contingent, or, as it may be called, constructive injury which a person causes to society, by conduct which neither violates any specific duty to the public, nor occasions perceptible hurt to any assignable individual except himself; the inconvenience is one which society can afford to bear, for the sake of the greater good of human freedom. If grown persons are to be punished for not taking proper care of themselves, I would rather it were for their own sake, than under the pretence of preventing them from impairing their capacity of rendering to society benefits which society does not pretend it has a right to exact. But I cannot consent to argue the point as if society had no means of bringing its weaker members up to its ordinary standards of rational conduct, except waiting till they do something irrational, and then punishing them, legally or morally, for it. Society has had absolute power over them during all the early portion of their existence: it has had the whole period of childhood and nonage in which to try whether it could make them capable of rational conduct in life. The existing generation is master both of the training and the entire circumstances of the generation to come; it cannot indeed make them perfectly wise and good, because it is itself so lamentably deficient in goodness and wisdom; and its best efforts are not always, in individual cases, its most successful ones; but it is perfectly well able to make the rising generation, as a whole, as good as, and a little better than, itself. If society lets any considerable number of its members grow up mere children, incapable of being acted on by rational consideration of distant motives, society has itself to blame for the consequences. Armed not only with all the powers of education, but with the ascendancy which the authority of a received opinion always exercises over the minds who are least fitted to judge for themselves; and aided by the *natural* penalties which cannot be prevented from falling on those who incur the distaste or the contempt of those who know them; let not society pretend that it needs, besides all this, the power to issue commands and enforce obedience in the personal concerns of individuals, in which, on all principles of justice and policy, the decision ought to rest with those who are to abide the consequences. Nor is there anything which tends more to discredit and frustrate the better means of influencing conduct, than a resort to the worse. If there be among those whom it is attempted to coerce into prudence or temperance, any of the material of which vigorous and independent characters are made, they will infallibly rebel against the yoke. No such person will ever feel that others have a right to control him in his concerns, such as they have to prevent him from injuring them in theirs; and it easily comes to be considered a mark of spirit and courage to fly in the face of such usurped authority, and do with ostentation the exact opposite of what it enjoins; as in the fashion of grossness which succeeded, in the time of Charles II, to the fanatical moral intolerance of the Puritans. With respect to what is said of the necessity of protecting society from the bad examples set to others by the vicious or the self-indulgent; it is true that bad example may have a pernicious effect, especially the example of doing wrong to others with impunity to the wrongdoer. But we are now speaking of conduct which, while it does no wrong to others, is supposed to do great harm to the agent himself: and I do not see how those who believe this, can think otherwise than that the example, on the whole, must be more salutary than hurtful, since, if it displays the misconduct, it displays also the painful or degrading consequences which, if the conduct is justly censured, must be supposed to be in all or most cases attendant on it.

But the strongest of all the arguments against the interference of the public with purely personal conduct, is that when it does interfere, the odds are that it interferes wrongly, and in the wrong place. On questions of social morality, of duty to others, the opinion of the public, that is, of an overruling majority, though often wrong, is likely to be still oftener right; because on such questions they are only required to judge of their own interests; of the manner in which some mode of conduct, if allowed to be practised, would affect themselves. But the opinion of a similar majority, imposed as a law on the minority, on questions of self-regarding conduct, is quite as likely to be wrong as right; for in these cases public opinion means, at the best, some people's opinion of what is good or bad for other people; while very often it does not even mean that; the public, with the most perfect indifference, passing over the pleasure or convenience of those whose conduct they censure, and considering only their own preference. There are many who consider as an injury to themselves any conduct which they have a distaste for, and resent it as an outrage to their feelings; as a religious bigot, when charged with disregarding the religious feelings of others, has been known to retort that they disregard his feelings, by persisting in their abominable worship or creed. But there is no parity between the feeling of a person for his own opinion, and the feeling of another who is offended at his holding it; no more than between the desire of a thief to take a purse, and the desire of the right owner to keep it. And a person's taste is as much his own peculiar concern as his opinion or his purse. It is easy for any one to imagine an ideal public, which leaves the freedom and choice of individuals in all uncertain matters undisturbed, and only requires them to abstain from modes of conduct which universal experience has condemned. But where has there been seen a public which set any such limit to its censorship? or when does the public trouble itself about universal experience? In its interferences with personal conduct it is seldom thinking of anything but the enormity of acting or feeling differently from itself; and this standard of judgment, thinly disguised, is held up to mankind as the dictate of religion and philosophy, by nine tenths of all moralists and speculative writers. These teach that things are right because they are right; because we feel them to be so. They tell us to search in our minds and hearts for laws of conduct binding on ourselves and on all others. What can the poor public do but apply these instructions, and make their own personal feelings of good and evil, if they are tolerably unanimous in them, obligatory on all the world?

The evil here pointed out is not one which exists only in theory; and it may perhaps be expected that I should specify the instances in which the public of this age and country improperly invests its own preferences with the character of moral laws. I am not writing an essay on the aberrations of existing moral feeling. That is too weighty a subject to be discussed parenthetically, and by way of illustration. Yet examples are necessary, to show that the principle I maintain is of serious and practical moment, and that I am not endeavoring to erect a barrier against imaginary evils. And it is not difficult to show, by abundant instances, that to extend the bounds of what may be called moral police, until it encroaches on the most unquestionably legitimate liberty of the individual, is one of the most universal of all human propensities.

As a first instance, consider the antipathies which men cherish on no better grounds than that persons whose religious opinions are different from theirs, do not practise their religious observances, especially their religious abstinences. To cite a rather trivial example, nothing in the creed or practice of Christians does more to envenom the hatred of Mahomedans against them, than the fact of their eating pork. There are few acts which Christians and Europeans regard with more unaffected disgust, than Mussulmans regard this particular mode of satisfying hunger. It is, in the first place, an offence against their religion; but this circumstance by no means explains either the degree or the kind of their repugnance; for wine also is forbidden by their religion, and to partake of it is by all Mussulmans accounted wrong, but not disgusting. Their aversion to the flesh of the "unclean beast" is, on the contrary, of that peculiar character, resembling an instinctive antipathy, which the idea of uncleanness, when once it thoroughly sinks into the feelings, seems always to excite even in those whose personal habits are anything but scrupulously cleanly, and of which the sentiment of religious impurity, so intense in the Hindoos, is a remarkable example. Suppose now that in a people, of whom the majority were Mussulmans, that majority should insist upon not permitting pork to be eaten within the limits of the country. This would be nothing new in Mahomedan countries. Would it be a legitimate exercise of the moral authority of public opinion? and if not, why not? The practice is really revolting to such a public. They also sincerely think that it is forbidden and abhorred by the Deity. Neither could the prohibition be censured as religious persecution. It might be religious in its origin, but it would not be persecution for religion, since nobody's religion makes it a duty to eat pork. The only tenable ground of condemnation would be, that with the personal tastes and self-regarding concerns of individuals the public has no business to interfere.

To come somewhat nearer home: the majority of Spaniards consider it a gross impiety, offensive in the highest degree to the Supreme Being, to worship him in any other manner than the Roman Catholic; and no other public worship is lawful on Spanish soil. The people of all Southern Europe look upon a married clergy as not only irreligious, but unchaste, indecent, gross disgusting. What do Protestants think of these perfectly sincere feelings, and of the attempt to enforce them against non-Catholics? Yet, if mankind are justified in interfering with each other's liberty in things which do not concern the interests of others, on what principle is it possible consistently to exclude these cases? or who can blame people for desiring to suppress what they regard as a scandal in the sight of God and man? No stronger case can be shown for prohibiting anything which is regarded as a personal immorality, than is made out for suppressing these practices in the eyes of those who regard them as impieties; and unless we are willing to adopt the logic of persecutors, and to say that we may persecute others because we are right, and that they must not persecute us because they are wrong, we must be aware of admitting a principle of which we should resent as a gross injustice the application to ourselves.

The preceding instances may be objected to, although unreasonably, as drawn from contingencies impossible among us: opinion, in this country, not being likely to enforce abstinence from meats, or to interfere with people for worshipping, and for either marrying or not marrying, according to their creed or inclination. The next example, however, shall be taken from an interference with liberty which we have by no means passed all danger of. Wherever the puritans have been sufficiently powerful, as in New England, and in Great Britain at the time of the Commonwealth, they have endeavored, with considerable success, to put down all public, and nearly all private, amusements: especially music, dancing, public games, or other assemblages for purposes of diversion, and the theatre. There are still in this country large bodies of persons by whose notions of morality and religion these recreations are condemned; and those persons belonging chiefly to the middle class, who are the ascendant power in the present social and political condition of the kingdom, it is by no means impossible that persons of these sentiments may at some time or other command a majority in Parliament. How will the remaining portion of the community like to have the amusements that shall be permitted to them regulated by the religious and moral sentiments of the stricter Calvinists and Methodists? Would they not, with considerable peremptoriness, desire these intrusively pious members of society to mind their own business? This is precisely what should be said to every government and every public, who have the pretension that no person shall enjoy any pleasure which they think wrong. But if the principle of the pretension be admitted, no one can reasonably object to its being acted on in the sense of the majority, or other preponderating power in the country; and all persons must be ready to conform to the idea of a Christian commonwealth, as understood by the early settlers in New England, if a religious profession similar to theirs should ever succeed in regaining its lost ground, as religions supposed to be declining have so often been known to do.

To imagine another contingency, perhaps more likely to be realized than the one last mentioned. There is confessedly a strong tendency in the modern world towards a democratic constitution of society, accompanied or not by popular political institutions. It is affirmed that in the country where this tendency is most completely realized—where both society and the government are most democratic—the United States—the feeling of the majority, to whom any appearance of a more showy or costly style of living than they can hope to rival is disagreeable, operates as a tolerably effectual sumptuary law, and that in many parts of the Union it is really difficult for a person possessing a very large income, to find any mode of spending it, which will not incur popular disapprobation. Though such statements as these are doubtless much exaggerated as a representation of existing facts, the state of things they describe is not only a conceivable and possible, but a probable result of democratic feeling, combined with the notion that the public has a right to a veto on the manner in which individuals shall spend their incomes. We have only further to suppose a considerable diffusion of Socialist opinions, and it may become infamous in the eyes of the majority to possess more property than some very small amount, or any income not earned by manual labor. Opinions similar in principle to these, already prevail widely among the artisan class, and weigh oppressively on those who are amenable to the opinion chiefly of that class, namely, its own members. It is known that the bad workmen who form the majority of the operatives in many branches of industry, are decidedly of opinion that bad workmen ought to receive the same wages as good, and that no one ought to be allowed, through piecework or otherwise, to earn by superior skill or industry more than others can without it. And they employ a moral police, which occasionally becomes a physical one, to deter skilful workmen from receiving, and employers from giving, a larger remuneration for a more useful service. If the public have any jurisdiction over private concerns, I cannot see that these people are in fault, or that any individual's particular public can be blamed for asserting the same authority over his individual conduct, which the general public asserts over people in general.

But, without dwelling upon supposititious cases, there are, in our own day, gross usurpations upon the liberty of private life actually practised, and still greater ones threatened with some expectation of success, and opinions proposed which assert an unlimited right in the public not only to prohibit by law everything which it thinks wrong, but in order to get at what it thinks wrong, to prohibit any number of things which it admits to be innocent.

Under the name of preventing intemperance, the people of one English colony, and of nearly half the United States, have been interdicted by law from making any use whatever of fermented drinks, except for medical purposes: for prohibition of their sale is in fact, as it is intended to be, prohibition of their use. And though the impracticability of executing the law has caused its repeal in several of the States which had adopted it, including the one from which it derives its name, an attempt has notwithstanding been commenced, and is prosecuted with considerable zeal by many of the professed philanthropists, to agitate for a similar law in this country. The association, or "Alliance" as it terms itself, which has been formed for this purpose, has acquired some notoriety through the publicity given to a correspondence between its Secretary and one of the very few English public men who hold that a politician's opinions ought to be founded on principles. Lord Stanley's share in this correspondence is calculated to strengthen the hopes already built on him, by those who know how rare such qualities as are manifested in some of his public appearances, unhappily are among those who figure in political life. The organ of the Alliance, who would "deeply deplore the recognition of any principle which could be wrested to justify bigotry and persecution," undertakes to point out the "broad and impassable barrier" which divides such principles from those of the association. "All matters relating to thought, opinion, conscience, appear to me," he says, "to be without the sphere of legislation; all pertaining to social act, habit, relation, subject only to a discretionary power vested in the State itself, and not in the individual, to be within it." No mention is made of a third class, different from either of these, viz., acts and habits which are not social, but individual; although it is to this class, surely, that the act of drinking fermented liquors belongs. Selling fermented liquors, however, is trading, and trading is a social act. But the infringement complained of is not on the liberty of the seller, but on that of the buyer and consumer; since the State might just as well forbid him to drink wine, as purposely make it impossible for him to obtain it. The Secretary, however, says, "I claim, as a citizen, a right to legislate whenever my social rights are invaded by the social act of another." And now for the definition of these "social rights." "If anything invades my social rights, certainly the traffic in strong drink does. It destroys my primary right of security, by constantly creating and stimulating social disorder. It invades my right of equality, by deriving a profit from the creation of a misery, I am taxed to support. It impedes my right to free moral and intellectual development, by surrounding my path with dangers, and by weakening and demoralizing society, from which I have a right to claim mutual aid and intercourse." A theory of "social rights," the like of which probably never before found its way into distinct language—being nothing short of this—that it is the absolute social right of every individual, that every other individual shall act in every respect exactly as he ought; that whosoever fails thereof in the smallest particular, violates my social right, and entitles me to demand from the legislature the removal of the grievance. So monstrous a principle is far more dangerous than any single interference with liberty; there is no violation of liberty which it would not justify; it acknowledges no right to any freedom whatever, except perhaps to that of holding opinions in secret, without ever disclosing them: for the moment an opinion which I consider noxious, passes any one's lips, it invades all the "social rights" attributed to me by the Alliance. The doctrine ascribes to all mankind a vested interest in each other's moral, intellectual, and even physical perfection, to be defined by each claimant according to his own standard.

Another important example of illegitimate interference with the rightful liberty of the individual, not simply threatened, but long since carried into triumphant effect, is Sabbatarian legislation. Without doubt, abstinence on one day in the week, so far as the exigencies of life permit, from the usual daily occupation, though in no respect religiously binding on any except Jews, it is a highly beneficial custom. And inasmuch as this custom cannot be observed without a general consent to that effect among the industrious classes, therefore, in so far as some persons by working may impose the same necessity on others, it may be allowable and right that the law should guarantee to each, the observance by others of the custom, by suspending the greater operations of industry on a particular day. But this justification, grounded on the direct interest which others have in each individual's observance of the practice, does not apply to the self-chosen occupations in which a person may think fit to employ his leisure; nor does it hold good, in the smallest degree, for legal restrictions on amusements. It is true that the amusement of some is the day's work of others; but the pleasure, not to say the useful recreation, of many, is worth the labor of a few, provided the occupation is freely chosen, and can be freely resigned. The operatives are perfectly right in thinking that if all worked on Sunday seven days' work would have to be given for six days' wages: but so long as the great mass of employments are suspended, the small number who for the enjoyment of others must still work, obtain a proportional increase of earnings; and they are not obliged to follow those occupations, if they prefer leisure to emolument. If a further remedy is sought, it might be found in the establishment by custom of a holiday on some other day of the week for those particular classes of persons. The only ground, therefore, on which restrictions on Sunday amusements can be defended, must be that they are religiously wrong; a motive of legislation which never can be too earnestly protested against. "Deorum injuriæ Diis curæ." It remains to be proved that society or any of its officers holds a commission from on high to avenge any supposed offence to Omnipotence, which is not also a wrong to our fellow-creatures. The notion that it is one man's duty that another should be religious, was the foundation of all the religious persecutions ever perpetrated, and if admitted, would fully justify them. Though the feeling which breaks out in the repeated attempts to stop railway travelling on Sunday, in the resistance to the opening of Museums, and the like, has not the cruelty of the old persecutors, the state of mind indicated by it is fundamentally the same. It is a determination not to tolerate others in doing what is permitted by their religion, because it is not permitted by the persecutor's religion. It is a belief that God not only abominates the act of the misbeliever, but will not hold us guiltless if we leave him unmolested.

I cannot refrain from adding to these examples of the little account commonly made of human liberty, the language of downright persecution which breaks out from the press of this country, whenever it feels called on to notice the remarkable phenomenon of Mormonism. Much might be said on the unexpected and instructive fact, that an alleged new revelation, and a religion founded on it, the product of palpable imposture, not even supported by the *prestige* of extraordinary qualities in its founder, is believed by hundreds of thousands, and has been made the foundation of a society, in the age of newspapers, railways, and the electric telegraph. What here concerns us is, that this religion, like other and better religions, has its martyrs; that its prophet and founder was, for his teaching, put to death by a mob; that others of its adherents lost their lives by the same lawless violence; that they were forcibly expelled, in a body, from the country in which they first grew up; while, now that they have been chased into a solitary recess in the midst of a desert, many of this country openly declare that it would be right (only that it is not convenient) to send an expedition against them, and compel them by force to conform to the opinion of other people. The article of the Mormonite doctrine which is the chief provocative to the antipathy which thus breaks through the ordinary restraints of religious tolerance, is its sanction of polygamy; which, though permitted to Mahomedans, and Hindoos, and Chinese, seems to excite unquenchable animosity when practised by persons who speak English, and profess to be a kind of Christians. No one has a deeper disapprobation than I have of this Mormon institution; both for other reasons, and because, far from being in any way countenanced by the principle of liberty, it is a direct infraction of that principle, being a mere riveting of the chains of one half of the community, and an emancipation of the other from reciprocity of obligation towards them. Still, it must be remembered that this relation is as much voluntary on the part of the women concerned in it, and who may be deemed the sufferers by it, as is the case with any other form of the marriage institution; and however surprising this fact may appear, it has its explanation in the common ideas and customs of the world, which teaching women to think marriage the one thing needful, make it intelligible that many a woman should prefer being one of several wives, to not being a wife at all. Other countries are not asked to recognize such unions, or release any portion of their inhabitants from their own laws on the score of Mormonite opinions. But when the dissentients have conceded to the hostile sentiments of others, far more than could justly be demanded; when they have left the countries to which their doctrines were unacceptable, and established themselves in a remote corner of the earth, which they have been the first to render habitable to human beings; it is difficult to see on what principles but those of tyranny they can be prevented from living there under what laws they please, provided they commit no aggression on other nations, and allow perfect freedom of departure to those who are dissatisfied with their ways. A recent writer, in some respects of considerable merit, proposes (to use his own words) not a crusade, but a *civilizade,* against this polygamous community, to put an end to what seems to him a retrograde step in civilization. It also appears so to me, but I am not aware that any community has a right to force another to be civilized. So long as the sufferers by the bad law do not invoke assistance from other communities, I cannot admit that persons entirely unconnected with them ought to step in and require that a condition of things with which all who are directly interested appear to be satisfied, should be put an end to because it is a scandal to persons some thousands of miles distant, who have no part or concern in it. Let them send missionaries, if they please, to preach against it; and let them, by any fair means (of which silencing the teachers is not one), oppose the progress of similar doctrines among their own people. If civilization has got the better of barbarism when barbarism had the world to itself, it is too much to profess to be afraid lest barbarism, after having been fairly got under, should revive and conquer civilization. A civilization that can thus succumb to its vanquished enemy must first have become so degenerate, that neither its appointed priests and teachers, nor anybody else, has the capacity, or will take the trouble, to stand up for it. If this be so, the sooner such a civilization receives notice to quit, the better. It can only go on from bad to worse, until destroyed and regenerated (like the Western Empire) by energetic barbarians.

JAMES FITZJAMES STEPHEN
The Doctrine of Liberty in Its Application to Morals

These explanations enable me to restate without fear of misapprehension the object of morally intolerant legislation. It is to establish, to maintain, and to give power to that which the legislator regards as a good moral system or standard. For the reasons already assigned I think that this object is good if and in so far as the system so established and maintained is good. How far any particular system is good or not is a question which probably does not admit of any peremptory final decision; but I may observe that there are a considerable number of things which appear good and bad, though no doubt in different degrees, to all mankind. For the practical purpose of legislation refinements are of little importance. In any given age and nation virtue and vice have meanings which for that purpose are quite definite enough. In England at the present day many theories about morality are current, and speculative men differ about them widely, but they relate not so much to the question whether particular acts are right or wrong, as to the question of the precise meaning of the distinction, the manner in which the moral character of particular actions is to be decided, and the reasons for preferring right to wrong conduct. The result is that the object of promoting virtue and preventing vice must be admitted to be both a good one and one sufficiently intelligible for legislative purposes.

If this is so, the only remaining questions will be as to the efficiency of the means at the disposal of society for this purpose, and the cost of their application. Society has at its disposal two great instruments by which vice may be prevented and virtue promoted—namely, law and public opinion; and law is either criminal or civil. The use of each of these instruments is subject to certain limits and conditions, and the wisdom of attempting to make men good either by Act of Parliament or by the action of public opinion depends entirely upon the degree in which those limits and conditions are recognized and acted upon.

First, I will take the case of criminal law. What are the conditions under which and the limitations within which it can be applied with success to the object of making men better? In considering this question it must be borne in mind that criminal law is at once by far the most powerful and by far the roughest engine which society can use for any purpose. Its power is shown by the fact that it can and does render crime exceedingly difficult and dangerous. Indeed, in civilized society it absolutely prevents avowed open crime committed with the strong hand, except in cases where crime rises to the magnitude of civil war. Its roughness hardly needs illustration. It strikes so hard that it can be enforced only on the gravest occasions, and with every sort of precaution against abuse or mistake. Before an act can be treated as a crime, it ought to be capable of distinct definition and of specific proof, and it ought also to be of such a nature that it is worth while to prevent it at the risk of inflicting great damage, direct and indirect, upon those who commit it. These conditions are seldom, if ever, fulfilled by mere vices. It would obviously be impossible to indict a man for ingratitude or perfidy. Such charges are too vague for specific discussion and distinct proof on the one side, and disproof on the other. Moreover, the expense of the investigations necessary for the legal punishment of such conduct would be enormous. It would be necessary to go into an infinite number of delicate and subtle inquiries which would tear off all privacy from the lives of a large number of persons. These considerations are, I think, conclusive reasons against treating vice in general as a crime.

The excessive harshness of criminal law is also a circumstance which very greatly narrows the range of its application. It is the *ratio ultima* of the majority against persons whom its application assumes to have renounced the common bonds which connect men together. When a man is subjected to legal punishment, society appeals directly and exclusively to his fears. It renounces the attempt to work upon his affections or feelings. In other words, it puts itself into distinct, harsh, and undisguised opposition to his wishes; and the effect of this will be to make him rebel against the law. The violence of the rebellion will be measured partly by the violence of the passion the indulgence of which is forbidden, and partly by the degree to which the law can count upon an ally in the man's own conscience. A law which enters into a direct contest with a fierce imperious passion, which the person who feels it does not admit to be bad, and which is not directly injurious to others, will generally do more harm than good; and this is perhaps the principal reason why it is impossible to legislate directly against unchastity, unless it takes forms which every one regards as monstrous and horrible. The subject is not one for detailed discussion, but any one who will follow out the reflections which this hint suggests will find that they supply a striking illustration of the limits which the harshness of criminal law imposes upon its range.

If we now look at the different acts which satisfy the conditions specified, it will, I think, be found that criminal law in this country actually is applied to the suppression of vice and so to the promotion of virtue to a very considerable extent; and this I say is right.

The punishment of common crimes, the gross forms of force and fraud, is no doubt ambiguous. It may be justified on the principle of self-protection, and apart from any question as to their moral character. It is not, however, difficult to show that these acts have in fact been forbidden and subjected to punishment not only because they are dangerous to society, and so ought to be prevented, but also for the sake of gratifying the feeling of hatred—call it revenge, resentment, or what you will—which the contemplation of such conduct excites in healthily constituted minds. If this can be shown, it will follow that criminal law is in the nature of a persecution of the grosser forms of vice, and an emphatic assertion of the principle that the feeling of hatred and the desire of vengeance above-mentioned are important elements of human nature which ought in such cases to be satisfied in a regular public and legal manner.

The strongest of all proofs of this is to be found in the principles universally admitted and acted upon as regulating the amount of punishment. If vengeance affects, and ought to affect, the amount of punishment, every circumstance which aggravates or extenuates the wickedness of an act will operate in aggravation or diminution of punishment. If the object of legal punishment is simply the prevention of specific acts, this will not be the case. Circumstances which extenuate the wickedness of the crime will often operate in aggravation of punishment. If, as I maintain, both objects must be kept in view, such circumstances will operate in different ways according to the nature of the case.

A judge has before him two criminals, one of whom appears, from the circumstances of the case, to be ignorant and depraved, and to have given way to very strong temptation, under the influence of the other, who is a man of rank and education, and who committed the offence of which both are convicted under comparatively slight temptation. I will venture to say that if he made any difference between them at all every judge on the English bench would give the first man a lighter sentence than the second.

What should we think of such an address to the prisoners as this? You, A, are a most dangerous man. You are ignorant, you are depraved, and you are accordingly peculiarly liable to be led into crime by the solicitations or influence of people like your accomplice B. Such influences constitute to men like you a temptation practically all but irresistible. The class to which you belong is a large one, and is accessible only to the coarsest possible motives. For these reasons I must put into the opposite scale as heavy a weight as I can, and the sentence of the court upon you is that you be taken to the place from whence you came and from thence to a place of execution, and that there you be hanged by the neck till you are dead. As to you, B, you are undoubtedly an infamous wretch. Between you and your tool A there can, morally speaking, be no comparison at all. But I have nothing to do with that. You belong to a small and not a dangerous class. The temptation to which you gave way was slight, and the impression made upon me by your conduct is that you really did not care very much whether you committed this crime or not. From a moral point of view, this may perhaps increase your guilt; but it shows that the motive to be overcome is less powerful in your case than in A's. You belong, moreover, to a class, and occupy a position in society, in which exposure and loss of character are much dreaded. This you will have to undergo. Your case is a very odd one, and it is not likely that you will wish to commit such a crime again, or that others will follow your example. Upon the whole, I think that what has passed will deter others from such conduct as much as actual punishment. It is, however, necessary to keep a hold over you. You will therefore be discharged on your own recognizance to come up and receive judgment when called upon, and unless you conduct yourself better for the future, you will assuredly be so called upon, and if you do not appear, your recognizance will be inexorably forfeited.

Caricature apart, the logic of such a view is surely unimpeachable. If all that you want of criminal law is the prevention of crime by the direct fear of punishment, the fact that a temptation is strong is a reason why punishment should be severe. In some instances this actually is the case. It shows the reason why political crimes and offences against military discipline are punished so severely. But in most cases the strength of the temptation operates in mitigation of punishment, and the reason of this is that criminal law operates not merely by producing fear, but also indirectly, but very powerfully, by giving distinct shape to the feeling of anger, and a distinct satisfaction to the desire of vengeance which crime excites in a healthy mind.

Other illustrations of the fact that English criminal law does recognize morality are to be found in the fact that a considerable number of acts which need not be specified are treated as crimes merely because they are regarded as grossly immoral.

I have already shown in what manner Mr. Mill deals with these topics. It is, I venture to think, utterly unsatisfactory. The impression it makes upon me is that he feels that such acts ought to be punished, and that he is able to reconcile this with his fundamental principles only by subtleties quite unworthy of him. Admit the relation for which I am contending between law and morals, and all becomes perfectly clear. All the acts referred to are unquestionably wicked. Those who do them are ashamed of them. They are all capable of being clearly defined and specifically proved or disproved, and there can be no question at all that legal punishment reduces them to small dimensions, and forces the criminals to carry on their practices with secrecy and precaution. In other words, the object of their suppression is good, and the means adequate. In practice this is subject to highly important qualifications, of which I will only say here that those who have due regard to the incurable weaknesses of human nature will be very careful how they inflict penalties upon mere vice, or even upon those who make a trade of promoting it, unless special circumstances call for their infliction. It is one thing however to tolerate vice so long as it is inoffensive, and quite another to give it a legal right not only to exist, but to assert itself in the face of the world as an 'experiment in living' as good as another, and entitled to the same protection from law.

I now pass to the manner in which civil law may and does, and as I say properly, promote virtue and prevent vice. This is a subject so wide that I prefer indicating its nature by a few illustrations to attempting to deal with it systematically. It would, however, be easy to show that nearly every branch of civil law assumes the existence of a standard of moral good and evil which the public at large have an interest in maintaining, and in many cases enforcing—a proceeding which is diametrically opposed to Mr. Mill's fundamental principles.*

The main subject with which law is conversant is that of rights and duties, and all the commoner and more important rights and duties presuppose some theory of morals. Contracts are one great source of rights and duties. Is there any country in the world the courts of which would enforce a contract which the Legislature regarded as immoral? and is there any country in which there would be much difficulty in specific cases in saying whether the object or the consideration of a contract was or was not immoral? Other rights are of a more general nature, and are liable to be violated by wrongs. Take the case of a man's right to his reputation, which is violated by defamation. How, without the aid of some sort of theory of morals, can it be determined whether the publication of defamatory matter is justifiable or not?

Perhaps the most pointed of all illustrations of the moral character of civil law is to be found in the laws relating to marriage and inheritance. They all proceed upon an essentially moral theory as to the relation of the sexes. Take the case of illegitimate children. A bastard is *filius nullius*—he inherits nothing, he has no claim on his putative father. What is all this except the expression of the strongest possible determination on the part of the Legislature to recognize, maintain, and favour marriage in every possible manner

---

*Mr. Morley says on this: 'A good deal of rather bustling ponderosity is devoted to proving that the actual laws do in many points assume the existence of a standard of moral good and evil, and that this proceeding is diametrically opposed to Mr. Mill's fundamental principles. To this one would say first that the actual existence of laws of any given kind is wholly irrelevant to Mr. Mill's contention, which is that it would be better if laws of such a kind did not exist. Secondly, Mr. Mill never says, nor is it at all essential to his doctrine to hold, that a government ought not to have "a standard of moral good and evil which the public at large have an interest in maintaining, and in many instances enforcing." He only set apart a certain class of cases to which the right or duty of enforcement of the criminal standard does not extend—self-regarding cases.'

As to the first point, surely it is not irrelevant to show that Mr. Mill is at issue with the practical conclusions to which most nations have been led by experience. Those to whom I address myself may be disposed to doubt whether a principle which condemns so many of the institutions under which they live can be right.

As to the second point, Mr. Mill says in express words: 'Society, as society, has no right to decide anything to be wrong which concerns only the individual.' This I think is equivalent to denying that society ought to have a moral standard, for by a moral standard I understand a judgment that certain acts are wrong, whoever they concern. Whether they concern the agent only or others as well, is and must be an accident. Mr. Morley, however, thinks that Mr. Mill's opinion was that society may and ought to have a moral standard, but ought not to enforce it in the case of self-regarding acts. I say, and attempt throughout the whole of this chapter to prove, that as regards the 'moral coercion of public opinion' this is neither possible nor desirable, and that as regards legal coercion, the question whether it is possible and desirable depends upon considerations drawn from the nature of law, civil and criminal. Whether I am right or wrong I cannot see that I have not understood Mr. Mill, or that I have not contradicted him.

as the foundation of civilized society? It has been plausibly maintained that these laws bear hardly upon bastards, punishing them for the sins of their parents. It is not necessary to my purpose to go into this, though it appears to me that the law is right. I make the remark merely for the sake of showing to what lengths the law does habitually go for the purpose of maintaining the most important of all moral principles, the principle upon which one great department of it is entirely founded. It is a case in which a good object is promoted by efficient and adequate means.

These illustrations are so strong that I will add nothing more to them from this branch of the law, but I may refer to a few miscellaneous topics which bear on the same subject. Let us take first the case of sumptuary laws. Mr. Mill's principles would no doubt condemn them, and, as they have gone out of fashion, it may be said, that unless my principle does so too, it is the worse for my principle. I certainly should not condemn sumptuary laws on the principle that the object in view is either bad or improper for legislation. I can hardly imagine a greater blessing to the whole community than a reduction in the lavish extravagance which makes life so difficult and laborious. It is difficult for me to look at a lace machine with patience. The ingenuity which went to devise it might have made human life materially happier in a thousand ways, and its actual effect has been to enable a great number of people to wear an imitation of an ornament which derives what little merit it has principally from its being made by hand. If any one could practically solve the problem of securing the devotion of the higher forms of human ingenuity to objects worthy of them, he would be an immense benefactor to his species. Life, however, has become so complicated, vested interests are so powerful and so worthy of respect, it is so clear that the enforcement of any conceivable law upon such a subject would be impossible, that I do not think anyone in these days would be found to propose one. In a simpler age of the world and in a smaller community such laws may have been very useful. The same remarks apply to laws as to the distribution of property and to the regulation of trade.

Laws relating to education and to military service and the discipline of the army have a moral side of the utmost importance. Mr. Mill would be the first to admit this; indeed, in several passages of his book he insists on the fact that society has complete control over the rising generation as a reason why it should not coerce adults into morality. This surely is the very opposite of the true conclusion. How is it possible for society to accept the position of an educator unless it has moral principles on which to educate? How, having accepted that position and having educated people up to a certain point, can it draw a line at which education ends and perfect moral indifference begins? When a private man educates his family, his superiority over them is founded principally on his superior age and experience; and as this personal superiority ceases, the power which is founded upon it gradually ceases also. Between society at large and individuals the difference is of another kind. The fixed principles and institutions of society express not merely the present opinions of the ruling part of the community, but the accumulated results of centuries of experience, and these constitute a standard by which the conduct of individuals may be tried, and to which they are in a variety of ways, direct and indirect, compelled to conform. This, I think, is one of the meanings which may be attached to the assertion that education never ceases. As a child grows into a man, and as a young man grows into an old man, he is brought under the influence of successive sets of educators, each of whom sets its mark upon him. It is no uncommon thing to see aged parents taught by their grown-up children lessons learned by the children in their intercourse with their own generation. All of us are continually educating each other, and in every instance this is and must be a process at once moral and more or less coercive.*

As to Mr. Mill's doctrine that the coercive influence of public opinion ought to be exercised only for self-protective purposes, it seems to me a paradox so startling that it is almost impossible to argue against it. A single consideration on the subject is sufficient to prove this. The principle is one which it is impossible to carry out. It is like telling a rose that it ought to smell sweet only for the purpose of affording pleasure to the owner of the ground in which it grows. People form and express their opinions on each other, which, collectively, form public opinion, for a thousand reasons; to amuse themselves; for the sake of something to talk about; to gratify this or that momentary feeling; but the effect of such opinions, when formed, is quite independent of the grounds of their formation. A man is tried for murder, and just escapes conviction. People read the trial from curiosity; they discuss it for the sake of discussion; but if, by whatever means, they are brought to think that the man was in all probability guilty, they shun his society as they would shun any other hateful thing. The opinion produces its effect in precisely the same way whatever was its origin.

The result of these observations is that both law and public opinion do in many cases exercise a powerful coercive influence on morals, for objects which are good in the sense explained above, and by means well calculated

---

*Mr. Morley says in reference to this passage and the preceding passages from pp. [29–30]: 'Mr. Stephen . . . proves the contradictory of assertions which his adversary never made, as when he cites judicial instances which imply the recognition of morality by the law.' I think Mr. Morley misunderstands my argument, which nevertheless appears to me very plain. It is simply this: I say laws can and do promote virtue and diminish vice by coercion in the cases and in the ways specified, and their interference does more good than harm. The contradictory of this proposition would be that in the cases specified legal interference does more harm than good. Surely if Mr. Mill's general principle is true, this must follow from it. Therefore in denying it I deny a necessary inference from the principle which I attack.

to attain those objects, to a greater or less extent at a not inadequate expense. If this is so, I say law and public opinion do well, and I do not see how either the premises or the conclusion are to be disproved.

Of course there are limits to the possibility of useful interference with morals, either by law or by public opinion; and it is of the highest practical importance that these limits should be carefully observed. The great leading principles on the subject are few and simple, though they cannot be stated with any great precision. It will be enough to mention the following:

(1) Neither legislation nor public opinion ought to be meddlesome. A very large proportion of the matters upon which people wish to interfere with their neighbors are trumpery little things which are of no real importance at all. The busybody and world-betterer who will never let things alone, or trust people to take care of themselves, is a common and a contemptible character. The commonplaces directed against these small creatures are perfectly just, but to try to put them down by denying the connection between law and morals is like shutting all light and air out of a house in order to keep out gnats and blue-bottle flies.

(2) Both legislation and public opinion, but especially the latter, are apt to be most mischievous and cruelly unjust if they proceed upon imperfect evidence. To form and express strong opinions about the wickedness of a man whom you do not know, the immorality or impiety of a book you have not read, the merits of a question on which you are uninformed, is to run a great risk of inflicting a great wrong. It is hanging first and trying afterwards, or more frequently not trying at all. This, however, is no argument against hanging after a fair trial.

(3) Legislation ought in all cases to be graduated to the existing level of morals in the time and country in which it is employed. You cannot punish anything which public opinion, as expressed in the common practice of society, does not strenuously and unequivocally condemn. To try to do so is a sure way to produce gross hypocrisy and furious reaction. To be able to punish, a moral majority must be overwhelming. Law cannot be better than the nation in which it exists, though it may and can protect an acknowledged moral standard, and may gradually be increased in strictness as the standard rises. We punish, with the utmost severity, practices which in Greece and Rome went almost uncensured. It is possible that a time may come when it may appear natural and right to punish adultery, seduction, or possibly even fornication, but the prospect is, at present, indefinitely remote, and it may be doubted whether we are moving in that direction.

(4) Legislation and public opinion ought in all cases whatever scrupulously to respect privacy. To define the province of privacy distinctly is impossible, but it can be described in general terms. All the more intimate and delicate relations of life are of such a nature that to submit them to unsympathetic observation, or to observation which is sympathetic in the wrong

way, inflicts great pain, and may inflict lasting moral injury. Privacy may be violated not only by the intrusion of a stranger, but by compelling or persuading a person to direct too much attention to his own feelings and to attach too much importance to their analysis. The common usage of language affords a practical test which is almost perfect upon this subject. Conduct which can be described as indecent is always in one way or another a violation of privacy. . . .

These, I think, are the principal forms in which society can and actually does promote virtue and restrain vice. It is impossible to form any estimate of the degree in which it succeeds in doing so, but it may perhaps be said that the principal importance of what is done in this direction by criminal law is that in extreme cases it brands gross acts of vice with the deepest mark of infamy which can be impressed upon them, and that in this manner it protects the public and accepted standard of morals from being grossly and openly violated. In short, it affirms in a singularly emphatic manner a principle which is absolutely inconsistent with and contradictory to Mr. Mill's— the principle, namely, that there are acts of wickedness so gross and outrageous that, self-protection apart, they must be prevented as far as possible at any cost to the offender, and punished, if they occur, with exemplary severity. . . .

3   Community and Rights

RONALD DWORKIN

Liberal Community

It is widely thought that liberalism as a political theory is hostile to, or anyway not sufficiently appreciative of, the value or importance of community, and that liberal tolerance, which insists that it is wrong of government to use its coercive power to enforce ethical homogeneity, undermines community.[1] I shall try to test these assumptions.

Very different arguments, using very different concepts of community, have been used to attack liberal tolerance in different ways. I distinguish four such arguments: The first is an argument from democratic theory which associates community with majority. In *Bowers,* Justice White suggested that the community has a right to use the law to support its vision of ethical decency:[2] it has a right to impose its views about ethics just because it is the majority. The second is an argument of *paternalism.* It holds that in a genuine political community each citizen has a responsibility for the well-being of other members and should therefore use his political power to reform those whose defective practices will ruin their lives. The third is an argument of *self-interest,* broadly conceived. It condemns atomism, the view that individuals are self-sufficient unto themselves, and emphasizes the wide variety of ways—material, intellectual, and ethical—in which people need community. It insists that liberal tolerance undermines the community's ability to serve these needs. The fourth, which I shall call *integration,* argues that liberal tolerance depends on an illegitimate distinction between the lives of individual people within the community and the life of the community as a whole. According to this argument, the value or goodness of any individual citizen's life is only a reflection and function of the value of the life of the community in which he lives. So citizens, in order to make their own lives successful, must vote and work to make sure that their fellow citizens lead decent lives.

Each of these arguments uses the concept of community in an increasingly more substantial and less reductive way. The first argument, that a democratic majority has a right to define ethical standards for all, uses community only as a shorthand symbol for a particular, numerically defined, political grouping. The second argument, which encourages paternalism, gives the concept more substance: It defines community not as just a political group, but as the dimensions of a shared and distinct responsibility. The third argument, that people need community, recognizes community as an entity in its own right, as a source of a wide variety of influences and benefits not reducible to the contributions of particular people one by one. The fourth argument, about identification, further personifies community and describes a sense in which a political community is not only independent of, but prior to, individual citizens. In this Article, I focus on this fourth argument, partly because I have not discussed it before, but also because I find its root idea, that people should identify their own interests with those of their political community, true and valuable. Properly understood, the idea furnishes no argument against liberal tolerance, and no support for *Bowers*. On the contrary, liberalism supplies the best interpretation of this concept of community, and liberal theory the best account of its importance.

I
Community and Democracy

Some liberals have thought that liberal tolerance can be fully justified by John Stuart Mill's harm principle, which holds that the state may properly restrain someone's liberty only to prevent his harming others, not himself. In *Law, Liberty and Morality*, H. L. A. Hart argued that this rules out legislation making homosexual acts criminal. But Hart's argument is sound only if we limit harm to physical injury to person or property. Every community has an ethical environment, and that environment makes a difference to the lives its members can lead. A community that tolerates homosexuality, and in which homosexuality has a strong presence, provides a different ethical environment from one in which homosexuality is forbidden, and some people believe themselves harmed by the difference. They find it much harder, for example, to raise their children to instincts and values of which they approve.

The first argument against liberal tolerance declares that questions about the shape of a democratic community's ethical environment should be decided in accordance with the majority's will. It argues not merely that whatever decisions the political officials elected by the majority make should be accepted as law, but that these political officials should make decisions that reflect the preferences of a majority rather than any minority.[3] This is substantive rather than merely procedural majoritarianism. The argument does not assume that any minority's moral views are base or wicked, but only that when opinion divides about the proper ethical environment for a community, it is unfair to allow a minority to dictate to majority will.

This assumes, however, that the contours of a community's ethical environment must be decided collectively, in a winner-take-all fashion, so that either the majority or some minority must determine, exclusively, its shape. If that assumption were true, then the argument would plainly be powerful. Some issues must, indeed, be decided in close to a winner-take-all way, and in those instances, one group's view must prevail entirely, to the total exclusion of any other. For example, whether the nation should adopt a particular version of a Strategic Defense Initiative (SDI). But democracy does not demand that all political decisions be winner-take-all. On the contrary, in one central sphere of life—the economic environment—justice requires exactly the opposite.

The economic environment in which we live—the distribution of property and preferences that creates supply, demand, and price—affects us even more obviously than our ethical environment does. I am harmed by the fact that I own less property than I might, and that others have different tastes than I might want them to have. The economic environment may frustrate my efforts to raise my children to have the values I might wish them to have; I cannot, for example, raise them to have the skills and experience of collecting Renaissance masterpieces. But even if a majority of citizens wanted to assign all economic resources to themselves, it would not be just for them to do so. Justice requires that property be distributed in fair shares, allowing each individual person his or her fair share of influence over the economic environment. People disagree, of course, about what constitutes a fair share, and a good part of modern political argument reflects that disagreement.[4] But my present point does not depend on any particular conception of distributive justice because any remotely plausible theory will reject the principle of exclusive majoritarian control.

If we take a parallel view of the ethical environment, then we must reject the claim that democratic theory assigns a majority complete control of that environment. We must insist that the ethical environment, like the economic, be the product of the choices individual people make. Of course neither of these environments should be left completely to unregulated individual choices. We need laws to protect the economic environment from theft and monopolization, for example, and zoning regulations that respond to market externalities. These laws help insure, so far as possible, that the economic environment has the shape it would have if resources were fairly distributed and markets were perfect.

The ethical environment requires regulation in the same spirit, to limit a minority's impact on the ethical environment to the impact its numbers and tastes justify. Zoning regulations which restrict the practice of potentially offensive acts to special or private places serve that purpose, for example. But restricting a minority's impact on the ethical environment through zoning is very different from cheating a minority of any impact at all, which is what the majoritarian argument proposes.

If we treat the ethical environment in the same way we treat the economic environment—allowing it to be fixed by individual decisions made against the background of a fair distribution of resources—then we reject the majoritarian claim that the majority has a right to eliminate whatever it finds harmful in the ethical environment. Each member of the majority has a right only to a fair impact on his environment—the same impact as any other single individual. He has no right to the environment that would make it easiest for him to raise his children to hold his favored opinions. He must try to do his best, to that end, in the environment fairness provides.

Can we find any reason to treat the ethical environment differently from the economic environment? Some economic issues, such as SDI, must be decided collectively, all one way or the other, rather than as a resultant of individual forces. And our sense of integrity and fairness require us to decide some issues of principle in the same way for everyone.[5] For example, officials should not aim to execute some proportion of convicted murderers to match the proportion of citizens who favor capital punishment. But neither of these reasons for making some political decisions collectively provides any argument for fixing a community's ethical environment that way. There is no practical reason why that environment must be exactly what some group thinks best. And since the various individual acts and decisions that contribute to forming an ethical environment are no more the acts of government than the various individual economic decisions that fix the economic environment are, there is no question of government violating integrity by letting individuals make these decisions in different ways.

We should not subject the ethical and economic environments to different regimes of justice because they are not two distinct environments, but interdependent aspects of the same one. The value of the resources someone controls is not fixed by laws of property alone, but also by other departments of law, stipulating how he can use that property. So moralistic legislation, which discriminates amongst some uses of property or leisure, always affects price and value to some degree. In some circumstances that effect is significant: morally inspired prohibition laws, for example. Any plausible regime of distributive justice must therefore take into account the degree of liberty citizens have in judging when resources are fairly distributed.[6] If we insist that the value of the resources people hold must be fixed by the interaction of individual choices rather than by the collective decisions of a majority, then we have already decided that the majority has no right to decide what kinds of lives everyone must lead. Once we accept that the economic and ethical environments are unified, in other words, we must accept liberal tolerance in matters of ethics because any contrary view denies the unity.

The majoritarian argument we have been considering is politically the most powerful argument against liberal tolerance. It was allowed a conspicuous place in the majority opinion in *Bowers*. This part of our overall discussion is therefore of considerable practical importance. But it is important to bear in mind its limits. It is aimed only at the majoritarian argument; it should not be taken as a statement of the exclusive ground of liberal tolerance, or as resting the entire value of liberty on an economic analogy. Nor does it purport to define any special rights to particularly important liberties, like freedom of speech or association. It only denies the majoritarian argument's essential premise that the shape of the ethical environment as a whole must be fixed winner-take-all by the majority's wishes. If the concept of community has an important role in the criticism of liberal tolerance, it must be in a more robust sense than simply as a name for a political unity over which majority rule roams.

II
Community and Concern

The second communitarian argument, the argument of paternalism, appeals to the idea of community in a more robust sense. It begins in the attractive idea that a true political community must be more than a Hobbesian association for mutual benefits in which each citizens regards all others as useful means to his or her own ends; it must be an association in which each takes some special interest in the well-being of others for its own sake. The argument adds that people who are genuinely concerned about others take an interest in their *critical* as well as their *volitional* well-being. I must explain that distinction, because it is crucial to the argument of paternalism.[7]

There are two senses in which people have interests, two ways in which their lives can go better or worse. Someone's volitional well-being is improved whenever he has or achieves something he wants.[8] But his critical well-being is improved only by his having or achieving those things that he should want, that is, achievements or experiences that it would make his life a worse one not to want. We can make this distinction subjectively, as a distinction between two ways in which a person might understand or regard his own interests. I myself, for example, consider some of the things I want very much as falling under my volitional interests. I want good food, and fewer visits to the dentist, and to sail better than I do, and my life therefore goes better when I have them. But I do not think that I ought to want these things, or that my life would be a poorer one if for some reason I did not. But I take a different view of other things I want: such as having a close relationship with my children, and achieving some success in my work. I do not think that having a close relationship with my children is important just because I happen to want it; on the contrary, I want it because I believe a life without such relationships is impoverished. We make the same distinction objectively, that is, as a distinction not between two ways in which people might regard these interests, but between two classes of interests people actually have. People can fail to recognize their own critical interests. It makes sense to say that someone who has no regard for friendship or religion or challenging work, for example, leads a poorer life for that reason, whether he agrees or not. We also make critical judgments about ourselves; people all too often come to think, toward the end, that they have ignored what they only then realize is really important to their lives.[9]

The distinction is complex and can be explored and criticized in many different ways. Some, for example, will be skeptical about the whole idea of critical interests or well-being. They may think that since no one can prove that it is in anyone's critical interests to want something he does not, then the whole idea of critical well-being is mistaken. I shall not try to answer that skeptical objection here. I shall assume, as I believe most of us do in our ordinary lives, that we all have both kinds of interests. We can use the distinction between volitional and critical interests to distinguish two forms of paternalism. Volitional paternalism supposes that coercion can sometimes help people achieve what they already want to achieve, and is for that reason in their volitional interests. Critical paternalism supposes that coercion can sometimes provide people with lives that are better than the lives they now think good and coercion is therefore sometimes in their critical interests.

The second communitarian argument appeals to critical rather than volitional paternalism. It forces us to confront a philosophical issue about critical well-being. We can evaluate someone's life in two ways. We can look, first, at the components of that life: the events, experiences, associations, and achievements that make it up, and ask whether in our view these components, in the combination we find them, make a life good. We can look, second, at the attitudes of the person whose life it is. We can ask how he judges those components; we can ask whether he sought them or regards them as valuable, in short *endorses* them as serving his critical interests.

What view should we take about the relationship between these two ways of looking at the critical value of a life? We should distinguish two answers. The *additive* view holds that components and endorsements are separate elements of value. If someone's life has the components of a good life, then it has critical value. If he endorses these components, then their value increases. The endorsement is frosting on the cake. But if he does not, the value of the components remains. The *constitutive* view, on the other hand, argues that no component contributes to the value of a life without endorsement: If a misanthrope is much loved, but disdains the love as worthless, his life is not much more valuable for the affection of others.

The constitutive view is preferable for a variety of reasons. The additive view cannot explain why a good life is distinctively valuable for or to the person whose life it is. And it is implausible to think that someone can lead a better life against the grain of his most profound ethical convictions than at peace with them. If we accept the constitutive view, then we can answer the argument from critical paternalism in what we might call its crude or direct form. Suppose someone who would lead a homosexual life does not, out of fear of punishment. If he never endorses the life he leads as superior to the life he would otherwise have led, then his life has not been improved, even in the critical sense, by the paternalistic constraints he hates.

We must recognize a more subtle aim of critical paternalism, however. Suppose the state deploys a combination of constraints and inducements such that a homosexual is converted and does in the end endorse and appreciate the conversion. Has his life then been improved? The answer turns on an issue I have so far neglected: the conditions and circumstances of genuine endorsement. There must be some constraints on endorsement; otherwise critical paternalism could always justify itself by adding chemical or electrical brainwashing to its regime.

We must distinguish acceptable from unacceptable circumstances of endorsement. The distinction, as we know from the history of liberal theories of education, is a difficult one to draw, but any adequate account of acceptable circumstances would, I believe, include the following proposition. We would not improve someone's life, even though he endorsed the change we brought about, if the mechanisms we used to secure the change lessened his ability to consider the critical merits of the change in a reflective way. Threats of criminal punishment corrupt rather than enhance critical judgment, and even if the conversions they induce are sincere, these conversions cannot be counted as genuine in deciding whether the threats have improved someone's life. The second communitarian argument is therefore self-defeating.

Notes

1. Throughout this essay I distinguish ethics from morality. Ethics, as I use the term, includes convictions about which kinds of lives are good or bad for a person to lead, and morality includes principles about how a person should treat other people. So the question I consider is whether a political community should use criminal law to force its members to lead what a majority deems good lives, not whether it should use the law to force them to behave justly to others.

2. 478 U.S. 186 (1986).

3. We might object to procedural as well as substantive majoritarianism in the case of enforcing morals; we might say that such questions should be decided not by elected officials but by a constitutional court like the Supreme Court. I am not considering that procedural question in this lecture, however. *See* Dworkin, *What is Equality, Part 4: Political Equality,* 22 U.S.F. L. Rev. 28–30 (1987): Dworkin, *Democracy: Equality and Constitution,* forthcoming in the Alberta Law Review.

4. In my view, fair shares are those that equalize, so far as this is possible, the opportunity costs to others of the material resources each person holds. *See* Dworkin, *What is Equality? Part 2: Equality of Resources,* 10 PHIL. & PUB. AFF. 283 (1981). I restrict the opportunity-cost test to material (or, as I have sometimes said, impersonal) resources, because that test is not appropriate for personal resources like talents and health.

5. For an account of the requirement of integrity, and of the issues of principle it demands be decided the same for everyone, see R. DWORKIN, LAW'S EMPIRE (1987), especially Chapter 6. For a more extended discussion of the distinction between matters of principle like those cited in the text, and matters of policy like SDI, see R. DWORKIN, A MATTER OF PRINCIPLE (1986), especially Chapter 3.

6. This argument is developed at considerable length, and its consequences for liberalism described, in Dworkin, *What is Equality? Part 3: The Place of Liberty,* 73 IOWA L. REV. 1 (1988).

7. This discussion of this section draws on material in lectures I gave last spring at Stanford University under the auspices of the Tanner Foundation. These will appear in a forthcoming collection of Tanner Foundation lectures to be published by the Foundation. Readers who wish to see an expanded discussion of the distinction between volitional and critical interests, and reasons for preferring the constitutive to the additive view of critical interests, should consult those lectures.

8. That characterization of volitional interests ignores the fact that some of the things a person wants may conflict with other things he wants. But the refinements needed to take account of that fact are not necessary for the general distinction between coalitional and critical interests I make in the text.

9. The distinction between critical and volitional well-being is not the distinction between what is really in my interests and what I only think is. My volitional interests are genuine, real interests, not merely reflections of my present judgments, which I may later decide are mistakes, about where my critical interests lie. The two kinds of interests, the two modes of well-being are distinct. I can intelligibly want something without thinking it makes my life a better life to have; indeed a life in which someone only wanted what he thought it in his critical interests to have would be a sad, preposterous mess of a life. I should add (because the question was raised at the conference) that I use the term "critical interests" rather than "real interests" to avoid suggesting what this footnote denies, that the contrasting "volitional" interests are in some way illusory or bogus.

JOHN FINNIS

Rights and Equality of Concern and Respect

It is sometimes argued that to prefer, and seek to embody in legislation, some conception or range of conceptions of human flourishing is unjust because it is necessarily to treat with unequal concern and respect those members of the community whose conceptions of human good fall outside the preferred range and whose activities are or may therefore be restricted by the legislation. As an argument warranting opposition to such legislation this argument cannot be justified; it is self-stultifying. Those who put forward the argument prefer a conception of human good, according to which a person is entitled to equal concern and respect and a community is in bad shape in which that entitlement is denied; moreover, they act on this preference by seeking to repeal the restrictive legislation which those against whom they are arguing may have enacted. Do those who so argue and so act thereby necessarily treat with unequal concern and respect those whose preferences and legislation they oppose? If they do, then their own argument and action is itself equally unjustified, and provides no basis for political preferences or action. If they do not (and this must be the better view), then neither do those whom they oppose. Nor can the argument be rescued by proposing that it escapes self-stultification by operating at a different 'level of discourse': for example, by being an argument about entitlements rather than about good. For there is no difficulty in translating any 'paternalist' political preference into the language of entitlement, by postulating an entitlement of every member of a community to a milieu that will support rather than hinder his own pursuit of good and the well-being of his children, or an entitlement of each to be rescued from his own folly. Whether or not such entitlements can be made out, they certainly pertain to the same 'level of discourse'. Nor, finally, can the argument we are considering be saved by a stipulation that arguments and political programmes motivated, as it is, by concern for 'equal respect and concern for other people' must be regarded as showing equal concern and respect for everyone, even those people whose (paternalist) arguments and legislation they reject and override. For, on the one hand, such a stipulation is merely an *ad hoc* device for escaping self-stultification; if overriding someone's political preferences and compelling him to live in a society whose ways he detests were *ipso facto* to show unequal concern and respect for him in one context, so it would be in any other. And, on the other hand, there is no difficulty in supposing that a 'paternalist' political programme may be based on a conception of what is required for equal concern and respect for all; for paternalists may well consider that, for example, to leave a person to succumb to drug addiction on the plea that it is 'his business' is to deny him the active concern one would show for one's friend in like situation; or that to fail to forbid teachers to form sexual attachments with their pupils is to deny the children of negligent or 'wrong-headed' parents the protection that the paternalist legislator would wish for his own children, and is thus again a failure in 'equal concern and respect'. 'I wish someone had stopped me from . . .': if this can rationally be said (as it can), it follows necessarily that even the most extensive and excessive programme of paternalism might be instituted without denial of equal concern and respect to anybody.

The pursuit of any form of human community in which human rights are protected by the imposition of duties will necessarily involve both selection of some and rejection of other conceptions of the common good, and considerable restrictions on the activities of everyone (including the legislators themselves, in their private capacities as persons subject to egoism and indifference to the real well-being of others). Some ways of pursuing the common good through legislation do indeed err by forgetting that personal authenticity, self-direction, and privacy for contemplation or play or friendship are aspects and important adjuncts of human well-being. Paternalist programmes guilty of this oversight should be criticized for that—a failure in commutative justice—and not for the quite different vice of discrimination, group bias, denial of equal concern and respect, a kind of refined selfishness, a failure in distributive justice. To judge another man mistaken, and to act on that judgment, is not to be equated, in any field of human discourse and judgment, with despising that man or preferring oneself. . . .

4 Liberalism: Objections and Defenses

IRVING KRISTOL

*Pornography, Obscenity, and
the Case for Censorship*

Being frustrated is disagreeable, but the real disasters in life begin when you get what you want. For almost a century now, a great many intelligent, well-meaning, and articulate people—of a kind generally called liberal or intellectual, or both—have argued eloquently against any kind of censorship of art and/or entertainment. And within the past ten years, the courts and the legislatures of most Western nations have found these arguments persuasive—so persuasive that hardly a man is now alive who clearly remembers what the answers to these arguments were. Today, in the United States and other democracies, censorship has to all intents and purposes ceased to exist.

Is there a sense of triumphant exhilaration in the land? Hardly. There is, on the contrary, a rapidly growing unease and disquiet. Somehow, things have not worked out as they were supposed to, and many notable civil libertarians have gone on record as saying this was not what they meant at all. They wanted a world in which "Desire Under the Elms" could be produced, or "Ulysses" published, without interference by philistine busybodies holding public office. They have got that, of course; but they have also got a world in which homosexual rape takes place on the stage, in which the public flocks during lunch hours to witness varieties of professional fornication, in which Times Square has become little more than a hideous market for the sale and distribution of printed filth that panders to all known (and some fanciful) sexual perversions.

But disagreeable as this may be, does it really matter? Might not our unease and disquiet be merely a cultural hangover—a "hangup," as they say? What reason is there to think that anyone was ever corrupted by a book?

This last question, oddly enough, is asked by the very same people who seem convinced that advertisements in magazines or displays of violence on television do indeed have the power to corrupt. It is also asked, incredibly enough and in all sincerity, by people—e.g., university professors and school teachers—whose very lives provide all the answers one could want. After all, if you believe that no one was ever corrupted by a book, you have also to believe that no one was ever improved by a book (or a play or a movie). You have to believe, in other words, that all art is morally trivial and that, consequently, all education is morally irrelevant. No one, not even a university professor, really believes that.

To be sure, it is extremely difficult, as social scientists tell us, to trace the effects of any single book (or play or movie) on an individual reader or any class of readers. But we all know, and social scientists know it too, that the ways in which we use our minds and imaginations do shape our characters and help define us as persons. That those who certainly know this are nevertheless moved to deny it merely indicates how a dogmatic resistance to the idea of censorship can—like most dogmatism—result in a mindless insistence on the absurd.

I have used these harsh terms—"dogmatism" and "mindless"—advisedly. I might also have added "hypocritical." For the plain fact is that none of us is a complete civil libertarian. We all believe that there is some point at which the public authorities ought to step in to limit the "self-expression" of an individual or a group, even where this might be seriously intended as a form of artistic expression, and even where the artistic transaction is between consenting adults. A playwright or theatrical director might, in this crazy world of ours, find someone willing to commit suicide on the stage, as called for by the script. We would not allow that—any more than we would permit scenes of real physical torture on the stage, even if the victim were a willing masochist. And I know of no one, no matter how free in spirit, who argues that we ought to permit gladiatorial contests in Yankee Stadium, similar to those once performed in the Colosseum at Rome—even if only consenting adults were involved.

The basic point that emerges is one that Prof. Walter Berns has powerfully argued: No society can be utterly indifferent to the ways its citizens publicly entertain themselves. Bearbaiting and cockfighting are prohibited only in part out of compassion for the suffering animals; the main reason they were abolished was because it was felt that they debased and brutalized the citizenry who flocked to witness such spectacles. And the question we face with regard to pornography and obscenity is whether, now that they have such strong legal protection from the Supreme Court, they can or will brutalize and debase our citizenry. We are, after all, not dealing with one passing incident—one book, or one play, or one movie. We are dealing with a general tendency that is suffusing our entire culture.

I say pornography *and* obscenity because, though they have different dictionary definitions and are frequently distinguishable as "artistic" genres, they are nevertheless in the end identical in effect. Pornography is not objectionable simply because it arouses sexual desire or lust or prurience in the mind of the reader or spectator; this is a silly Victorian notion. A great many nonpornographic works—including some parts of the Bible—excite sexual desire very successfully. What is distinctive about pornography is that, in the words of D. H. Lawrence, it attempts "to do dirt on [sex] . . . [It is an] insult to a vital human relationship."

In other words, pornography differs from erotic art in that its whole purpose is to treat human beings obscenely, to deprive human beings of their specifically human dimension. That is what obscenity is all about. It is light years removed from any kind of carefree sensuality—there is no continuum between Fielding's "Tom Jones" and the Marquis de Sade's "Justine." These works have quite opposite intentions. To quote Susan Sontag: "What pornographic literature does is precisely to drive a wedge between one's existence as a full human being and one's existence as a sexual being—while in ordinary life a healthy person is one who prevents such a gap from opening up." This definition occurs in an essay *defending* pornography—Miss Sontag is a candid as well as gifted critic—so the definition, which I accept, is neither tendentious nor censorious.

Along these same lines, one can point out—as C. S. Lewis pointed out some years back—that it is no accident that in the history of all literatures obscene words—the so-called "four-letter words"—have always been the vocabulary of farce or vituperation. The reason is clear—they reduce men and women to some of their mere bodily functions—they reduce man to his animal component, and such a reduction is an essential purpose of farce or vituperation.

Similarly, Lewis also suggested that it is not an accident that we have no offhand, colloquial, neutral terms—not in any Western European language at any rate—for our most private parts. The words we do use are either (a) nursery terms, (b) archaisms, (c) scientific terms or (d) a term from the gutter (that is, a demeaning term). Here I think the genius of language is telling us something important about man. It is telling us that man is an animal with a difference: he has a unique sense of privacy, and a unique capacity for shame when this privacy is violated. Our "private parts" are indeed private, and not merely because convention prescribes it. This particular convention is indigenous to the human race. In practically all primitive tribes, men and women cover their private parts; and in practically all primitive tribes, men and women do not copulate in public.

It may well be that Western society, in the latter half of the 20th century, is experiencing a drastic change in sexual mores and sexual relationships. We have had many such "sexual revolutions" in the past—and the bourgeois family and bourgeois ideas of sexual propriety were themselves established in the course of a revolution against 18th century "licentiousness"—and we shall doubtless have others in the future. It is, however, highly improbable (to put it mildly) that what we are witnessing is the Final Revolution which will make sexual relations utterly unproblematic, permit us to dispense with any kind of ordered relationships between the sexes, and allow us freely to redefine the human condition. And so long as humanity has not reached that utopia, obscenity will remain a problem. . . .

JOEL FEINBERG
Harmless Wrongdoing

The most characteristic argument for the strict moralistic position in its pure form involves the imaginative use of examples. The strict moralist must find actual or hypothetical examples of actions or states of affairs that are not only "evil in the generic sense" but *morally* evil as judged by "natural" objective standards, and perfectly free-floating, that is not evil simply because harmful (in the liberal's sense), offensive, or exploitatively unfair, but *evil in any case*. Then, if the example is such that the liberal, reacting spontaneously, would be embarrassed to have to oppose criminal prohibition, the example has telling probative impact. Indeed such arguments, while technically *ad hominem* in form, have as much force as can normally be expected in ethical discourse. This strategy requires that the strict moralist cite some plausible (though admittedly uncharacteristic) free-floating moral evils that are such great evils that the need to prevent them *as such* is likely to be accepted by the reader as a weightier reason than the case for individual liberty on the other side of the scales. All the legal moralist can do at this point is present relevant examples in a vivid and convincing way, pointedly reminding the reader of certain principles of critical morality that he holds in common with the legal moralist and takes equally seriously. The relative "weight" of acknowledged reasons is not otherwise amenable to proof. More exactly, the legal moralist offers *counterexamples* to the liberal thesis that personally harmless transactions between consenting adults in private cannot be evils of sufficient magnitude to justify preventive coercion.

Let us begin with the standard liberal example of the pornographic film or the nude stage show. Imagine that the advertising for these entertainments is perfectly honest and straightforward. On the one hand, it is not lurid or titillating in a way that would offend passersby; on the other hand, it does not conceal the nature of the shows in a way that would mislead customers into expecting something that is not pornographic. Imagine further that children are not permitted entrance. Since neither compulsion nor deception is used to dragnet audiences, everyone who witnesses the show does so voluntarily, knowing full well what he is in for. No one then can complain that he has been harmed or offended by what he sees. The shows therefore can be banned only on the ground that the erotic experiences in the minds of the spectators are inherent evils of a free-floating kind.

The playfully skeptical legal moralist can now begin to alter these hypothetical paradigms until his liberal adversary begins to squirm. He asks us to suppose, for example, that the voluntary audience is thrilled to watch the explicit portrayal on the stage of sexual intercourse, or even "sodomy and other sexual aberrations." Imagine live actors and actresses performing live sex for the delectation of live voyeurs. Well, surely this would be degrading and dehumanizing for the actors, protests the liberal. In that case, the state has a right to make sure that the actors too, and not only the audience, are voluntary participants. But why shouldn't some contracts between producers and actors be capable of passing the test of voluntariness? No doubt the actors' work would be unpleasant, but let us suppose that it is well paid. People have been known to put up, quite voluntarily, with great discomfort for the sake of earning money. Could sexual exhibitionism be that much worse than coal mining? Maybe it could. But should it not be up to the free choice of the actor to decide whether a certain amount of public degradation is worth ten thousand dollars a week? It would be paternalistic to prevent him from doing what he wants to do on the ground that we know better than he what is good for him. Liberal principles, then, offer no grounds to justify the legal prohibition of such diversions. That may not embarrass the liberal (very much), but other counterexamples lie in wait for him.

Imagine a really kinky live sex show primarily for voluntary spectators who prefer their sex with sadomasochistic seasoning. William Buckley eagerly takes up the argument from here:

> Does an individual have the right to submit to sadistic treatment? To judge from the flotsam that sifts up in the magazine racks, there is a considerable appetite for this sort of thing. Let us hypothesize an off-Broadway show featuring an SM production in which the heroine is flailed—real whips, real woman, real blood—for the depraved. One assumes that the ACLU would defend the right of the producers to get on with it, trotting out the argument that no one has the right to interfere with the means by which others take their pleasure.
>
> The opposing argument is that the community has the right first to define, then to suppress, depravity. Moreover, the community legitimately concerns itself over the coarsening effect of depravity.[1]

That the community has the right to define and suppress depravity as an inherent evil is, of course, the moralist thesis here at issue. That the community can be concerned with "coarsening effects," on the other hand, is the sort of consideration a proponent of the harm principle might invoke if he thought on empirical grounds that people with coarsened characters tend to cause harm to unwitting victims, so it is a consideration that can be put aside here.

Vicarious sexual pleasures of a "depraved" sort are not the only examples of private enjoyments found repugnant by some legal moralists. Professional boxing matches are another case in point. Here some of the liberals themselves are among the most denunciatory. *The New York Times* published an editorial demanding the abolition of professional boxing altogether shortly after the bloody first Frazier-Ali fight. One of the many indignant letters to the editor that followed denounced *The New York Times,* in turn, on familiar liberal principles:

> Ali and Frazier fought of their own free choice. Neither of them has complained that he was forced to submit to brutal and dehumanizing treatment. Those who paid money to see the fight did so willingly and most of them thought they got their money's worth. . . . [W]hat was immoral about this fight? No rights were transgressed. Those who disapprove of professional boxing were not forced to watch.
> . . . The parallel to declining civilizations of the past referred to in your editorial is without any basis in fact. The contestants in the cruel sports that were practiced in the dying days of the Roman Empire, for example, were not free men with free choice. . . .[2]

The liberal author of that letter is set up for the last of the ingenious moralistic counterexamples to be considered here. Irving Kristol has us consider the possibility of gladiatorial contests in Yankee Stadium before consenting adult audiences, of course, and between well-paid gladiators who are willing to risk life or limb for huge stakes. The example is not far-fetched. We can imagine that, with closed circuit television, the promoter could offer twenty million dollars to the winners and ten million to the estates of the losers. How could we advocate legal prohibition without abandoning the liberal position that only the harm and offense principles can provide reasons of sufficient strength to override the case for liberty? Kristol has no doubts that the liberal is stuck with his huge free-floating evil and can urge prohibition only at the cost of hypocrisy:

> I might also have [used the word] . . . "hypocritical." For the plain fact is that none of us is a complete civil libertarian. We all believe that there is some point at which the public authorities ought to step in to limit the "self-expression" of an individual or a group even where this might be seriously intended as a form of artistic expression, and even where the artistic transaction is between consenting adults. A playwright or theatrical director might, in this crazy world of ours, find someone willing to commit suicide on the stage, as called for by the script. We would not allow that—any more than we would permit scenes of

real physical torture on the stage, even if the victim were a willing masochist. And I know of no one, no matter how free in spirit, who argues that we ought to permit gladiatorial contests in Yankee Stadium, similar to those once performed in the Colosseum of Rome—even if only consenting adults were involved.[3]

The example of the gladiatorial show, at first sight, satisfies the requirements for argumentative cogency. Almost anyone would concede that the bloody contest would be an evil, and most would be willing to concede (at least at first) that the evil would be in the non-grievance category, since in virtue of the careful observance of the *Volenti* maxim, there would be no aggrieved victim. Moreover, the evil involved, in all of its multiple faces, would be a moral one. It is morally wrong for thousands of observers to experience pleasure at the sight of maiming and killing. It is an obscenely immoral spectacle they voluntarily observe, made even worse by their blood-thirsty screams and vicarious participation. If we reserve the term "immoral," as some have suggested, for *actions,* then the immoralities are compounded and multiplied, for the promoter acts immorally in arranging the contest, advertising it, and selling tickets; each gladiator acts immorally by voluntarily participating; and millions of voluntary spectators share the guilt. If all these individual moral failings can be coherently combined, they add up to a social evil of great magnitude indeed. And yet it seems at first sight that the evil is a non-grievance one, since no one can complain in a personal grievance that he has been wronged.

From liberals who are determined to avoid hypocrisy, Kristol's examples will elicit at least three types of reply. First, Kristol is entirely too complacent about the problem of determining genuine "willingness" and "voluntary consent." The higher the risk of harm involved, the stricter must be the standards, one would think, for voluntariness. When it is a person's very life that is at issue, the standards would have to be at their strictest, especially when the life involved is clearly of great value to its possessor, unlike the life of the would-be suicide suffering from a painful terminal illness. Perhaps, as we have seen, the state would have the right, on liberal principles, to require such things as psychiatric interviews, multiple witnessing, cooling-off periods, and the like, before accepting a proffered consent as fully voluntary. Kristol talks glibly of finding "willing" public suicides in "this crazy world of ours," not noticing that an agreement is hardly consensual if one of the parties is "crazy." To exploit a crazy person in the way he describes is not distinguishable from murder and equally condemned by the harm principle. On the other hand, we must admit that a self-confident and powerful gladiator need not be "crazy" to agree to risk his life before the howling mobs for twenty million dollars. There could be a presumption that such a person doesn't fully understand what he is doing, or is not fully free of neurotic influences on his choice, but these hypotheses are rebuttable in principle, and in some cases that we can easily imagine, with only minor difficulty and expense rebuttable in fact. The liberal's second and third responses (below), then, are the more pertinent ones.

In conceding to the legal moralist that the wholly voluntary contest *is* an "evil" we are not making that judgment primarily because of the injury or death, the utterly "defeated interest," of the losing contestant. That result is an "evil," one might say, because it is regrettable that anyone had to be injured in that way, but so long as we adhere to the doctrine of the absolute priority of personal autonomy that sort of evil is always more than counterbalanced (indeed it is as if cancelled out) by prior consent to the risk. The primary evil relied upon by the legal moralist is not that anyone was harmed (i.e., injured *and* wronged), for no one was, and not that anyone was injured even without being wronged, since that "otherwise evil" is nullified by consent, and there would be an even greater evil, indeed a wrong, if consent were overruled. The fatal maiming of the loser was an "evil" (regrettable state) that he had an absolute right to risk. In reaffirming that right we are making it clear that we are not backtracking on our opposition to paternalism. The acknowledged evil that makes this case a hard one for the liberal is apparently a free-floating one, an evil not directly linked to human interests and sensibilities. That evil consists in the objective regrettability of millions deriving pleasure from brutal bloodshed and others getting rich exploiting their moral weakness. The universe would be an intrinsically better place, the strict legal moralist insists, if that did not occur, even though no one actually was wronged by it, and there is no one to voice a personal grievance at it.

The liberal who is sensitive to the charge of hypocrisy may, in the end, have to reply as follows. Gladiatorial contests and "voluntary" submission to torture are among the most extreme hypothetical examples of non-grievance evils that the legal moralist's imagination can conjure. There seems little likelihood that they will ever occur, at least in the foreseeable future. Yet they seem to be convincing hypothetical examples of very great evils. A liberal might treat them as the limiting case of the "bloated mouse" that has more weight than the undernourished human being. The need to prevent them would be, in his view, one of the very weightiest reasons for coercion that one could plausibly imagine from the category of (merely) free-floating evils. He could then concede that the question of whether they could legitimately be prevented by state coercion is a difficult and close one, and admit this without hypocrisy or inconsistency. He would still hesitate to resort to legal coercion even to prevent the greatest of free-floating evils, simply because he cannot say who is *wronged* by the evils. At any rate, he can concede that the case is close. But the actual examples that people quarrel over:

pornographic films, bawdy houses, obscene books, homosexuality, prostitution, private gambling, soft drugs, and the like, are at most very minor free-floating evils, and at the least, not intuitively evils at all. The liberal can continue to oppose legal prohibitions of them, while acknowledging that the wildly improbable evils in the hypothetical examples of Buckley and Kristol are other kettles of fish. The liberal position least vulnerable to charges of inconsistency and hypocrisy would be the view that the prevention of free-floating evils, while always a relevant reason for coercion, is nevertheless a reason in a generally inferior category, capable of being weighed on the same scale as the presumptive case for liberty only in its most extreme—and thus far only hypothetical—forms.

The preceding paragraph describes a rather uncomfortable fallback position for the liberal who wishes to preserve without hypocrisy what he can of his liberal principles in the face of Kristol's vivid counterexample. Before he settles in to that position, however, he would be well advised to look more carefully at the complex of images and associations we experience when we ponder the example that is supposed to appeal to our "intuitions." What exactly is it about that example that we are responding to when it inclines us toward Kristol's conclusion? Inevitably, I think, we import into the example a nightmare of unconsented-to indirect harms. We naturally set the example in a brutal society full of thugs and bullies who delight in human suffering, whose gladiatorial rituals concentrate and reenforce their callous insensitivity and render it respectable. We cannot hold an image of these wretches in our minds without recoiling, for each of them alone will seem threatening or dangerous, and thousands or millions of them together will be downright terrifying. It is highly difficult, if not plain impossible, to think of widespread indifference to suffering as a mere private moral failing unproductive of further individual and social harm. And so we move quickly (too quickly) in the direction of Kristol's conclusion, ready to endorse with enthusiasm his judgment that the gladiatorial contest would be a huge evil, and to accept uncritically at the same time that the evil would be free-floating.

The immorality of the participants in Kristol's story, then, is not like that of the solitary taboo-breakers or other harmless wrongdoers who can righteously rebuff our interference with the claim that what they do is none of our business. Rather it is an inseparable component of our spontaneous reaction to the story that the wrongdoing and "wrongfeeling" in it powerfully threaten basic human interests and are therefore quite assuredly everybody's business. I have insisted that moral corruption as such is not a relevant ground for preventive criminalization, but when the moral dispositions that are corrupted include concern about the sufferings of others, then the interests of others become vulnerable, and the corrupting activity can no longer be thought to be exclusively self-regarding. Nor are we considering here the mere "speculative tendency" of actions to endanger others, short of a clear and present danger that they will. When the bloody maiming and slaughtering of a human being is considered so thrilling and enjoyable that thousands will pay dearly to witness it, it would seem to follow that thousands are already so brutalized that there is a clear and present danger that some innocent parties (identities now unknown) will suffer at *their* hands. Indeed, it may be too late, in Kristol's gladiator example, to prevent such harms by prohibiting the show. If seventy thousand people will fill Yankee Stadium and enough others will attend closed television showings in theaters to permit the producer to pay thirty million dollars (my example) to the gladiators and still make a profit, then we are as a people already brutalized, and legal coercion, at best, can only treat the symptoms and slow their speed.

Kristol might reply to the above argument as follows. "*I* am writing the story," he might say, "in order to make *my* point. And in *my* version of the story, the spectators, for all their love of gory thrills, are not dangerous to other people. None of them would ever be likely to commit battery, mayhem, or homicide. Perhaps providing them with an orderly outlet for their savage passions makes them even less dangerous than they would otherwise be." In any case, he might say, they resemble in their motives and actions the dutiful wife of the dying invalid who secretly welcomes his sufferings but would never do anything to cause them herself or the honorable bigot who values whites more than blacks but would never intentionally violate the rights of a black. The participating spectators then are, *ex hypothesi*, harmless to others. They all witness the spectacle voluntarily, and the gladiators themselves participate voluntarily, and no third parties are endangered or directly offended, so no one has a grievance. Yet it remains a monstrous moral evil that people should get pleasure in this way from the suffering of others, an evil whose prevention justifies prohibition, even though it is free-floating.

So might Kristol rejoin. But then the liberal reader might reply: "I never thought to interpret your example in *that* way. Indeed, it is highly unlikely that one could cultivate genuine joy at others' suffering without himself becoming more of a danger to others, and it is wildly improbable that hundreds and thousands of spectators could come to be bloodthirsty without constituting a threat to at least *some* of the rest of us. Perhaps what you ask us to assume is psychologically impossible. But never mind; I agree that it is at least *logically* possible that people should be capable of such decompartmentalization in their responses. So have it your way. But now my problem is that the original intuition to which you appealed, that the gladiator show is a sufficiently great evil to counterbalance autonomous liberty on the scales, is now substantially weakened. I can still acknowledge it *is* a free-floating evil that a person derives pleasure from the suffering of others, while now denying that it is the business of the law to interfere." The example of a free-floating evil is now a purer one, but what it has gained in purity it has lost in intuitive forcefulness. Kristol's new mouse would no longer be as bloated as it was.

*   *   *

Kristol's Gladiatorial Contest

The counterexample that gave me the most trouble in the category of free-floating evils (non-grievance evils that are not welfare-connected) was the gladiatorial contest story proposed by Irving Kristol. In Chapter 30, where I considered this proposed counterexample, I wavered in my response between cautious and bold liberalism. There is especially strong incentive to affirm the bold position in the face of arguments that purely free-floating evils should be criminalized, and it is a tribute to the ingenuity of this example that it caused me to waver at all. A *pure* free-floating evil, after all, is nothing that anyone needs protection from in any sense. It neither violates any one's rights nor causes any setback to interests the risk of which had not already been voluntarily accepted by the interest-holder. If the "evil" in question, nevertheless, truly is an evil, then its occurrence is regrettable and the universe as a whole would be a better place without it, but it is nothing that anyone has a right to make a personal complaint (or feel personally aggrieved) about. *I* don't have a right, for example, that *you* think only pure thoughts. That is your business, no one else's. I am not harmed either with or without my consent by your thoughts, and neither are you (necessarily) harmed either. It is better, perhaps, that you not have such thoughts, and regrettable that you do, but no one is made worse off by them, so why bring the law into it at all (one might naturally ask)?

Kristol's example, however, is impure. There is a sense in which the voluntarily produced and witnessed contest *is* a free-floating evil. It is objectively regrettable (to put it mildly) that several hundred thousand adults should derive great pleasure from gory bloodshed, human suffering, and the sight of savage cruelty. When we isolate that grossly inappropriate mass response we find it *very* regrettable indeed and morally revolting even to think about. But who would need protection from it, given that no children are exposed to it and there are no unwilling participants or spectators? To us disapproving outsiders the spectators might all say "It is none of your business." If the isolated free-floating evil (the morally inappropriate response of the audience) were all there was to consider in the example, the slightly fazed liberal might maintain some of his boldness. He might concede that the free-floating evil has some weight on the scales, if only because the moral responses of so many people are so extremely distorted, but he might still deny that preventing the evil has substantial weight, given that it is freely chosen and harmless to the disapproving "others." He can boldly insist, therefore, that the law be kept from interfering, and thereby reject the force of the story as a counterexample.

The free-floating evil in the example, however, is not so easily isolable. The story is drenched in ominous danger. The imagery in the reader's mind includes excited, savage mobs thirsting after the blood of those who have been paid to take extreme risks, but how easily contained or limited is their bloodlust to those who consent? One tries to think of the sorts of people who would enjoy such an experience, and it is hard to bring into focus the image of a "fan" whom one would be prepared to trust outside the arena. The sensitive reader then feels threatened in his imagination as well as re-pelled, and reasons of the harm principle type are on his mind when he judges that "there ought to be a law against it." If one argued against him that for the enthusiastic spectators the contest is a mere healthy catharsis leaving them less prone to violence in ordinary life, he will probably reply not that the contest should be prohibited despite its innocuous character, but rather that the prohibition should hold because he doesn't believe for a minute that it is "innocuous."

Kristol's example is also impure in another way. It not only brings in harm principle considerations, it also naturally implicates legal paternalism and in-cites the paternalist to defend his favored sorts of reasons. The evils in the story include not only free-floating moral evils in the response of the specta-tors and the enrichment of the pandering promoter, but also welfare-con-nected non-grievance evils in the injuries to the gladiators themselves. Taken as an argument in favor of paternalism the example has more initial force. Its form is quite the same as the argument from voluntary slavery in Volume three (pp. 71–81) and the bold liberal will respond in similar ways. The gladiators in principle have a right to risk their lives if they truly wish to do so, but the humane element in the liberal spirit rises to the fore when the liberal thinks about it, and he is moved to ask: "Do they really know what they are doing?" In the end, he will find nonpaternalistic grounds—doubts about voluntariness and appeals to the prevention of public dangers—for refusing permission to the promoter.

Think of how a legalized fight to the death before paying spectators would work. The state would insist on a licensing procedure to confirm voluntariness and protect innocents from indirect dangers. In the begin-ning, the criminal law need not be involved at all. It would be reserved as a back-up sanction to enforce the prohibition of unlicensed promotions. The explicit aim of the contest in the promoter's application for a license would not be the vindication of the combatants' honor, as in a duel; nor would it be to put one of them out of his misery, as in legalized euthanasia. Rather the aim of the combat would be to establish the dominance of one of the combatants, to establish once and for all which of them is the more formidable gladiator, and incidentally to give thrills of the most basic animal kind to the audience. If the combat is to achieve these aims, if it is to be a *contest* at all (as opposed, for example, to a public mugging), it must be governed by fair rules impartially administered. Both wary gladiators would want to insist on that in advance, and most spectators would agree. Without such rules the spectacle might be a mere homicide committed with impunity by a cheater. It might also occur to the contracting contestants, and certainly to the state licensors, that there would be just as much excitement of the primordial thrilling kind if the rule-governed contest were permitted to last only until one party has clearly established his superiority. At that point it could be stopped by an impartial referee appointed by the licensing commission. This would surely make the deal more attractive to the gladiators, and because it would be no less exciting to the spectators, it would be no less remunerative to the promoter and the participants. It might even be *more* attractive to the audience because it is less gruesome, shocking, and heart-breaking. And the appeal of the contest would be not just primitive thrills but also the spectacle of skill and technique, and even strategy and tactics. It would be no less thrilling but much more interesting than a mutual bashing with clubs. In fact, its appeal would be more effective if the weapons that could be used were restricted. The contest would also last longer that way. Just as a pornographic show will be more exciting if more subtle, the performers teasing their audiences along rather than being unrestrained and fully naked from the start, so the fighting match will be more thrilling if the battlers are less destructive.

Given the greater reasonableness all around of the sublimated type of contest, and especially its lesser risks to the pugilists themselves, it would bring into question how truly voluntary the participants' insistence on combat to the death with lethal weapons would be. Unreasonableness is not the same thing as involuntariness, of course, but extreme unreasonableness creates a strong presumption of nonvoluntariness that would be difficult to rebut, and the state might even be justified in making the presumption conclusive for practical reasons. The sublimated form of contest would also be less likely to cause harm to others by leading to a general coarsening of sympathies and a sharpening of lethal impulses in real life. In short, the arrangement most appealing to promoter, participants, audience, and the state in its role as protector of the public, would resemble our own boxing, wrestling, and fencing matches, not the barbarous killings in Kristol's example, and a liberal state would have many reasons for refusing to license the latter. Liberalism might remain bold in the face of the Kristol example, even though the liberal concedes some weight to preventing the evil of exploitation by pandering and the evil of inappropriate thrills at the sight of injuries being inflicted on a human being.

Notes

1. William F. Buckley, Jr., "Death for Gilmore?" *New York Times Magazine,* December 7, 1976, p. 32.

2. *The New York Times,* editorial, March 10, 1971.

3. Irving Kristol, "Pornography, Obscenity, and the Case for Censorship," *The New York Times Magazine,* March 28, 1971.

5 Impartiality and Standing

THOMAS NAGEL

Moral Conflict and Political Legitimacy

I

Robert Frost defined a liberal as someone who can't take his own side in an argument. A bit harsh, but there is something paradoxical about liberalism, at least on the surface, and something obscure about the foundations of the sort of impartiality that liberalism professes. That is what I want to discuss.

Ethics always has to deal with the conflict between the personal standpoint of the individual and some requirement of impartiality. The personal standpoint will bring in motives derived not only from the individual's interests but also from his attachments and commitments to people, projects, and particular things. The requirement of impartiality can take various forms, but it usually involves treating or counting everyone equally in some respect—according them all the same rights, or counting their good or their welfare or some aspect of it the same in determining what would be a desirable result or a permissible course of action. Since personal motives and impartiality can conflict, an ethical theory has to say something about how such conflicts are to be resolved. It may do this by according total victory to the impartial side in case of conflict, but that is only one solution.

The clash between impartiality and the viewpoint of the individual is compounded when we move from personal ethics to political theory. The reason is that in politics, where we are all competing to get the coercive power of the state behind the institutions we favor—institutions under which all of us will have to live—it is not only our personal interests, attachments, and commitments that bring us into conflict, but our different moral conceptions. Political competitors differ as to both the form and the content of the impartial component of morality. They differ over what is good and bad in human life, and what kind of equal respect or consideration we owe each other. Their political disagreements therefore reflect not only conflicts of interest but conflicts over the values that public institutions should serve, impartially, for everyone.

Is there a higher-order impartiality that can permit us to come to some understanding about how such disagreements should be settled? Or have we already gone as far as necessary (and perhaps even as far as possible) in taking up other people's point of view when we have accepted the impartial component of our own moral position? I believe that liberalism depends on the acceptance of a higher-order impartiality, and that this raises serious problems about how the different orders of impartiality are to be integrated. To some extent this parallels the familiar problem in moral theory of integrating impartiality with personal motives; but the problem here is more complicated, and the motive for higher-order impartiality is more obscure.[1]

It is so obscure that critics of liberalism often doubt that its professions of impartiality are made in good faith. Part of the problem is that liberals ask of everyone a certain restraint in calling for the use of state power to further specific, controversial moral or religious conceptions—but the results of that restraint appear with suspicious frequency to favor precisely the controversial moral conceptions that liberals usually hold.

For example, those who argue against the restriction of pornography or homosexuality or contraception on the ground that the state should not attempt to enforce contested personal standards of morality often don't think there is anything wrong with pornography, homosexuality, or contraception. They would be against such restrictions even if they believed it *was* the state's business to enforce personal morality, or if they believed that the state could legitimately be asked to prohibit anything simply on the ground that it was wrong.

More generally, liberals tend to place a high value on individual freedom, and limitations on state interference based on a higher-order impartiality among values tends to promote the individual freedom to which liberals are partial. This leads to the suspicion that the escalation to a higher level of impartiality is a sham, and that all the pleas for toleration and restraint really disguise a campaign to put the state behind a secular, individualistic, and libertine morality—against religion and in favor of sex, roughly.

Yet liberalism purports to be a view that justifies religious toleration not only to religious skeptics but to the devout, and sexual toleration not only to libertines but to those who believe extramarital sex is sinful. Its good faith is to some degree attested in the somewhat different area of free expression, for there liberals in the United States have long defended the rights of those they detest. The American Civil Liberties Union is usually glad of the chance to defend the Nazis when they want to demonstrate somewhere. It shows that liberals are willing to restrain the state from stopping something that they think is wrong—for we can assume most supporters of the ACLU think both that it is wrong to be a Nazi and that it is wrong for the Nazis to demonstrate in Skokie.

Another current example is that of abortion. At least some who oppose its legal prohibition believe that it is morally wrong, but that their reasons for this belief cannot justify the use of state power against those who are convinced otherwise. This is a difficult case, to which I shall refer again.

Of course liberalism is not merely a doctrine of toleration, and liberals all have more specific interests and values, some of which they will seek to support through the agency of the state. But the question of what kind of impartiality is appropriate arises there as well. Both in the prohibition of what is wrong and in the promotion of what is good, the point of view from which state action and its institutional framework are supposed to be justified is complex and in some respects obscure. I shall concentrate on the issue of toleration, and shall often use the example of religious toleration. But the problem also arises in the context of distributive justice and promotion of the general welfare—for we have to use some conception of what is good for people in deciding what to distribute and what to promote, and the choice of that conception raises similar questions of impartiality.[2]

II

This question is part of the wider issue of political legitimacy—the history of attempts to discover a way of justifying coercively imposed political and social institutions to the people who have to live under them, and at the same time to discover what those institutions must be like if such justification is to be possible. "Justification" here does not mean "persuasion." It is a normative concept: arguments that justify may fail to persuade, if addressed to an unreasonable audience; and arguments that persuade may fail to justify. Nevertheless, justifications hope to persuade the reasonable, so these attempts have a practical point: political stability is helped by wide agreement to the principles underlying a political order. But that is not all: for some, the possibility of justifying the system to as many participants as possible is of independent moral importance. Of course this is an ideal. Given the actual range of values, interests, and motives in a society, and depending on one's standards of justification, there may not be a legitimate solution, and then one will have to choose between illegitimate government and no government.

The practical and the moral issues of political motivation are intertwined. On the one hand, the motivations that are morally required of us must be practically and psychologically possible, otherwise our political theory will be utopian in the bad sense. On the other hand, moral argument and insight can reveal and explain the possibility of political motivations which cannot be assumed in advance of moral discussion. In this way, political theory may have an effect on what motives are practically available to ground legitimacy, and therefore stability.

Defenses of political legitimacy are of two kinds: those which discover a possible *convergence* of rational support for certain institutions from the separate motivational standpoints of distinct individuals; and those which seek a *common standpoint* that everyone can occupy, which guarantees agreement on what is acceptable. There are also political arguments that mix the convergence and common standpoint methods.

A convergence theory may begin from motives that differ widely from person to person, or it may begin from a single type of motive, like self-interest, which differs from person to person only because it is self-referential. In either case, the difference of starting points means that the motivational base itself does not guarantee that there is a social result which everyone will find desirable. A common standpoint theory, by contrast, starts from a single desire that is not self-referential, and this guarantees a common social aim, provided people can agree on the facts.

Hobbes, the founder of modern political theory, is a convergence theorist par excellence. Starting from a premoral motive that each individual has, the concern for his own survival and security, Hobbes argues that it is rational for all of us to converge from this self-referential starting point on the desirability of a system in which general obedience to certain rules of conduct is enforced by a sovereign of unlimited power. This is a convergence theory because the motive from which each of us begins refers only to his own survival and security, and it is entirely contingent that there should be any outcome that all of us can accept equally on those grounds: our personal motives could in principle fail to point us toward a common goal. And as is generally true of convergence theories, the political result is thought to be right because it is rationally acceptable to all, rather than being rationally acceptable to all because it is by some independent standard right.

Utilitarianism, on the other hand, is an example of a common standpoint theory. It asks each person to evaluate political institutions on the basis of a common moral motive which makes no reference to himself.[3] If all do take up this point of view of impartial benevolence, it will automatically follow that they have reason to accept the same solutions—since they are judging in light of a common desire for everyone's happiness. A political result is then rationally acceptable to everyone because by the utilitarian standard it is right; it is not right because it is universally acceptable.

There are other types of convergence theories—notably those which find political legitimacy in a compromise among conflicting economic, social, and religious interests, acceptable to all as an alternative to social breakdown. And common standpoint theories can be based on motives other than general benevolence—commitment to the protection of certain individual rights, rejection of severe social and economic inequalities, even nationalism or a shared religious commitment.

But what I want to concentrate on is a type of mixed theory that is characteristic of contemporary liberalism. Recent political philosophy has seen the development of a new type of liberal theory, exemplified by the work of

Rawls and others, whose distinctive feature is that it bases the legitimacy of institutions on their conformity to principles which it would be reasonable for disparate individuals to agree on, where the standard of individual reasonableness is not merely a premoral rationality, but rather a form of reasoning that includes moral motives. In contrast with Hobbesian convergence, reasonable agreement is in these theories sought by each person as an end and not merely as a means, necessary for social stability. At the same time, the moral motives which contribute to convergence are not sufficient by themselves to pick out an acceptable result: more individual motives also enter into the process. So the principles converged on are right because they are acceptable—not generally acceptable because they are by independent standards morally right.

With regard to Rawls, I am referring here not to the reasoning inside the Original Position (from which moral motives are excluded), but to the wider argument within which the Original Position plays a subsidiary role, the argument that we should regulate our claims on our common institutions by the principles that *would* be chosen in the Original Position.

It may seem surprising to characterize Rawl's theory as a mixed theory, for in asking us all to enter the Original Position to choose principles of justice, he seems simply to be proposing a common standpoint of impartiality which guarantees that we will all approve of the same thing. But an important element of Rawl's argument is his reference to the strains of commitment: even in the Original Position, not knowing his own conception of the good, each person can choose only such principles of justice as he believes he will be able to live under and continue to affirm in actual life, when he knows the things about himself and his position in society that are concealed by the Veil of Ignorance.[4] This introduces an element of convergence.[5]

True principles of justice are those which can be affirmed by individuals motivated both by the impartial sense of justice as fairness and by their fundamental personal interests, commitments, and conceptions of the good. As with other convergence theories, it is not logically guaranteed that there are such principles, but if there are, they will be shaped by the requirement of such convergence, and their rightness will not be demonstrable independent of that possibility. That is what Rawls means by describing the theory as a form of constructivism.

The other position I would like to mention is T. M. Scanlon's. The criterion of moral wrongness he proposes in "Contractualism and Utilitarianism" employs the notion of a rule which no one could reasonably reject, provided he had among his motives a desire to live under rules which no one who also had that motive could reasonably reject. This notion can be used to construct a mixed theory of political legitimacy, where the common standpoint is represented by the said harmonious desire and convergence enters because what people can and cannot reasonably reject is determined in part by their other, divergent motives as well.

Note that the standard is not what principles or institutions people will *actually accept,* but what it would be unreasonable for them not to accept, given a certain common moral motivation in addition to their more personal, private, and communal ends. As with Rawls, there would be no standard of political legitimacy or rightness independent of this possibility of convergence.

It is a distinctive feature of both these theories that they set moral limits to the use of political power to further not only familiar social and economic interest, but also moral convictions. They are mixed theories based not just on a mixture of benevolence and self-concern, but on limits to the *content* of benevolence. They distinguish between the values a person can appeal to in conducting his own life and those he can appeal to in justifying the exercise of political power.

III

What I want to know is whether a position of this type is coherent and defensible. I am concerned less with the specific views of Rawls or Scanlon than with the fundamental moral idea behind such a position, which is that we should not impose arrangements, institutions, or requirements on other people on grounds that they could reasonably reject (where reasonableness is not simply a function of the independent rightness or wrongness of the arrangements in question, but genuinely depends on the point of view of the individual to some extent). The question is whether an interpretation of this condition, or something like it, can be found which makes it plausible, despite an initial appearance of paradox.

It is not clear why the possibility of this kind of convergence should be the standard of political legitimacy at all. Why should I care whether others with whom I disagree can accept or reject the grounds on which state power is exercised? Why shouldn't I discount their rejection if it is based on religious or moral or cultural values that I believe to be mistaken? Why allow my views of the legitimate use of state power to become hostage to what it would be reasonable for *them* to accept or reject? Can't I instead base those views on the values that I believe to be correct?

An antiliberal critic of Rawls could put the point by asking why he should agree to be governed by principles that he would choose if he did not know his own religious beliefs, or his conception of the good. Isn't that being *too* impartial, giving too much authority to those whose values conflict with yours—betraying your own values, in fact? If I believe something, I believe it to be *true,* yet here I am asked to refrain from acting on that belief in deference to beliefs I think are false. What possible moral motivation could I have for doing that? Impartiality among persons is one thing, but impartiality among conceptions of the good is quite another. Why isn't true justice giving everyone the best possible chance of salvation, for example, or of a good life? In other words, don't we have to start from the values that we ourselves accept in deciding how state power may legitimately be used?

And it might be added, are we not doing that anyway if we adopt the liberal standard of impartiality? Not everyone believes that political legitimacy depends on this condition, and if we forcibly impose political institutions because they do meet it (and block the imposition of institutions that do not), why are we not being just as partial to our own values as someone who imposes a state religion? It has to be explained why this is a form of impartiality at all.

To answer these questions we have to identify the moral conception involved and see whether it has the authority to override those more particular moral conceptions that divide us—and if so, to what extent or in what respects. Rawls has said in a recent article that if liberalism had to depend on a commitment to comprehensive moral ideals of autonomy and individuality, it would become just "another sectarian doctrine."[6] The question is whether its claim to be something else has any foundation.

IV

If liberalism is to be defended as a higher-order theory rather than just another sectarian doctrine, it must be shown to result from an interpretation of impartiality itself, rather than from a particular conception of the good that is to be made impartially available. Of course any interpretation of impartiality will be morally controversial—it is not a question of rising to a vantage point above all moral disputes—but the controversy will be at a different level.

In the versions of liberalism formulated by Rawls, Ronald Dworkin, and Bruce Ackerman, exclusion of appeal to particular conceptions of the good at the most basic level of political argument is one of the ways in which it is required that social institutions should treat people equally or impartially. But since this is much less obvious than the requirements of impartiality with respect to race, sex, social class, or even natural endowments, it requires a special explanation by reference to more fundamental moral ideas. The requirement itself may be modified as a result of the explanation: the proposal I end up with does not correspond perfectly to the views from which I begin.[7]

What form should impartiality take, in the special conditions which are the province of political theory? The specialness of the conditions is important. We have to be impartial not just in the conferring of benefits, but in the imposition of burdens, the exercise of coercion to ensure compliance with a uniform set of requirements, and the demand for support of the institutions that impose those requirements and exercise that coercion. (Even if the support is not voluntarily given, it will to some degree be exacted, if only through payment of taxes and passive conformity to certain institutional arrangements.) I suggest that this element of coercion imposes an especially stringent requirement of objectivity in justification.[8]

If someone wishes simply to benefit others, there can in my view be no objection if he gives them what is good by his own lights (so long as he does them no harm by theirs). If someone wants to pray for the salvation of my soul, I can't really complain on the ground that I would rather he gave me a subscription to *Playboy*. The problem arises when he wants to force me to attend church or pay for its upkeep instead of staying home and reading *Playboy*. The real problem is how to justify making people do things against their will.

We can leave aside the familiar and unproblematic Hobbesian basis for coercion: I may want to be forced to do something as part of a practice whereby everyone else is forced to do the same, with results that benefit us all in a way that would not be possible unless we could be assured of widespread compliance. This is not really forcing people to do what they don't want to do, but rather enabling them to do what they want to do by forcing them to do it.

There are two other types of coercion whose justification seems clear: prevention of harm to others and certain very basic forms of paternalism. In both these types of case, we can make an impersonal appeal to values that are generally shared: people don't want to be injured, robbed, or killed, and they don't want to get sick. The nature of those harms and the impersonal value of avoiding them are uncontroversial, and can be appealed to to justify forcibly preventing their infliction. From an impersonal standpoint I can agree that anyone, myself included, should be prevented from harming others in those ways.

I can also agree that under some conditions I should be prevented from harming myself in those ways, as should anyone else. The clear conditions include my being crazy or seriously demented, or radically misinformed about the likely results of what I am doing. Paternalism is justified in such cases because when we look at them from outside, we find no impersonal value competing with the values of health, life, and safety. If I say I would want to be prevented from drinking lye during a psychotic episode, it is not because the dangers of internal corrosion outweigh the value of self-expression. We are not faced here with a conflict of impartialities.

But in other cases we are. I have gone over these familiar examples for the sake of contrast. There are cases where forcing someone to do what he doesn't want to do is problematic—not just because he doesn't want to do it, but because of his reasons for not wanting to do it. The problematic cases are those in which either the impersonal value to which I appeal to justify coercion would not be acknowledged by the one coerced, or else it conflicts with another impersonal value to which he subscribes but which I do not acknowledge, though I would if I were he. In such a case it seems that I shall have failed in some respect to be impartial whether I coerce him or not.

An example may help. I am not a Christian Scientist. If I ask myself whether, thinking of it from outside, I would want to be forced to undergo medical treatment if I *were* a Christian Scientist and had a treatable illness, it is hard to know what to say. On the one hand, given my beliefs, I am inclined to give no impersonal weight to the reasons I would offer for refusing treatment if I were a Christian Scientist, and substantial weight to the medical reasons in favor of treatment. After all, if I believe Christian Science is false, I believe it would be false even if I believed it was true. On the other hand, I am inclined to give considerable impersonal weight to the broader consideration of not wanting others to ride roughshod over my beliefs on the subject of religion, whatever they may be.

Or suppose a Roman Catholic who believes that outside the Church there is no salvation asks himself whether if he were not a Catholic he would want to be given strong incentives to accept the Catholic faith, perhaps by state support of the Church and legal discouragement of other religions.[9] He may be torn between the impartial application of his actual religious values and the impartial application of a more general value that he also holds, of not wanting other people's religious convictions to be imposed on him.

Which of these should dominate? It is really a problem about the interpretation of the familiar role-reversal argument in ethics: "How would you like it if someone did that to you?" The answer that has to be dealt with is "How would I like it if someone did *what* to me?" There is often more than one way of describing a proposed course of action, and much depends on which description is regarded as relevant for the purpose of moral argument.

V

This general problem is familiar in the context of interpreting universalizability conditions in ethics, but I am thinking of a particular version of it. Should a Catholic, considering restriction of freedom of worship and religious education for Protestants from an impersonal standpoint, think of it as

    (1) preventing them from putting themselves and others in danger of eternal damnation;

    (2) promoting adherence to the true faith;

    (3) promoting adherence to the Catholic faith;

    (4) preventing them from practicing their religion; or

    (5) preventing them from doing something they want to do?

For the purpose of argument, let me suppose that as far as he is concerned, he would be doing all of these things. The question then is, which of them determines how he should judge the proposed restriction from an impersonal standpoint?

The defense of liberalism depends on rejecting (5) as the relevant description, and then stopping with (4) rather than going on to (2) or (1). Roughly, the liberal position avoids two contrary errors. To accept as an authoritative impersonal value everyone's interest in doing what he wants to do, for whatever reason (that is, to rely on description [5]), is to give too much authority to other people's preferences in determining their claims on us. To accord impersonal weight to our own values, whatever they are (that is, to rely on descriptions [1] and [2]), is on the other hand not to give others enough authority over what we may require of them.

The characteristic of description (4) that the others lack is that it has some chance of both (a) being accepted by all parties concerned as a true description of what is going on (something it shares with [3] and [5]), and (b) being accorded the same kind of impersonal value by all parties concerned (something it shares, more or less, with [1] and [2]).

This makes (4) a natural choice for the morally relevant description which provides a basis for impartial assessment. However several objections have to be dealt with.

First, why isn't (5) at least as impartial as (4)? No one wants to be prevented from doing what he wants to do. Why can't we all agree that impersonal value should be assigned to people's doing or getting what they want, rather than to something more restricted like freedom of worship?

But the fact is that we cannot. To assign impersonal value to the satisfaction of all preferences is to accept a particular view of the good—a component of one form of utilitarianism—which many would find clearly unacceptable and which they would not be unreasonable to reject.[10] The objection to making it the basis of political legitimacy parallels the objection to making any other comprehensive individual conception of the good the basis of political and social institutions. A liberal who is a utilitarian should no more impose his conception of the good on others than should a liberal who is a Roman Catholic or a devotee of aesthetic perfection—that is, he should pursue the good so conceived for himself and others only within the limits imposed by a higher-order impartiality.

This reply, however, leads to another objection: If (5) is ruled out, why shouldn't (4) be ruled out for parallel reasons? The value of liberty seems more neutral than the value of preference-satisfaction, but perhaps it is not. The problem with assigning impersonal value to the satisfaction of preferences per se (description [5]) is that if a nonutilitarian is asked, "How would you like to be prevented from doing something you want to do?" he can reply, "That depends on what it is, and why I want to do it." A similar move might be made against assigning uniform impersonal value to religious toleration (description [4]). If a Catholic is asked, "How would you like to be prevented from practicing your religion?" why can't he reply, "That depends on whether it's the true religion or not"?

But in that case we are left with no version of what is going on that permits a common description resulting in a common impersonal assessment. If the description can be agreed on the assessment cannot be, and vice versa. Impartiality has been ruled out.

VI

A solution to this impasse requires that we find a way of being impartial not only in the allocation of benefits or harms but in their identification. The defense of liberalism requires that a limit somehow be drawn to appeals to *the truth* in political argument, and that a standpoint be found from which to draw that limit. It may seem paradoxical that a general condition of impartiality should claim greater authority than more special conceptions which one believes to be, simply, true—and that it should lead us to defer to conceptions which we believe to be false—but that is the position.

Gerald Dworkin discusses this issue in an essay called "Non-neutral Principles." He means principles like "The true religion should be taught in the public schools"—whose application to particular cases "is a matter of controversy for the parties whose conduct is supposed to be regulated by the principle in question."[11]

Dworkin argues that the liberal position has to rest on a skeptical epistemological premise—"that one cannot arrive at justified belief in religious matters."[12] That, he claims, is the only possible justification for suppressing knowledge of the parties' religious beliefs in Rawls's Original Position—a condition essential to Rawls's argument for tolerance. "If there were a truth and it could be ascertained," asks Dworkin, "would those in the original position who contemplated the possibility that they would be holders of false views regard their integrity as harmed by choosing that it [sic] should be suppressed?"[13]

Rawls, however, claims that his position depends on no such skepticism.[14] "We may observe," he says, "that men's having an equal liberty of conscience is consistent with the idea that all men ought to obey God and accept the truth. The problem of liberty is that of choosing a principle by which the claims men make on one another in the name of their religion are to be regulated. Granting that God's will should be followed and the truth recognized does not as yet define a principle of adjudication."[15]

He intends to put forward not a skeptical position about religious knowledge but a restriction on the sorts of convictions that can be appealed to in political argument. In his recent discussion he says: "It is important to stress that from other points of view, for example, from the point of view of personal morality, or from the point of view of members of an association, or of one's religious or philosophical doctrine, various aspects of the world and one's relation to it, may be regarded in a different way. But these other points of view are not to be introduced into political discussion."[16]

I believe that true liberalism requires that something like Rawls's view be correct, that is, that exclusion of the appeal to religious convictions not rely on a skeptical premise about individual belief. Rather it must depend on a distinction between what justifies individual belief and what justifies appealing to that belief in support of the exercise of political power. As I have said, liberalism should provide the devout with a reason for tolerance.

But is Rawls right? It is not sufficient to exclude knowledge of one's religious beliefs from the Original Position on the ground that this is needed to make agreement possible. The question is whether there is a viable form of impartiality that makes it possible to exclude such factors from the basis of one's acceptance of political institutions, or whether, alternatively, we have to give up the hope of liberal legitimacy.

I believe that the demand for agreement, and its priority in these cases over a direct appeal to the truth, must be grounded in something more basic. Though it has to do with epistemology, it is not skepticism but a kind of epistemological restraint: the distinction between what is needed to justify belief and what is needed to justify the employment of political power depends on a higher standard of objectivity, which is ethically based.

The distinction results, I believe, if we apply the general form of moral thought that underlies liberalism to the familiar fact that while I cannot maintain a belief without implying that what I believe is true, I still have to acknowledge that there is a big difference, looking at it from the outside, between my believing something and its being true.

On the view I would defend, there is a highest-order framework of moral reasoning (not the whole of morality) which takes us outside ourselves to a standpoint that is independent of who we are. It cannot derive its basic premises from aspects of our particular and contingent starting points within the world, though it may authorize reliance on such specialized points of view if this is justified from the more universal perspective. Since individuals are very different from one another and must lead complex individual lives, the universal standpoint cannot reasonably withhold this authorization lightly. But it is most likely to be withheld from attempts to claim the authority of the impersonal standpoint for a point of view that is in fact that of a particular individual or party, against that of other individuals or parties who reject that point of view. This happens especially in the political or social imposition of institutions that control our lives, that we cannot escape, and that are maintained by force.

Morality can take us outside ourselves in different ways or to different degrees. The first and most familiar step is to recognize that what we want

should not depend only on our own interests and desires—that from outside, other people's interests matter as much as ours do, and we should want
to reconcile our interests with theirs as far as possible. But liberal impartiality
goes beyond this, by trying to make the epistemological standpoint of
morality impersonal as well.

The idea is that when we look at certain of our convictions from outside,
however justified they may be from within, the appeal to their truth must be
seen merely as an appeal to our beliefs, and should be treated as such unless
those beliefs can be shown to be justifiable from a more impersonal standpoint. If not, they have to remain, for the purpose of a certain kind of moral
argument, features of a personal perspective—to be respected as such but no
more than that.

This does not mean we have to stop believing them—that is, believing
them to be *true*. Considered as individual beliefs they may be adequately
grounded, or at least not unreasonable: the standards of individual rationality are different from the standards of epistemological ethics. It means
only that from the perspective of political argument we may have to regard
certain of our beliefs, whether moral or religious or even historical or scientific, simply as someone's beliefs, rather than as truths—unless they can be
given the kind of impersonal justification appropriate to that perspective, in
which case they may be appealed to as truths without qualification.

We accept a kind of epistemological division between the private and the
public domains: in certain contexts I am constrained to consider my beliefs
merely as beliefs rather than as truths, however convinced I may be that they
are true, and that I know it. This is not the same thing as skepticism. Of
course if I believe something I believe it to be true. I can recognize the
possibility that what I believe may be false, but I cannot with respect to any
particular present belief of mine think that possibility is realized. Nevertheless, it is possible to separate my attitude toward my belief from my attitude
toward the thing believed, and to refer to my belief alone rather than to its
truth in certain contexts of justification.

The reason is that unless there is some way of applying from an impersonal standpoint the distinction between my believing something and its
being true, an appeal to its truth is equivalent to an appeal to my belief in its
truth. To show that the two are not equivalent I would have to show how
the distinction could be applied, in political argument, in a way that did not
surreptitiously assume my personal starting point—by, for example, defining
objective truth in terms of the religion to which I adhere, or the beliefs I
now hold. I have to be able to admit that I might turn out to be wrong, by
some standards that those who disagree with me but are also committed to
the impersonal standpoint can also acknowledge. The appeal to truth as opposed to belief is compatible with disagreement among the parties—but it

must imply the possibility of some standard to which an impersonal appeal can be made, even if it cannot settle our disagreement at the moment.

VII

The real difficulty is to make sense of this idea, the idea of something which is neither an appeal to my own beliefs nor an appeal to beliefs that we all share. It cannot be the latter because it is intended precisely to justify the forcible imposition in some cases of measures that are not universally accepted. We need a distinction between two kinds of disagreement—one whose grounds make it all right for the majority to use political power in the service of their opinion, and another whose grounds are such that it would be wrong for the majority to do so.

For this purpose we cannot appeal directly to the distinction between reasonable and unreasonable beliefs. It would be an impossibly restrictive condition on political power to say that its exercise may be justified only by appeal to premises that others could not reasonably reject (though less restrictive than the condition that the premises be *actually* accepted by all). If the impossibility of reasonable rejection comes in at all, it must come in at a higher level, in justifying some less stringent standard for the justification of particular employments of political power.

Reasonable persons can disagree not only over religious doctrines and ultimate conceptions of the good life, but over levels of public provision of education and health care, social security, defense policy, environmental preservation, and a host of other things that liberal societies determine by legislative action. What distinguishes those disagreements from the ones where liberalism rejects majority rule? When can I regard the grounds for a belief as objective in a way that permits me to appeal to it in political argument, and to rely on it even though others do not in fact accept it and even though they may not be unreasonable not to accept it? What kinds of grounds must those be, if I am not to be guilty of appealing simply to my belief, rather than to a common ground of justification?

By a common ground I do not mean submerged agreement on a set of premises by which the claim could in principle be settled in a way that all parties would recognize as correct. Public justification in a context of actual disagreement requires, first, preparedness to submit one's reasons to the criticism of others, and to find that the exercise of a common critical rationality and consideration of evidence that can be shared will reveal that one is mistaken. This means that it must be possible to present to others the basis of your own beliefs, so that once you have done so, *they have what you have,* and can arrive at a judgment on the same basis. That is not possible if part of the source of your conviction is personal faith or revelation—because to report your faith or revelation to someone else is not to give him what you have, as you do when you show him your evidence or give him your arguments.

Public justification requires, second, an expectation that if others who do not share your belief are wrong, there is probably an explanation of their error which is not circular. That is, the explanation should not come down to the mere assertion that they do not believe the truth (what you believe), but should explain their false belief in terms of errors in their evidence, or identifiable errors in drawing conclusions from it, or in argument, judgment, and so forth. One may not always have the information necessary to give such an account, but one must believe there is one, and that the justifiability of one's own belief would survive a full examination of the reasons behind theirs. These two points may be combined in the idea that a disagreement which falls on objective common ground must be open-ended in the possibility of its investigation and pursuit, and not come down finally to a bare confrontation between incompatible personal points of view. I suggest that conflicts of religious faith fail this test, and most empirical and many moral disagreements do not.

The large question I have not addressed is whether there are significant differences of fundamental moral opinion which also fail the test—and if so, how the line is to be drawn between those cases and others, which fall into the public domain. My sense is that the sort of liberal restraint I have been describing should apply, in the present state of moral debate, to certain matters besides the enforcement of religious views. I would include abortion, sexual conduct, and the killing of animals for food, for example. Admittedly, if we refrain from enforcing any moral position on these matters, it has the same effect as we would get if the law were based on the positive position that whatever people choose to do in these areas is permissible. But the two justifications for restraint are very different, and if I am right, the first is available to those who may not accept the second.

To defend this claim would require serious analysis of the issues. I would try to argue that such disagreements come down finally to a pure confrontation between personal moral convictions, and that this is perceptibly different from a disagreement in judgment over the preponderant weight of reasons bearing on an issue. Of course there are reasons and arguments on both sides, but they come to an end in a different and more personal way than arguments about welfare payments or affirmative action, for example. This does not mean that such disagreements cannot move into the public category through further development of common grounds of argument. But at any given stage, the justifications on opposite sides of an issue may come to an end with moral instincts which are simply internal to the points of view of the opposed parties—and this makes them more like conflicts of personal religious conviction.

I realize that this is vague. It also raises a further problem: Why can't the same be said of some fundamental issues that clearly fall within the public domain? Aren't people's disagreements about the morality of nuclear deterrence and the death penalty just as ultimate and personal as their disagreements over abortion?

The question requires much more discussion than I can give it here. Briefly, these issues are poor candidates for liberal toleration because they are not matters of individual conduct, which the state may or may not decide to regulate. So no conclusion about what the state should do can be derived from the refusal to justify the use of state power by reference to any particular position on the moral issue. The application of the death penalty or the possession by the military of nuclear weapons cannot be left to the private conscience of each individual citizen: the state *must* decide.[17]

The same question might also be raised about fundamental issues of social justice—the conflicts of economic liberals with radical libertarians, or with radical collectivists who regard individualism as an evil. Here I would give a more complex answer. I do not believe these moral oppositions are as "personal" as the others: even radical disagreements about freedom and distributive justice are usually part of some recognizable public argument. On the other hand, social provision is not so essentially the function of the state as is warfare: voluntary collective action is certainly possible. So to the extent that some of these disagreements are like religious disagreements, there would be a place for liberal toleration in the economic sphere—for example, toleration of private ownership even by those who think it is an evil. . . .

Notes

1. Leading contemporary examples of philosophical liberalism are: John Rawls, *A Theory of Justice* (Cambridge: Harvard University Press, 1971); Ronald Dworkin, "Liberalism," in *Public and Private Morality*, ed. Stuart Hampshire (Cambridge: Cambridge University Press, 1978); Bruce Ackerman, *Social Justice in the Liberal State* (New Haven: Yale University Press, 1980); T. M. Scanlon, "Contractualism and Utilitarianism," in *Utilitarianism and Beyond*, ed. Amartya Sen and Bernard Williams (Cambridge: Cambridge University Press, 1982).

2. See T. M. Scanlon, "Preference and Urgency," *Journal of Philosophy* 72 (1975)—an essay to which I am much indebted.

3. I am thinking of utilitarianism in a modern version, associated with Sidgwick. In Bentham and Mill, the motives that lead to compliance with the principle of utility are various, and not related to its truth.

4. *A Theory of Justice*, p. 176.

5. This observation comes from Scanlon, "Contractualism and Utilitarianism," p. 126. Another interpretation has been suggested to me, however, by Warren Quinn. Perhaps the strains of commitment are simply strains it is unfair to impose on people, and this is shown by our unwillingness, in the Original Position, to choose principles which carry the risk of subjecting us to those strains. This would restore Rawls to the common standpoint category.

6. "Justice as Fairness: Political not Metaphysical," *Philosophy & Public Affairs*, vol. 14, no. 3 (Summer 1985): 246.

7. Rawls himself treats these issues from a somewhat different point of view in the article just mentioned and in his H. L. A. Hart Lecture, "The Idea of an Overlapping Consensus," *Oxford*

Journal of Legal Studies, in press. I shall not try to compare our approaches here, except to say that mine seems to depend less on actual consensus, and seeks an independent moral argument that can be offered to those holding widely divergent values.

8. This would be implied, on one reading, by the second formulation of Kant's categorical imperative—that one should treat humanity never merely as a means, but always also as an end. If you force someone to serve an end that he cannot share, you are treating him as a mere means— even if the end is his own good, as you see it (*Foundations of the Metaphysics of Morals,* Prussian Academy edition, pp. 429–30). See Onora O'Neill, "Between Consenting Adults," *Philosophy & Public Affairs,* vol. 14, no. 3 (Summer 1985): 261–63; and Christine M. Korsgaard, "The Right to Lie: Kant on Dealing with Evil," *Philosophy and Public Affairs,* vol. 15, no. 4 (Fall 1986): 330–34.

9. "He would want," in these examples, is not a conditional prediction of what his desires would be in those circumstances; rather, it refers to what he *now* wants to happen should those counterfactual circumstances obtain—as in the statement "I would want to be restrained if I tried to drink lye during a psychotic episode." The "want" goes outside rather than inside the conditional.

10. See Scanlon, "Preference and Urgency."

11. *Journal of Philosophy* 71 (1974): 492.

12. Ibid., p. 505.

13. Ibid., pp. 503–4.

14. *A Theory of Justice,* pp. 214–15.

15. Ibid., pp. 217–18.

16. "Justice as Fairness: Political not Metaphysical," p. 231.

17. Conscientious objection is another matter: its legal acceptance can probably be explained by the liberal principle I am defending.

GERALD J. POSTEMA

Public Faces—Private Places: Liberalism and the Enforcement of Morality

> *Private faces in public places*
> *Are wiser and nicer*
> *Than public faces in private places.*
> —W. H. Auden

1   Introduction

Liberals insist on a distinction between public and private departments of morality. While both departments, according to liberals, make valid claims on our behaviour and attitudes, only public morality can legitimately call on the law to underwrite and enforce its demands. They insist on the importance of public morality, publicly recognized and enforced by law, existing alongside a realm of private morality, jealously guarded by law against intrusion by government. Joel Feinberg recently expressed the liberal view well: "The question [for the liberal] is not whether society can pass judgment at all in matters of morals, but rather which matters of morals are its proper business."

In contrast, conservative critics of liberalism hold the stronger thesis that there is no matter of genuine moral concern that is not, in principle at least, a proper basis for legislation. They reject any deep distinction between 'departments' of morality. According to Devlin, it is "no more possible to define a sphere of private morality than it is to define one of private subversive activity."[1] Morality, on this view, is a seamless web. Thus, if society can with justification legally enforce *any* part of morality, they believe, it is justified in principle in enforcing every part of it. There are "no theoretical limits to the legislation against immorality."[2] Only pragmatic reasons stand in the way of *global* enforcement, that is, legal enforcement of all of morality. I will call this 'globalist legal moralism,' 'globalism' for short.

Liberals resist 'globalism.' They hold *both* that private morality is valid and binding on us in just the way all morality is valid and binding, *and yet* that private morality may not be enforced by law or society. It is one thing to show that something is morally incumbent on you or me as individuals, or on us as a group, but it is quite another thing to say that society is *entitled to enforce* these moral demands. To justify enforcement is to justify a certain kind of *public response* to actual or potential violations of moral obligations and responsibilities. Only matters of genuinely public moral concern, they insist, can justify such a public response.

This directly challenges the strict legal moralist, who believes that the law's proper mission is to prevent or punish immorality *as such,* but it does not yet effectively distinguish the liberal's from the moral conservative's position. For conservatives are willing to admit that it is in virtue of its public character that morality is a fit basis for engaging the law's enforcement machinery. They differ with liberals only about whether this argument puts any limits in principle on what the law can be used to enforce. That is, they disagree about what makes morality 'public' and so about the *limits* of public morality.

Thus, liberals and their conservative critics agree that society is entitled, at least in some cases, to enforce morality. They also agree that there is such a thing as public morality. The issue over which they differ is how to understand the nature, force, and particularly *the limits* of public morality. Liberals insist there are *principled* limits to the reach of public morality; their conservative critics allow only pragmatic limits, defined case by case. I propose here to defend the liberal position as I have outlined it. I will suggest a way of drawing the limits of public morality by taking seriously its claim to being *public.*

Properly understood, public morality has definite limits which correspond in many respects to those traditionally defended by liberals. However, the liberalism that emerges from my argument is a revision of traditional liberalism in at least two respects. First, its focus is different: it seeks to draw the boundaries of public morality not in terms of respect for autonomy of individuals, but rather in terms of the nature of political community. Second, the boundaries of public morality, and thus the limits of legitimate enforcement of morality, to the extent they are clear from my general characterization, are likely to differ in certain important respects from the traditional liberal definition. Whether they draw inspiration from Kant or Mill, liberals seem to agree that public morality is strictly limited to matters of what Feinberg calls "grievance morality." (Liberals inspired by Mill define the boundaries of public morality in terms of "harm" (to others). Kantian liberals tend to restrict public morality to the morality of rights and justice.) Critics have argued that this is an impoverished conception of public morality. I agree with this conclusion, although not always with the arguments given for it. While the boundaries of (enforceable) public morality, on my sketch, entail a certain neutrality with regard to competing comprehensive conceptions of the good life, they nevertheless allow appeals to "harmless wrongs" and considerations that cannot be squeezed into the category of "grievance morality" without distortion. The position I defend here takes seriously the liberal distinction between public and private (or as I shall insist later, *nonpublic*) morality, but draws the line in a somewhat different place.

2   The Moral Enforcement Thesis: A Defence

2.1 *The Moral Enforcement Thesis*

To begin the inquiry, consider the *Moral Enforcement Thesis:*

(MET)   If a society is ever justified in prohibiting or requiring conduct of its members, or imposing burdens on them, or distributing differential benefits or burdens among them, by means of its law, it is justified in doing so *on grounds that* the conduct in view is morally wrong, or morally required, or that the law is an effective means to achieving distinctively moral aims.

Note two features of this thesis. First, it presupposes a more general theory justifying a society's use of law to carry out its aims. MET is an addendum to, or qualification of, a general theory of legislation and punishment. Second, it clarifies that general theory by focusing on *the grounds on which* society decides to employ the law. While the second clause might be read to say that society is justified *if* or *as long as* the conduct in view is morally wrong, etc., the intent of MET is different. MET focuses on the *reasons for which* the laws are adopted. It maintains that lawmakers are justified in *making laws for the reason that* certain moral aims will thereby be advanced.

It is useful to formulate in terms of MET the dispute between liberals and conservatives I introduced in the preceding section. Liberals and conservatives alike accept the Moral Enforcement Thesis, albeit in different versions. Conservatives accept the MET without qualification; liberals accept a qualified MET. Liberals insist that *only some* moral grounds provide a justification for society's use of the law to achieve its purposes and, thus, that some reasons drawn from morality, while sound and valid for other purposes, nevertheless do not provide, even in principle, sound reasons for legal regulation of behavior.

The enforcement of morals literature rarely questions MET. That literature focuses solely on the merits of globalist or qualified versions of it. However, MET needs defense. A persuasive defense is available, I believe, but once it is clearly put on the table, the outlines of the debate between liberals and conservatives change. The best argument for MET, I believe, will force us also to articulate the boundaries of (enforceable) public morality. My defense of MET proceeds in three stages. First, I defend MET against a substantial challenge. Second, I discuss two unsuccessful defenses of MET. Finally, I offer a positive argument for the thesis which draws on lessons from our criticism of the previous attempts.

2.2 A Challenge to the Moral Enforcement Thesis

The challenge comes from the 'Moral Disestablishment Thesis':

(MDT)   The law must never use state power to enforce moral values. Defenders of MDT hold that the fact that actions are morally wrong or morally obligatory, or that policies are necessary to achieve morally worthy aims, must never figure as reasons for legislation. The law must not be in the business of promoting or protecting moral values.

Before we assess MDT we must clear up two ambiguities in this formulation. First, law can be said to 'promote or protect moral values' in either of two ways. (a) Legislation (that is, legislators through the laws they make) might seek to direct individual behaviour or regulate the operation of social institutions so that they conform to certain moral standards or achieve certain moral goals. It can 'enforce moral values' by punishing their violation. Alternatively, (b) legislation might seek further to *inculcate* certain standards or goals in those subject to the law; it might seek to 'teach virtue.' Since MDT sets out to challenge MET, we need to formulate MDT in a way that is inconsistent with MET. However, while some defenders of MET might *also* believe law may, or even must, 'teach virtue' to citizens, this is not part of the MET. So to deny the legitimacy of the law's 'teaching virtue' is not to reject MET. If MDT is to challenge MET, it must be understood to reject 'promotion' of moral values not only in sense (b) but also, and more pointedly, in sense (a).

Second, the exclusion of moral values from the repertoire of legislative justifications advocated by MDT can be either broad or narrow. Narrow exclusion would first distinguish *moral* values and standards from other, notably *political,* values and standards, and would only block legislative consideration of the former. Broad exclusion would ban *all* moral considerations, including considerations of political morality. Again, once attention is drawn to this ambiguity, it becomes clear that only MDT under a broad interpretation is a direct challenge to MET. Narrow exclusion represents not a *rejection,* but only a *qualification,* of MET along the lines of the liberal version of MET, which excludes *private* but not *public* morality. MDT represents a challenge to MET only if MDT excludes *all* moral standards and values from legislative consideration.

However, MDT thus clarified is either radically implausible or simply confused. Moral reasons may not be the *only* reasons for introducing the laws we have. Mere convenience, or enhancement of the aesthetics of our communities may occasionally provide reason enough to justify a law. However, these reasons alone will only rarely be sufficient to justify incurring the substantial moral and other costs of working the law's heavy machinery. Thus, if moral considerations may not figure among the grounds of law, justification of most of our laws, indeed the laws of any conceivable society, would fail.

Of course, defenders of MDT do not want us to limit our attention to aesthetic considerations. Typically, they insist on the legitimacy of what would seem to be *moral* considerations, gratuitous harm, for example. But, they argue, it is the *harm* caused by certain behaviour, not the fact that such harm is morally wrong, that alone provides the ground for legal interference. This is confused. It *may* be possible logically to distinguish the harm from the wrong (if, for example, the wrong is supervenient upon the harm), but the harm commands the lawmaker's attention and supplies a justification only insofar as it is *wrong*. Gratuitous harm is *wrong* and that is why we have a powerful reason to prohibit it. For MDT to embrace, for example, prevention of harm to others as an appropriate justifying ground of law, but to deny its moral significance is simply incoherent. The justificatory force of prevention of harm to others is strictly a function of its moral significance. Since the strongest case *against* legal interference is a powerful *moral* case, it could not be otherwise.

Defenders of MDT might be tempted to reply that this is all true, but the problem with MET is that it treats *the mere fact* that an act is immoral as a sufficient ground for legal interference. But this, again, is confused. To say a piece of behaviour is morally wrong is to express a conclusory judgement which purports to rest on reasons. No piece of behaviour is morally wrong and nothing more. It is morally wrong because it is harmful, or irresponsible, or a violation of trust, or unfair, or exploitative, or some other of a thousand different things. No one who endorses MET, whether liberal or conservative, need endorse the bad argument that any claim of moral wrongfulness of behavior is sufficient *in itself* to justify legal prohibition of it, without further argument showing why the behaviour is wrongful. MET holds that moral reasons are often sound reasons for law. MDT denies this only as a result of confusion.

In fairness, liberals must accept responsibility for this last mentioned confusion. They often complain that conservatives believe that the 'mere immorality' of an act is a sufficient basis for legally prohibiting it. But no conservative need hold this view, and liberals know this. The issue between them is not whether something *in addition* to moral wrongfulness is necessary to justify legal prohibition, but whether *all*, or *only some*, moral wrongs are fair game for legal prohibition. Liberals might distinguish between rape and sex for hire, on the ground that these are different *kinds* of moral wrong, but not on the ground that the former involves something *more* or *other than* moral wrong, namely harm. Liberals believe this difference is relevant to the boundaries of legitimate legal interference whereas their conservative critics do not. The difference is not between moral reasons and *other* reasons, but between different kinds of moral reasons.

Thus, once we clearly distinguish MDT from MET, MDT stands convicted of confusion. Purged of confusion and more fully developed, MDT may challenge certain versions of MET (most notably, the globalist version, but possibly also the liberal version), but it does not challenge MET itself.

2.3 On the Moral Title to Enforce Morality: Two Arguments

2.3.1 The Question of Moral Standing. To defend MET it is necessary to address the following question: What *entitles* a political community to enact its moral convictions into law and to use its coercive machinery to enforce these enactments?

This question needs clarification. First, as we noted earlier, the question is not whether a society's regulating behaviour of its members or imposing burdens on them through the law is ever justified, rather it is whether society is ever entitled to do so *on* (what it regards to be) distinctively *moral grounds*. Secondly, the question is not whether evil-doers should ever suffer punishment, or whether virtue should ever be rewarded, or even whether it would be a good thing that people be prevented from carrying out morally evil intentions. Rather, it is to ask whether a *political community* ever has title to punish, reward, or prevent evil. This is a question of *standing*.

Thirdly, questions of *standing* must be distinguished from questions of *justification*. Questions of standing are threshold questions, questions about whether an agent is in a position (is entitled) to engage in certain kinds of actions, provided there are good reasons for doing so. To recognize the role of standing in morality is to accept that moral reasons are sometimes indexed to certain 'positions' or roles. We recognize that there is an important difference between its being a good thing that some event occurs, on the one hand, and a particular person's being entitled to bring it about, on the other hand. Perhaps, it would be good and right for the drunken driver to be forgiven for taking the life of the young mother in my neighborhood, but it is not *for me* to grant the forgiveness. I have no standing to forgive in this case. Similarly, while I may learn that my neighbor is about to betray his friend, I may be morally powerless—I may lack the moral authority or standing—to prevent him from doing so, or to make him suffer for it later. He could justly complain that I have no right to interfere.

By the same token, it is appropriate for us to ask, What standing does a political community have to enforce morality? Of course, usually we do not need special standing to *make* moral judgements, or even to express them, insofar as this is a natural and direct expression of our moral convictions. But we must have special standing to take action to *enact* and *enforce* these convictions—that is, to create structures of rules to encourage compliance with these convictions or to punish noncompliance. Some special claim to enforce the moral concerns in question must be defended. Questions of standing pose a special kind of moral issue and call for a special kind of moral argument. Credible claims to moral standing of an agent tend to rest on one or more of three bases: relative to the matter and the parties in question the party claiming standing (a) has some special wisdom, skill, or expertise, (b) bears some important relation to the parties, or (c) has some significant interest at stake.

As I see it, morality is very tight-fisted when it comes to distributing standing to *individuals* to enact and enforce its dictates. Perhaps it is a good thing, perhaps it is just and right, that MacBeth suffer for his sins, but it is not for you or me to inflict that suffering, to exact that justice. Parents, perhaps, may be in a position *with respect to their children* to enforce the dictates of morality. Relative to their children (at least their younger children), they usually can claim greater moral wisdom and a special *responsibility,* owed primarily to the children, for their moral nurture. But the scope of this authority is sharply limited, and it is accorded parents, not in the name of morality itself, but in the name of the good (moral and otherwise) of the children. With regard to the world of adult moral agents generally we have no analogous claim to moral authority.

The same must be said, I believe, about the right of a political community to enact and enforce morality. No political community, and no government, has any greater claim than individual moral agents to the wisdom, expertise, or special interest necessary to ground the title to enact and enforce morality *in general.* Against this Fitzjames Stephen wrote, "There are acts of wickedness so gross and outrageous that . . . they must be prevented . . . at any cost to the offender and punished, if they occur, with exemplary severity" [see p. 35 of this book]. The sentiment Fitzjames Stephen expresses is compelling. The moral universe in which such evil is left unpunished and wickedness prospers may seem a moral universe radically out of joint. But this fact provides no justification for legal attempts to prevent and punish. When it comes to such matters, it is hard to find anyone with a plausible claim to standing, except perhaps God. From the moral necessity of the prevention of evil and the punishment of wickedness nothing follows about the right to undertake such tasks, and without such title it is likely that the moral result is simply inaccessible to us.

This, it seems to me, provides us sufficient reason to reject the strict legal moralist's thesis that society is entitled to enact and enforce *any* concern of morality, just in virtue of its being a *true* concern of morality. Yet, liberals and conservatives alike are willing to recognize the standing of society to enact and enforce morality in at least *some* cases, namely when the morality in question is 'public morality.' On what does this title rest?

2.3.2 Liberalism and Moral Standing: Mill and Locke. Liberals seldom address this question directly. They spend all their time arguing for *limits* on this right. For example, in *On Liberty*, Mill *formulates* his Harm Principle in terms of standing:

> As soon as any part of a person's conduct affects prejudicially the interests of others, society *has jurisdiction* over it, and the question whether the general welfare will or will not be promoted by interfering with it becomes *open to discussion*. But there is *no room for entertaining* any such question when a person's conduct affects the interests of no persons besides himself. . . . (emphasis added) [See p. 12 of this book.]

Mill makes clear that having "jurisdiction" does not entail having sufficient *justification* to interfere. A case in point is his discussion of laws imposing a duty to rescue. Arguments falling properly within the *jurisdiction* of society can be made, he believed, but he thinks that in many such cases there are good utilitarian reasons for leaving rescue to the benevolent motivation of individual citizens.

Mill, of course, defends his Harm Principle on ultimately utilitarian grounds, but this argument is concerned entirely with the *boundaries* of society's jurisdiction to interfere, not with its ground. This, in a way, is not surprising, in view of the utilitarian background of Mill's theory. It is typical of utilitarian theory to treat particular questions of standing as questions of *local restrictions* on the otherwise universal *responsibility*, and so *standing*, of all competent moral agents to perform those actions which maximize the general welfare. For utilitarian theory no special argument needs to be given for standing to promote welfare. On the contrary, special arguments are needed for restrictions on this title. In *On Liberty,* Mill simply extends to government and society the courtesy utilitarian theory standardly accords to individual moral agents. But, while it may not be surprising that Mill does not directly address the question of standing of society to enforce morality, it is surprising that other liberals who do not share his commitment to utilitarianism similarly ignore the question.

Not all liberals ignore this question. Indeed the question is at the core of the contractarian tradition, especially its Lockean branch. Lockeans argue that the state has only those rights (actually or hypothetically) transferred to it by individuals. So the state has the right to punish rights violations as the designated *agent* of its individual citizens, exercising their rights in their behalf. This provides both *ground* and *limits* of the state's title to enforce morality, for it has such title only with regard to those matters of morality over which *individuals* themselves have jurisdiction—those matters for which individuals are entitled in their own name to demand (and exact) punishment—viz., vindication of their rights.

This argument is, of course, much challenged, not only for difficulties it has in explaining plausibly the transfer of individual rights to the state, but also for the rights it attributes to individuals, in particular the right to punish. The Lockean seems to confuse the right (i.e., title) to punish with the right to (i.e., justification of) self-defense. The latter, it is reasonable to believe, ultimately lies in the hands of the potential victim. But the right to punish is more problematic. The right is rooted in the direct and personal *stake* individuals have in the vindication of their own rights. This is a promising start. But the act of *punishing* wrongs, even when they are wrongs done *to oneself* (violations of one's rights), clearly has a *public* dimension which is not within the reach of individuals considered apart from the political communities of which they are members.

The contractarian scaffolding may not be essential to this argument, however. Taking a cue from a different part of Locke's theory of government, one could argue that a government's title to enact and enforce morality is rooted not so much in rights of individuals to do so, but rather in its office as a *trustee* of the interests and rights of its citizens. Both the title and its limits can be derived from this conception of trusteeship. This is in some ways more promising, but it is wedded to an individualism which many contemporary liberals no longer embrace. In particular, it ignores the fact that the good of individuals is frequently linked intrinsically (rather than merely instrumentally) to the good or values of communities of which they are members. So concern for the good or interests of individuals may involve concern for the good of the communities into which they are integrated. But to give any weight to this consideration seems to nudge the defense of

MET in a decidedly conservative direction. To see whether this is true, we should take a closer look at Devlin's argument for MET.

2.3.3 A Conservative Argument for Moral Standing: Devlin. Unlike the liberals, Devlin directly addresses the question of standing. He frames his discussion of the enforcement of morals around the questions: (1) "Has society the right to pass judgement at all on matters of morals?" (2) If so "has it also the right to use the weapon of law to enforce it?"[3] A society has the right to *pass* judgement on moral matters, Devlin argues, because the existence (survival) of that society depends on the existence in it of a recognized morality. Without "shared ideas on politics, morals and ethics no society can exist. . . . For society . . . is held [together] by the invisible bonds of common thought."[4] A society's right to "use the weapon of law" to enforce morality rests on two independent, albeit related, conditions: (1) its use is necessary to preserve something which is essential to the existence of that society; and (2) the moral standards enforced are matters of collective judgement in that society. Clearly, if the conditions for the right to pass judgement are met, the right to enforce that judgement are met. From this argument Devlin draws the globalist conclusion we noted earlier: that there are no theoretical limits to the power of the state to legislate against immorality.

This argument has been the target of devastating criticism from liberal quarters. The criticisms show Devlin's globalist conclusion to be unsupported, but they tend to leave intact the general *structure* of his argument for standing. The argument, reinterpreted and relying on substantially different assumptions, provides a sound basis for recognizing a community's title to enact and enforce its public morality. The version of the argument I shall sketch below differs from Devlin's not only in the interpretation it gives to its basic premises, but also in the *limits* to the entitlement to enforce which it suggests. Before turning to my argument, let us look again at Devlin's.

The basic strategy of Devlin's argument is to ground society's right to enact and enforce morality in the right of society to protect itself, to take necessary steps to prevent serious threats to its survival. The legal enactment and enforcement of the society's collective moral judgments is said to be one such necessary means of social self-protection. All citizens have a stake in this protective activity, because the good of each clearly depends on the survival of the society in which they undertake to pursue it. Moreover, it seems appropriate for citizens to look to the public, collective instruments provided by the law, because the survival of their social order is, if anything is, a public good, producible only through public, collective means.

This, it seems to me, is the (or at least *an*) appropriate kind of argument for a community's standing to enact and enforce morality. It identifies a recognizable human good to which exercise of the power is related (the survival of social order), the good, while no doubt a good *of* individual human beings, is nevertheless recognizably public, and so the use of distinctively public means of the law seems appropriate, and, if the integrity of a society's public morality and the survival of social order are related as Devlin maintains, it seems appropriate to accord society the right to use its law to enact and enforce this morality. The problem with the argument lies not in its general structure, but in the substantive assumptions on which it rests. I will mention only two problems.

The first has been pointed out frequently by critics: there is simply no reason to think that the *survival* of a given society depends on the continued adherence by members of that society to the particular set of moral ideas, values, and standards around which there may be consensus at a given time. From the fact that survival of *any* society depends on *some* body of shared moral beliefs (or other) it does not follow that the survival of Transylvania depends on Transylvanians continuing to practice the particular and perhaps elaborate and complex code actually practiced at present. Devlin fails to distinguish between threats to the *survival* of a society and prospects of *change in* a society.

This is, I think, a fair criticism of Devlin and the argument cannot survive as it stands. But what led him astray was a deeper and more interesting confusion. Sometimes Devlin worries about the *disintegration* of society. But 'disintegration' can refer either to a process of social *dissolution,* or to a process of social *degeneration.* The latter, but clearly not the former, involves a *qualitative* judgement.

The basic structure of Devlin's argument (especially as it is read by liberal critics) speaks the language of an external observer making non-qualitative judgements. In this language, Devlin's argument asserts that a society's recognized morality plays a *functional* role in the society: the end state is continued viability of particular social order, and widely shared moral beliefs are a necessary means to achieving this end. The problem with Devlin's argument construed in this way is that, while *some* shared moral beliefs may be functionally necessary, it is false that the entire set of currently held common moral beliefs are.

However, claims of social disintegration are far more likely to be plausible if taken as *qualitative* judgements, that is, as judgements about threats to the moral integrity or 'health' of the community, or judgements about the loss of valued social practices. But these judgements assume a *constitutive* rather than a *functional* relationship between the viability and availability of certain social practices, on the one hand, and the integrity or quality of the moral culture, on the other. The immediate rhetorical force of Devlin's argument depends on our reading 'social disintegration' in the key of qualitative judgements, but his argument in fact is written strictly in the key of non-qualitative judgements. So long as it stays in that key the argument will fail. A more plausible argument for a community's right to enforce its judgements of morality would pay serious attention to these *qualitative* judgements. After all, the moral ideals and principles around which a community rallies recommend themselves to its members in virtue of their *content*—in virtue of what they *are* and the grounds that can be given for them—not in virtue of the functional social role of members' beliefs about them. I propose, then, to transpose Devlin's argument into a key that takes qualitative judgements of a community's moral environment seriously.

2.3.4 A Defense of Moral Standing. In outline, the argument is that a community has standing to enact and enforce its public morality insofar as this is necessary to maintain the integrity of the moral life of that community. This right rests on the fact that the integrity of a community's moral life is an especially important public good in which members have a personal stake, and which, in virtue of its being a *public* good, often can only be protected through the essentially public means provided by the law. This argument needs an elaboration or defense at three key points. (1) I must explain what I mean by a community's *moral life;* (2) I must show that the integrity of a community's moral life is a public good in which its members have a stake; and (3) I must show why legal enactment and enforcement is an appropriate means for achieving this aim.

To begin: when I use the phrase 'the moral life of a community' I have in mind something more both concrete and active than a community's 'shared values' or 'recognized morality,' and more personally engaging than its 'moral environment.' A community's moral life is a typically complex matrix of social forms (activities, practices and relationships), widely practiced and valued in the community, the value and meaning of which depend on common, although often only imperfectly articulated, understandings. This matrix not only provides the environment *within which* members act, but it directly shapes their sense of the meaning and value of the actions about which they deliberate. It provides content, not just context, for their practical deliberation. Moreover, the interaction between matrix and member is reciprocal in two respects. First, the social forms shape the choices and actions of members, and those choices and actions, issuing from the more or less articulate understandings (and potential misunderstandings) of the social forms, continually reshape the social forms. Second, while the social forms provide criteria by which the actions of members are judged, at the same time the social forms themselves are judged. Social forms are *valued*— they are not merely 'the way things are done here.' And the widely shared view that they are valuable is itself open to evaluation. The *fact that* they are commonly believed to be valuable may be an important part of their value, but it is never by itself decisive (in the view of those who value them). Their valuing the social forms presupposes that there are *reasons* for regarding the social forms as worthy, and should these reasons turn out to be unsound, the social forms would lose their claim to value. This dimension of a community's moral life is evident in typical reactions of members to potential changes in constituent practices or structures of relationships. Some such changes may be regarded as *improvements* or *enhancements* of their moral life, others as *impoverishments* of it. Moreover, they might fully realize that after the change they might no longer see it as an impoverishment, but perhaps even as an improvement. But, especially if the change occurred through collective inattention, they would regard this prospect, not as evidence of its benign character, but as further reason to resist it. Not only would our moral life be impoverished, they might say, but even worse we would no longer be in a position to appreciate the loss. This shows that a shift in the shared sense of the value of some practice or relationship is not, from the point of view of members, sufficient for a shift in its actual value. Whether the shift is sufficient or not depends on how and in particular why (for what *reasons*) it occurred. Thus, this dimension of collective valuing enables members of the community to distinguish between improvements and impoverishments of their community's moral life. It enables them to make *qualitative* judgements about it, judgements of its 'moral health' or *integrity*.

Before we continue any further, note that I make only a very weak assumption about the existence or extent of such a moral life in any community. I suspect that Devlin is right that a community could exist without *any* such valued social forms and practiced moral commitments, but I see no reason to deny that a given community could subsist with only a very limited common moral life. We might judge such a community to be 'impoverished,' or 'morally bankrupt,' or 'debased.' But, as we have seen, these qualitative judgements do not entail that the community does not or cannot exist. Moreover, the credibility of these judgements depends in part on whether other, morally richer communities are available to members of this morally thin community. My argument for a community's standing to enforce morality does not *assume* that there always is an extensive moral life, it makes standing *conditional upon* the existence of such a moral life.

With this understanding of 'the moral life of a community' we can proceed with the argument for a community's standing to enforce its public morality. The case for standing turns on two theses: (1) that members of the community have a stake in the integrity of the moral life of their community and (2) that legal enactment and enforcement of the community's public morality is an appropriate method of protecting that stake.

The argument for the first of these theses proceeds from an understanding of certain conditions of human well-being and the relationship between the well-being of individual human beings and the 'well-being' or integrity of the communities to which they belong. First, our most important goals, those with the most pervasive influence in our lives, often depend on existing social forms, forms of behaviour and of relationships which are widely practiced and widely valued in the communities in which we live. The existence and integrity of these social forms is a necessary condition of the value which those pursuits which are most important to us have for us. Thus, we have a stake in the continued existence and integrity of these social forms, a stake which is not merely instrumental to the achievement of strictly personal, individual goals. Individuals have this stake in the community's moral life insofar as they continue to regard themselves as members of the community and active participants in that moral life.

Second, note that our well-being is both a function of our success in the pursuit of important goals, and a function of the value or worth of those goals. Many of our goals are adopted and pursued for the reason that they are worthy of our pursuit. Thus, members have a stake not only in the continued *existence* of such social forms, but also in their *integrity*. Persons who are integrated into the life of a community, who identify with it, will measure the moral quality of their lives at least in part in terms of the moral quality and integrity of that community. . . .

In virtue of this personal stake, which is a stake of members qua members, they may take as a proper focus of their collective concern the moral integrity of their common life. May this concern take the form of legal enactment and enforcement of this public morality? Yes, I maintain, because a community's moral life is a public good and is protected and maintained primarily (though perhaps never exclusively) through public and collective means. That the integrity of a community's moral life is a public good is obvious. It is public in at least three respects. (1) It is a matter of concern or importance potentially to all or nearly all members considered severally. It is not of exclusive interest or concern to a sub-set of the community. (2) It is a public good in the standard sense in which economists use the term. That is, it is the kind of good that, if it can be enjoyed by anyone in the community, it can be enjoyed by all. (3) It is public in the further sense that it is a common product, the result of common work. It involves activities in which all members participate to one extent or another both as 'producers' and as 'consumers' (and typically as 'producers' through their 'consumption').

Of course, a community's moral life is only in small portions the product of the explicit collective creation or *enactment* at a precise point in time. More typically it is the product of social evolutionary forces. Nevertheless, like other public goods, it often must be maintained by coordinated, collective efforts. This is due to the fact that evolutionary forces can be both creative and destructive, not only enhancing, but also impoverishing, a community's moral life. Since whether a potential change is an enhancement or an impoverishment is always a matter for reflective qualitative *judgement*, it is appropriate for the community to put into place mechanisms by which such reflective judgements can be made, expressed, and acted upon. Moreover, since the judgements are not merely judgements made by individual members for their own part only, but rather judgements of the community as a whole, the mechanisms must adequately express collective judgements in a fully public form. One such mechanism in a large and diverse community is the enactment and enforcement of laws designed to encourage respect for social forms constituting the community's moral life and the values which they make concrete. For these reasons, I conclude, a community has standing to enact and enforce its public morality, and more specifically, a political community has standing to legally enforce its public morality. . . .

Notes

1. Patrick Devlin, *The Enforcement of Morals* (Oxford University Press, 1965), p. 14.
2. Ibid.
3. Ibid., pp. 7–8.
4. Ibid., p. 10.

Part Two

Applications

6 Homosexuality

Bowers v. Hardwick

Justice WHITE delivered the opinion of the Court.

In August 1982, respondent Hardwick (hereafter respondent) was charged with violating the Georgia statute criminalizing sodomy by committing that act with another adult male in the bedroom of respondent's home. After a preliminary hearing, the District Attorney decided not to present the matter to the grand jury unless further evidence developed.

Respondent then brought suit in the Federal District Court, challenging the constitutionality of the statute insofar as it criminalized consensual sodomy. He asserted that he was a practicing homosexual, that the Georgia sodomy statute, as administered by defendants, placed him in imminent danger of arrest, and that the statute for several reasons violates the Federal Constitution. The District Court granted the defendants' motion to dismiss for failure to state a claim. . . .

A divided panel of the Court of Appeals for the Eleventh Circuit reversed. 760 F.2d 1202 (1985). . . . The court went on to hold that the Georgia statute violated respondent's fundamental rights because his homosexual activity is a private and intimate association that is beyond the reach of state regulation by reason of the Ninth Amendment and the Due Process Clause of the Fourteenth Amendment. . . . We agree with petitioner that the Court of Appeals erred, and hence reverse its judgment.

This case does not require a judgment on whether laws against sodomy between consenting adults in general, or between homosexuals in particular, are wise or desirable. It raises no question about the right or propriety of state legislative decisions to repeal their laws that criminalize homosexual sodomy, or of state-court decisions invalidating those laws on state constitutional grounds. The issue presented is whether the Federal Constitution confers a fundamental right upon homosexuals to engage in sodomy and hence invalidates the laws of the many States that still make such conduct illegal and have done so for a very long time. The case also calls for some judgment about the limits of the Court's role in carrying out its constitutional mandate.

We first register our disagreement with the Court of Appeals and with respondent that the Court's prior cases have construed the Constitution to confer a right of privacy that extends to homosexual sodomy and for all intents and purposes have decided this case. . . . We think it evident that none of the rights announced in those cases bears any resemblance to the claimed constitutional right of homosexuals to engage in acts of sodomy that is asserted in this case. No connection between family, marriage, or procreation on the one hand and homosexual activity on the other has been demonstrated, either by the Court of Appeals or by respondent. Moreover, any claim that these cases nevertheless stand for the proposition that any kind of private sexual conduct between consenting adults is constitutionally insulated from state proscription is unsupportable. Indeed, the Court's opinion in *Carey* twice asserted that the privacy right, which the *Griswold* line of cases found to be one of the protections provided by the Due Process Clause, did not reach so far.

Precedent aside, however, respondent would have us announce, as the Court of Appeals did, a fundamental right to engage in homosexual sodomy. This we are quite unwilling to do. It is true that despite the language of the Due Process Clauses of the Fifth and Fourteenth Amendments, which appears to focus only on the processes by which life, liberty, or property is taken, the cases are legion in which those Clauses have been interpreted to have substantive content, subsuming rights that to a great extent are immune from federal or state regulation or proscription. Among such cases are those recognizing rights that have little or no textual support in the constitutional language.

Striving to assure itself and the public that announcing rights not readily identifiable in the Constitution's text involves much more than the imposition of the Justices' own choice of values on the States and the Federal Government, the Court has sought to identify the nature of the rights qualifying for heightened judicial protection. In *Palko v. Connecticut,* it was said that this category includes those fundamental liberties that are "implicit in the concept of ordered liberty" such that "neither liberty nor justice would exist if [they] were sacrificed." . . . In *Moore v. East Cleveland,* (opinion of POWELL, J.) they are characterized as those liberties that are "deeply rooted in this Nation's history and tradition."

It is obvious to us that neither of these formulations would extend a fundamental right to homosexuals to engage in acts of consensual sodomy. Proscriptions against that conduct have ancient roots. Sodomy was a criminal offense at common law and was forbidden by the laws of the original thirteen States when they ratified the Bill of Rights. In 1868, when the Fourteenth Amendment was ratified, all but 5 of the 37 States in the Union had criminal sodomy laws. In fact, until 1961, all 50 States outlawed sodomy, and today, 24 States and the District of Columbia continue to provide criminal penalties for sodomy performed in private and between consenting adults. Against this background, to claim that a right to engage in such conduct is "deeply rooted in this Nation's history and tradition" or "implicit in the concept of ordered liberty" is, at best, facetious.

* * *

[4] Even if the conduct at issue here is not a fundamental right, respondent asserts that there must be a rational basis for the law and that there is none in this case other than the presumed belief of a majority of the electorate in Georgia that homosexual sodomy is immoral and unacceptable. This is said to be an inadequate rationale to support the law. The law, however, is constantly based on notions of morality, and if all laws representing essentially moral choices are to be invalidated under the Due Process Clause, the courts will be very busy indeed. Even respondent makes no such claim, but insists that majority sentiments about the morality of homosexuality should be declared inadequate. We do not agree, and are unpersuaded that the sodomy laws of some 25 States should be invalidated on this basis.

Accordingly, the judgment of the Court of Appeals is

Reversed

Chief Justice BURGER, concurring.

I join the Court's opinion, but I write separately to underscore my view that in constitutional terms there is no such thing as a fundamental right to commit sodomy.

As the Court notes, the proscriptions against sodomy have very "ancient roots." Decisions of individuals relating to homosexual conduct have been subject to state intervention throughout the history of Western civilization. Condemnation of those practices is firmly rooted in Judaeo-Christian moral and ethical standards. Homosexual sodomy was a capital crime under Roman law. During the English Reformation when powers of the ecclesiastical courts were transferred to the King's Courts, the first English statute criminalizing sodomy was passed. Blackstone described "the infamous crime against nature" as an offense of "deeper malignity" than rape, a heinous act "the very mention of which is a disgrace to human nature," and "a crime not fit to be named." The common law of England, including its prohibition of sodomy, became the received law of Georgia and the other Colonies. In 1816 the Georgia Legislature passed the statute at issue here, and that statute has been continuously in force in one form or another since that time. To hold that the act of homosexual sodomy is somehow protected as a fundamental right would be to cast aside millennia of moral teaching.

This is essentially not a question of personal "preferences" but rather of the legislative authority of the State. I find nothing in the Constitution depriving a State of the power to enact the statute challenged here.

Justice POWELL, concurring.

I join the opinion of the Court. I agree with the Court that there is no fundamental right—*i.e.,* no substantive right under the Due Process Clause—such as that claimed by respondent Hardwick, and found to exist by the Court of Appeals. This is not to suggest, however, that respondent may not be protected by the Eighth Amendment of the Constitution. The Georgia statute at issue in this case authorizes a court to imprison a person for up to 20 years for a single private, consensual act of sodomy. In my view, a prison sentence for such conduct—certainly a sentence of long duration— would create a serious Eighth Amendment issue. Under the Georgia statute a single act of sodomy, even in the private setting of a home, is a felony comparable in terms of the possible sentence imposed to serious felonies such as aggravated battery, first-degree arson, and robbery.

In this case, however, respondent has not been tried, much less convicted and sentenced.[1] Moreover, respondent has not raised the Eighth Amendment issue below. For these reasons this constitutional argument is not before us.

Justice BLACKMUN, with whom Justice BRENNAN, Justice MARSHALL, and Justice STEVENS join, dissenting.

This case is no more about "a fundamental right to engage in homosexual sodomy," as the Court purports to declare, than *Stanley v. Georgia* was about a fundamental right to watch obscene movies, or *Katz v. United States* was about a fundamental right to place interstate bets from a telephone booth. Rather, this case is about "the most comprehensive of rights most valued by civilized men," namely, "the right to be left alone."

The statute at issue, Ga. Code Ann. § 16–6–2 (1984), denies individuals the right to decide for themselves whether to engage in particular forms of private, consensual sexual activity. The Court concludes that § 16–6–2 is valid essentially because "the laws of . . . many States still make such conduct illegal and have done so for a very long time." But the fact that the moral judgments expressed by statutes like § 16–6–2 may be "'natural and familiar . . . ought not to conclude our judgment upon the question whether statutes embodying them conflict with the Constitution of the United States.'" Like Justice Holmes, I believe that "[i]t is revolting to have no better reason for a rule of law than that so it was laid down in the time of Henry IV. It is still more revolting if the grounds upon which it was laid down have vanished long since, and the rule simply persists from blind imitation of the past." Holmes, The Path of the Law, (1897). I believe we must analyze Hardwick's claim in the light of the values that underlie the constitutional right to privacy. If that right means anything, it means that, before Georgia can prosecute its citizens for making choices about the most intimate aspects of their lives, it must do more than assert that the choice they have made is an "'abominable crime not fit to be named among Christians.'"

I

In its haste to reverse the Court of Appeals and hold that the Constitution does not "confe[r] a fundamental right upon homosexuals to engage in sodomy," the Court relegates the actual statute being challenged to a foot-note and ignores the procedural posture of the case before it. A fair reading of the statute and of the complaint clearly reveals that the majority has dis torted the question this case presents.

The Court's almost obsessive focus on homosexual activity is particularly hard to justify in light of the broad language Georgia has used. Unlike the Court, the Georgia Legislature has not proceeded on the assumption that homosexuals are so different from other citizens that their lives may be con-trolled in a way that would not be tolerated if it limited the choices of those other citizens. Rather, Georgia has provided that "[a] person commits the offense of sodomy when he performs or submits to any sexual act involving the sex organs of one person and the mouth or anus of another." The sex or status of the persons who engage in the act is irrelevant as a matter of state law. In fact, to the extent I can discern a legislative purpose for Georgia's 1968 enactment of § 16–6–2, that purpose seems to have been to broaden the coverage of the law to reach heterosexual as well as homosexual activity. I therefore see no basis for the Court's decision to treat this case as an "as applied" challenge to § 16–6–2, or for Georgia's attempt, both in its brief and at oral argument, to defend § 16–6–2 solely on the grounds that it prohibits homosexual activity. Michael Hardwick's standing may rest in sig-nificant part on Georgia's apparent willingness to enforce against homosex-uals a law it seems not to have any desire to enforce against heterosexuals. But his claim that § 16–6–2 involves an unconstitutional intrusion into his privacy and his right of intimate association does not depend in any way on his sexual orientation. . . .

II

"Our cases long have recognized that the Constitution embodies a promise that a certain private sphere of individual liberty will be kept largely beyond the reach of government." In construing the right to privacy, the Court has proceeded along two somewhat distinct, albeit complementary, lines. First, it has recognized a privacy interest with reference to certain *decisions* that are properly for the individual to make. Second, it has recognized a privacy interest with reference to certain *places* without regard for the particular activities in which the individuals who occupy them are engaged. The case before us implicates both the decisional and the spatial aspects of the right to privacy.

A

The Court concludes today that none of our prior cases dealing with various decisions that individuals are entitled to make free of governmental interference "bears any resemblance to the claimed constitutional right of homosexuals to engage in acts of sodomy that is asserted in this case." While it is true that these cases may be characterized by their connection to protection of the family, the Court's conclusion that they extend no further than this boundary ignores the warning in *Moore v. East Cleveland,* against "clos[ing] our eyes to the basic reasons why certain rights associated with the family have been accorded shelter under the Fourteenth Amendment's Due Process Clause." We protect those rights not because they contribute, in some direct and material way, to the general public welfare, but because they form so central a part of an individual's life. "[T]he concept of privacy embodies the 'moral fact that a person belongs to himself and not others nor to society as a whole.'". . .

Only the most willful blindness could obscure the fact that sexual intimacy is "a sensitive, key relationship of human existence, central to family life, community welfare, and the development of human personality," *Paris Adult Theatre I v. Slaton.* The fact that individuals define themselves in a significant way through their intimate sexual relationships with others suggests, in a Nation as diverse as ours, that there may be many "right" ways of conducting those relationships, and that much of the richness of a relationship will come from the freedom an individual has to *choose* the form and nature of these intensely personal bonds. . . .

III

The Court's failure to comprehend the magnitude of the liberty interests at stake in this case leads it to slight the question whether petitioner, on behalf of the State, has justified Georgia's infringement on these interests. I believe that neither of the two general justifications for § 16–6–2 that petitioner has advanced warrants dismissing respondent's challenge for failure to state a claim.

First, petitioner asserts that the acts made criminal by the statute may have serious adverse consequences for "the general public health and welfare," such as spreading communicable diseases or fostering other criminal activity. Brief for Petitioner 37. Inasmuch as this case was dismissed by the District Court on the pleadings, it is not surprising that the record before us is barren of any evidence to support petitioner's claim. In light of the state of the record, I see no justification for the Court's attempt to equate the private, consensual sexual activity at issue here with the "possession in the home of drugs, firearms, or stolen goods," *ante,* at 2846, to which *Stanley* refused to extend its protection. None of the behavior so mentioned in *Stanley* can properly be viewed as [v]ictimless," drugs and weapons are inherently dangerous, and for property to be "stolen," someone must have been wrongfully deprived of it. Nothing in the record before the Court provides any justification for finding the activity forbidden by § 16–6–2 to be physically dangerous, either to the persons engaged in it or to others.[2]. . .

The core of petitioner's defense of § 16–6–2, however, is that respondent and others who engage in the conduct prohibited by § 16–6–2 interfere with Georgia's exercise of the "'right of the Nation and of the States to maintain a decent society.'" Essentially, petitioner argues, and the Court agrees, that the fact that the acts described in § 16–6–2 "for hundreds of years, if not thousands, have been uniformly condemned as immoral" is a sufficient reason to permit a State to ban them today. Brief for Petitioner 19; see *ante,* at 2843, 2844–2846, 2847.

I cannot agree that either the length of time a majority has held its convictions or the passions with which it defends them can withdraw legislation from this Court's scrutiny. As Justice Jackson wrote so eloquently for the Court in *West Virginia Board of Education v. Barnette,* "we apply the limitations of the Constitution with no fear that freedom to be intellectually and spiritually diverse or even contrary will disintegrate the social organization. . . . [F]reedom to differ is not limited to things that do not matter much. That would be a mere shadow of freedom. The test of its substance is the right to differ as to things that touch the heart of the existing order." It is precisely because the issue raised by this case touches the heart of what makes individuals what they are that we should be especially sensitive to the rights of those whose choices upset the majority.

The assertion that "traditional Judeo-Christian values proscribe" the conduct involved, cannot provide an adequate justification for § 16–6–2. That certain, but by no means all, religious groups condemn the behavior at issue gives the State no license to impose their judgments on the entire citizenry. The legitimacy of secular legislation depends instead on whether the State can advance some justification for its law beyond its conformity to religious doctrine. Thus, far from buttressing his case, petitioner's invocation of Leviticus, Romans, St. Thomas Aquinas, and sodomy's heretical status during the Middle Ages undermines his suggestion that § 16–6–2 represents a legitimate use of secular coercive power. A State can no more punish private behavior because of religious intolerance than it can punish such behavior because of racial animus. "The Constitution cannot control such prejudices, but neither can it tolerate them. Private biases may be outside the reach of the law, but the law cannot, directly or indirectly, give them effect." No matter how uncomfortable a certain group may make the majority of this Court, we have held that "[m]ere public intolerance or animosity cannot constitutionally justify the deprivation of a person's physical liberty."

Nor can § 16–6–2 be justified as a "morally neutral" exercise of Georgia's power to "protect the public environment." Certainly, some private behavior can affect the fabric of society as a whole. Reasonable people may differ about whether particular sexual acts are moral or immoral, but "we have ample evidence for believing that people will not abandon morality, will not think any better of murder, cruelty and dishonesty, merely because some private sexual practice which they abominate is not punished by the law."[3] Petitioner and the Court fail to see the difference between laws that protect public sensibilities and those that enforce private morality. Statutes banning public sexual activity are entirely consistent with protecting the individual's liberty interest in decisions concerning sexual relations: the same recognition that those decisions are intensely private which justifies protecting them from governmental interference can justify protecting individuals from unwilling exposure to the sexual activities of others. But the mere fact that intimate behavior may be punished when it takes place in public cannot dictate how States can regulate intimate behavior that occurs in intimate places.

This case involves no real interference with the rights of others, for the mere knowledge that other individuals do not adhere to one's value system cannot be a legally cognizable interest, cf. *Diamond v. Charles,* let alone an interest that can justify invading the houses, hearts, and minds of citizens who choose to live their lives differently.

IV

It took but three years for the Court to see the error in its analysis in *Minersville School District v. Gobitis* and to recognize that the threat to national cohesion posed by a refusal to salute the flag was vastly outweighed by the threat to those same values posed by compelling such a salute. I can only hope that here, too, the Court soon will reconsider its analysis and conclude that depriving individuals of the right to choose for themselves how to conduct their intimate relationships poses a far greater threat to the values most deeply rooted in our Nation's history than tolerance of nonconformity could ever do. Because I think the Court today betrays those values, I dissent.

Justice STEVENS, with whom Justice BRENNAN and Justice MAR-
SHALL join, dissenting.

Like the statute that is challenged in this case, the rationale of the Court's
opinion applies equally to the prohibited conduct regardless of whether the
parties who engage in it are married or unmarried, or are of the same or
different sexes. Sodomy was condemned as an odious and sinful type of behavior during the formative period of the common law. That condemnation
was equally damning for heterosexual sodomy. Moreover, it provided no
special exemption for married couples. The license to cohabit and to produce legitimate offspring simply did not include any permission to engage
in sexual conduct that was considered a "crime against nature."

The history of the Georgia statute before us clearly reveals this traditional
prohibition of heterosexual, as well as homosexual, sodomy. Indeed, at one
point in the 20th century, Georgia's law was construed to permit sexual
conduct between homosexual women even though such conduct was prohibited between heterosexuals. The history of the statutes cited by the
majority as proof for the proposition that sodomy is not constitutionally
protected similarly reveals a prohibition on heterosexual, as well as homosexual, sodomy.

Because the Georgia statute expresses the traditional view that sodomy is
an immoral kind of conduct regardless of the identity of the persons who
engage in it, I believe that a proper analysis of its constitutionality requires
consideration of two questions: First, may a State totally prohibit the described conduct by means of a neutral law applying without exception to all
persons subject to its jurisdiction? If not, may the State save the statute by
announcing that it will only enforce the law against homosexuals? The two
questions merit separate discussion.

I

Our prior cases make two propositions abundantly clear. First, the fact that
the governing majority in a State has traditionally viewed a particular practice as immoral is not a sufficient reason for upholding a law prohibiting the
practice; neither history nor tradition could save a law prohibiting miscegenation from constitutional attack. Second, individual decisions by married
persons, concerning the intimacies of their physical relationship, even when
not intended to produce offspring, are a form of "liberty" protected by the
Due Process Clause of the Fourteenth Amendment. Moreover, this protection extends to intimate choices by unmarried as well as married persons.

In consideration of claims of this kind, the Court has emphasized the individual interest in privacy, but its decisions have actually been animated by an even more fundamental concern. As I wrote some years ago:

> "These cases do not deal with the individual's interest in protection from unwarranted public attention, comment, or exploitation. They deal, rather, with the individual's right to make certain unusually important decisions that will affect his own, or his family's, destiny. The Court has referred to such decisions as implicating 'basic values,' as being 'fundamental,' and as being dignified by history and tradition." . . .

Society has every right to encourage its individual members to follow particular traditions in expressing affection for one another and in gratifying their personal desires. It, of course, may prohibit an individual from imposing his will on another to satisfy his own selfish interests. It also may prevent an individual from interfering with, or violating, a legally sanctioned and protected relationship, such as a marriage. And it may explain the relative advantages and disadvantages of different forms of intimate expression. But when individual married couples are isolated from observation by others, the way in which they voluntarily choose to conduct their intimate relations is a matter for them—not the State—to decide.[4] The essential "liberty" that animated the development of the law in cases like *Griswold, Eisenstadt,* and *Carey* surely embraces the right to engage in nonreproductive, sexual conduct that others may consider offensive or immoral.

Paradoxical as it may seem, our prior cases thus establish that a State may not prohibit sodomy within "the sacred precincts of marital bedrooms," *Griswold,* or, indeed, between unmarried heterosexual adults, *Eisenstadt.* In all events, it is perfectly clear that the State of Georgia may not totally prohibit the conduct proscribed by § 16–6–2 of the Georgia Criminal Code.

II

If the Georgia statute cannot be enforced as it is written—if the conduct it seeks to prohibit is a protected form of liberty for the vast majority of Georgia's citizens—the State must assume the burden of justifying a selective application of its law. Either the persons to whom Georgia seeks to apply its statute do not have the same interest in "liberty" that others have, or there must be a reason why the State may be permitted to apply a generally applicable law to certain persons that it does not apply to others.

The first possibility is plainly unacceptable. Although the meaning of the principle that "all men are created equal" is not always clear, it surely must mean that every free citizen has the same interest in "liberty" that the members of the majority share. From the standpoint of the individual, the homosexual and the heterosexual have the same interest in deciding how he will live his own life, and, more narrowly, how he will conduct himself in his personal and voluntary associations with his companions. State intrusion into the private conduct of either is equally burdensome.

The second possibility is similarly unacceptable. A policy of selective application must be supported by a neutral and legitimate interest—something more substantial than a habitual dislike for, or ignorance about, the disfavored group. Neither the State nor the Court has identified any such interest in this case. The Court has posited as justification for the Georgia statute "the presumed belief of a majority of the electorate in Georgia that homosexual sodomy is immoral and unacceptable." But the Georgia electorate has expressed no such belief—instead, its representatives enacted a law that presumably reflects the belief that *all sodomy* is immoral and unacceptable. Unless the court is prepared to conclude that such a law is constitutional, it may not rely on the work product of the Georgia Legislature to support its holding. For the Georgia statute does not single out homosexuals as a separate class meriting special disfavored treatment.

Nor, indeed, does the Georgia prosecutor even believe that all homosexuals who violate this statute should be punished. This conclusion is evident from the fact that the respondent in this very case has formally acknowledged in his complaint and in court that he has engaged, and intends to continue to engage, in the prohibited conduct, yet the State has elected not to process criminal charges against him. As Justice POWELL points out, moreover, Georgia's prohibition on private, consensual sodomy has not been enforced for decades. The record of nonenforcement, in this case and in the last several decades belies the Attorney General's representations about the importance of the State's selective application of its generally applicable law.

Both the Georgia statute and the Georgia prosecutor thus completely fail to provide the Court with any support for the conclusion that homosexual sodomy, *simpliciter,* is considered unacceptable conduct in that State, and that the burden of justifying a selective application of the generally applicable law has been met.

III

The Court orders the dismissal of respondent's complaint even though the State's statute prohibits all sodomy; even though that prohibition is concededly unconstitutional with respect to heterosexuals; and even though the State's *post hoc* explanations for selective application are belied by the State's own actions. At the very least, I think it is clear at this early stage of the litigation that respondent has alleged a constitutional claim sufficient to withstand a motion to dismiss.

I respectfully dissent.

Notes

1. It was conceded at oral argument that, prior to the complaint against respondent Hardwick, there had been no reported decision involving prosecution for private homosexual sodomy under this statute for several decades.

Moreover, the State has declined to present the criminal charge against Hardwick to a grand jury, and this is a suit for declaratory judgment brought by respondents challenging the validity of the statute. The history of nonenforcement suggests the moribund character today of laws criminalizing this type of private, consensual conduct. Some 26 States have repealed similar statutes. But the constitutional validity of the Georgia statute was put in issue by respondents, and for the reasons stated by the Court, I cannot say that conduct condemned for hundreds of years has now become a fundamental right.

2. Although I do not think it necessary to decide today issues that are not even remotely before us, it does seem to me that a court could find simple, analytically sound distinctions between certain private, consensual sexual conduct, on the one hand, and adultery and incest (the only two vaguely specific "sexual crimes" to which the majority points) on the other. For example, marriage, in addition to its spiritual aspects, is a civil contract that entitles the contracting parties to a variety of governmentally provided benefits. A State might define the contractual commitment necessary to become eligible for these benefits to include a commitment of fidelity and then punish individuals for breaching that contract. Moreover, a State might conclude that adultery is likely to injure third persons, in particular, spouses and children of persons who engage in extramarital affairs. With respect to incest, a court might well agree with respondent that the nature of familial relationships renders true consent to incestuous activity sufficiently problematical that a blanket prohibition of such activity is warranted. Notably, the Court makes no effort to explain why it has chosen to group private, consensual homosexual activity with adultery and incest rather than with private, consensual heterosexual activity by unmarried persons or, indeed, with oral or anal sex within marriage.

3. H.L.A. Hart, Immorality and Treason, reprinted in *The Law as Literature* 220, 225 (L. Blom-Cooper ed. 1964).

4. Indeed, the Georgia Attorney General concedes that Georgia's statute would be unconstitutional if applied to a married couple. See Tr. of Oral Arg. 8 (stating that application of the statute to a married couple "would be unconstitutional" because of the "right of marital privacy as identified by the Court in Griswold"). Significantly, Georgia passed the current statute three years after the Court's decision in *Griswold*.

Commonwealth of Kentucky v. Jeffrey Wasson

Opinion of the Court by Justice Leibson

Appellee, Jeffrey Wasson, is charged with having solicited an undercover Lexington policeman to engage in deviate sexual intercourse. KRS 510.100 punishes "deviate sexual intercourse with another person of the same sex" as a criminal offense, and specifies "consent of the other person shall not be a defense." Nor does it matter that the act is private and involves a caring relationship rather than a commercial one. It is classified as a Class A misdemeanor.

The appellee is actually charged under KRS 506.030, which covers "solicitation" to commit any criminal offense. If the offense solicited is a Class A misdemeanor, solicitation of the offense is punished as a Class B misdemeanor. KRS 506.030(2)(d). The issue here is whether KRS 510.100, which defines the underlying criminal offense, is constitutional.

The brief statement of facts upon which the District Court rendered judgment is as follows:

Lexington police were conducting a downtown undercover operation. Their modus operandi was to drive to a certain parking area, in plain clothes with microphones on their persons, and try to engage in conversation with persons passing by to see whether they would be solicited for sexual contact. The taped conversation between the undercover officer and Wasson covered approximately 20–25 minutes, toward the end of which Wasson invited the officer to "come home" to his residence. The officer then prodded Wasson for details, and Wasson suggested sexual activities which violated KRS 510.100. There was no suggestion that sexual activity would occur anyplace other than in the privacy of Wasson's home. The sexual activity was intended to have been between consenting adults. No money was offered or solicited.

[The commonwealth's] position is that the majority, speaking through the General Assembly, has the right to criminalize sexual activity it deems immoral, without regard to whether the activity is conducted in private between consenting adults and is not, in and of itself, harmful to the participants or to others; that, if not in all instances, at least where there is a Biblical and historical tradition supporting it, there are no limitations in the Kentucky Constitution on the power of the General United States Constitution. We stated: "The problem in this case is not whether the challenged statute passes muster under the federal constitution as interpreted by the United States Supreme Court, but whether it satisfies the much more detailed and explicit proscriptions of the Kentucky Constitution. It does not."

We view the United States Supreme Court decision in Bowers v. Hardwick as a misdirected application of the theory of original intent. To illustrate: as a theory of majoritarian morality, miscegenation was an offense with ancient roots. It is highly unlikely that protecting the rights of persons of different races to copulate was one of the considerations behind the Fourteenth Amendment. Nevertheless, in Loving v. Virginia, the United States Supreme Court recognized that a contemporary, enlightened interpretation of the liberty interest involved in the sexual act made its punishment constitutionally impermissible.

> The usual justification for laws against such conduct is that, even though it does not injure any identifiable victim, it contributes to moral deterioration of society. One need not endorse wholesale repeal of all 'victimless' crimes in

order to recognize that legislating penal sanctions solely to maintain widely held concepts of morality and aesthetics is a costly enterprise. It sacrifices personal liberty, not because the actor's conduct results in harm to another citizen but only because it is inconsistent with the majoritarian notion of acceptable behavior. Model Penal Code 8P. 371–2.

The Commonwealth has tried hard to demonstrate a legitimate governmental interest justifying a distinction, but has failed. Many of the claimed justifications are simply outrageous: that "homosexuals are more promiscuous than heterosexuals. . . . that homosexuals enjoy the company of children, and that homosexuals are more prone to engage in sex acts in public." The only proffered justification with superficial validity is that "infectious diseases are more readily transmitted by anal sodomy than by other forms of sexual copulation." But this statute is not limited to anal copulation, and this reasoning would apply to male-female anal intercourse the same as it applies to male-male intercourse. The growing number of females to whom AIDS (Acquired Immune Deficiency Syndrome) has been transmitted is stark evidence that AIDS is not only a male homosexual disease. The only medical evidence in the record before us rules out any distinction between male-male and male-female anal intercourse as a method of preventing AIDS. The act of sexual contact is not implicated, per se, whether the contact is homosexual or heterosexual. In any event, this statute was enacted in 1974 before the AIDS nightmare was upon us. It was 1982 or 1983 before AIDS was a recognized diagnostic entity.

In the final analysis we can attribute no legislative purpose to this statute except to single out homosexuals for different treatment for indulging their sexual preference by engaging in the same activity heterosexuals are now at liberty to perform. By 1974 there had already been a sea change in societal values insofar as attaching criminal penalties to extramarital sex. The question is whether a society that no longer criminalizes adultery, fornication, or deviate sexual intercourse between heterosexuals, has a rational basis to single out homosexual acts for different treatment. Is there a rational basis for declaring this one type of sexual immorality so destructive of family values as to merit criminal punishment whereas other acts of sexual immorality which were likewise forbidden by the same religious and traditional heritage of Western civilization are now decriminalized? If there is a rational basis for different treatment it has yet to be demonstrated in this case. We need not sympathize, agree with, or even understand the sexual preference of homosexuals in order to recognize their right to equal treatment before the bar of criminal justice.

To be treated equally by the law is a broader constitutional value than due process of law as discussed in the Bowers case. We recognize it as such under the Kentucky Constitution, without regard to whether the United States Supreme Court continues to do so in federal constitutional jurisprudence.

"Equal Justice Under Law" inscribed above the entrance to the United States Supreme Court, expresses the unique goal to which all humanity aspires. In Kentucky it is more than a mere aspiration.

Concurring Opinion by Justice Combs

I Concur in the majority opinion unreservedly.

Of necessity, we choose today between competing principles of political, jurisprudential, and (some would say) moral philosophy. Sworn to uphold and protect the Constitution of Kentucky, we seven aspire to perform that high absolute power, but a power of government (Section 27), a government instituted to ensure the "peace, safety, and happiness" of the people, in whom all power inheres (Section 4). Ordained as the jealous guardian of individual freedom, government wields legitimate power only in execution of the function. Its authority to interfere with one's liberty derives solely from its duty to preserve the liberty of another. Where one seeks happiness in private, removed from others (indeed unknown to others, absent prying), and where the conduct is not relational to the rights of another, state interference is per se overweening, arbitrary, and unconstitutional.

It may be asked whether a majority, believing its own happiness will be enhanced by another's conformity, may not enforce its moral code upon all. The answer is that, first, morality is an individual, personal—one might say, private—matter of conscience, and dwells inviolate within the fortress of Section 5: "No human authority shall, in any case whatsoever, control or interfere with rights of conscience." Second, the Constitution promotes no particular morality, however popular. Indeed, the New World having been sought out by those fleeing state and/or majoritarian persecution, our systems of government are predicated upon such imperatives as that recognized in Kentucky Constitution Section 2: "Absolute and arbitrary power over the lives, liberty and property of freemen exist nowhere in a republic, not even in the largest majority." Third, morality is a matter of values. Insofar as it comprises a moral code, the Constitution embraces—yea, embodies—the immutable values of individual freedom, liberty, and equality.

Those who decry today's result are quick to note the absence of the word "privacy" from the Constitution. To them I say, first, that Section 1, in enumerating certain inherent rights, does not purport to be exclusive. Its words are that those may be reckoned among every person's inalienable rights. The Constitution also omits mention of one's right to play checkers, to smile or frown, to rise or rest, to eat or fast, to look at a king. I have no doubt, as a citizen or as a jurist, that these rights exist. (Likely, neither is this list exhaustive.) Second, the right to privacy is a necessary concomitant to general natural freedom of conscience, as well as to the rights to enjoy life and liberty and to seek and pursue happiness. Third, given the nature, the purpose, the promise of our Constitution, and its institution of a government charged as the conservator of individual freedom, I suggest that the appropriate question is not "Whence comes the right to privacy?" but rather, "Whence comes the right to deny it?"

Dissent by: Lambert, Wintersheimer

The major premise in the majority opinion is that the Constitution forbids any legal restriction upon the private conduct of adults unless it can be shown that such conduct is harmful to another. This view represents the essence of the philosophy of John Stuart Mill in his essay on Liberty. While espousing such a view, however, Mill recognized the difficulty of distinguishing that part of a person's life which affected only himself from that which affected others. He recognized that one who by deleterious vices harmed himself indirectly harmed others and that society suffered indirect harm by the mere knowledge of immoral conduct. Nevertheless, Mill clung to his philosophy by insisting that society was without-power to punish gambling or drunkenness. He made a ringing defense of the right of persons so disposed to practice polygamy.

While the philosophy of John Stuart Mill as adopted by this Court in Campbell v. Commonwealth exalts individuality in the extreme, it has, nonetheless, a superficial appeal. It rejects majoritarian morality as a basis for law and imposes legal limits on the conduct of man only insofar as it may harm others. Unfortunately for the purposes of the majority, the philosophy of Mill and the views contained in the Campbell case, if logically applied, would necessarily result in the eradication of numerous other criminal statutes. For example, if majoritarian morality is without a role in the formulation of criminal law and the only standard is harm to another, all laws proscribing the possession and use of dangerous or narcotic drugs would fall.

Likewise, incest statutes which proscribe sexual intercourse between persons of close kinship regardless of age or consent would be rendered invalid. Laws prohibiting cruelty to animals, the abuse of dead human bodies, suicide and polygamy would be held unconstitutional. Despite the majority's disingenuous departure from Mill based on "an enlightened paternalism" to prevent self-inflicted harm, many prevailing criminal statutes would nevertheless fail the "harm to another" test. While the majority of this Court manifestly sees the proposition otherwise, the Supreme Court of the United States has addressed the role of morality as a rationale to support criminal law and found no impediment.

In the final analysis, the question is whether a rational distinction may be drawn between acts of sodomy committed by heterosexuals and homosexuals. As cases such as Griswold v. Connecticut, supra, Eisenstadt v. Baird, supra, Loving v. Virginia, supra, and Roe v. Wade, supra, demonstrate, there

is a heightened protection of the right of persons with respect to conduct in
the context of marriage, procreation, contraception, family relationships,
and child rearing and education. As such considerations are without any application as to acts of homosexual sodomy, the distinction is manifest.

MICHAEL J. SANDEL

Moral Argument and Liberal Toleration: Abortion and Homosexuality

People defend laws against abortion and homosexual sodomy in two different ways: Some argue that abortion and homosexuality are morally repre-
hensible and therefore worthy of prohibition; others try to avoid passing
judgment on the morality of these practices, and argue instead that, in a
democracy, political majorities have the right to embody in law their moral
convictions.

In a similar way, arguments against antiabortion and antisodomy laws take
two different forms: Some say the laws are unjust because the practices they
prohibit are morally permissible, indeed sometimes desirable; other oppose
these laws without reference to the moral status of the practices at issue, and
argue instead that individuals have a right to choose for themselves whether
to engage in them.

These two styles of argument might be called, respectively, the "naive"
and the "sophisticated." The naive view holds that the justice of laws depends on the moral worth of the conduct they prohibit or protect. The
sophisticated view holds that the justice of such laws depends not on a substantive moral judgment about the conduct at stake, but instead on a more
general theory about the respective claims of majority rule and individual
rights, of democracy on the one hand, and liberty on the other.

I shall try in this paper to bring out the truth in the naive view, which I
take to be this: The justice (or injustice) of laws against abortion and homosexual sodomy depends, at least in part, on the morality (or immorality) of
those practices.[1] This is the claim the sophisticated view rejects. In both its
majoritarian and its liberal versions, the sophisticated view tries to set aside
or "bracket" controversial moral and religious conceptions for purpose of
justice. It insists that the justification of laws be neutral among competing
visions of the good life.

In practice, of course, these two kinds of argument can be difficult to distinguish. In the debate over cases like *Roe v. Wade*[2] and *Bowers v. Hardwick*,[3] both camps tend to advance the naive view under cover of the sophisticated. (Such is the prestige of the sophisticated way of arguing.) For example, those who would ban abortion and sodomy out of abhorrence often argue in the name of deference to democracy and judicial restraint. Similarly, those who want permissive laws because they approve abortion and homosexuality often argue in the name of liberal toleration.

This is not to suggest that all instances of the sophisticated argument are disingenuous attempts to promote a substantive moral conviction. Those who argue that law should be neutral among competing conceptions of the good life offer various grounds for their claim, including most prominently the following:

> (1) the *relativist* view says law should not affirm a particular moral conception because all morality is relative, and so there are no moral truths to affirm; (2) the *utilitarian* view argues that government neutrality will, for various reasons, promote the general welfare in the long run; (3) the *voluntarist* view holds that government should be neutral among conceptions of the good life in order to respect the capacity of persons as free citizens or autonomous agents to choose their conceptions for themselves; and (4) the *minimalist,* or pragmatic view says that, because people inevitably disagree about morality and religion, government should bracket these controversies for the sake of political agreement and social cooperation.

In order to bring out the truth in the naive way of arguing, I look to the actual arguments judges and commentators have made in recent cases dealing with abortion and homosexuality. Their arguments, unfailingly sophisticated, illustrate the difficulty of bracketing moral judgments for purposes of law. Because their reasons for trying to be neutral among conceptions of the good life are drawn primarily from voluntarist and minimalist assumptions, I focus on these arguments. Finally, although much of my argument criticizes leading theories of liberal toleration, I do not think it offers any comfort to majoritarianism. The cure for liberalism is not majoritarianism, but a keener appreciation of the role of substantive moral discourse in political and constitutional argument.

I
Privacy Rights: Intimacy and Autonomy

In the constitutional right of privacy, the neutral state and the voluntarist conception of the person are often joined. In the case of abortion, for example, no state may, "by adopting one theory of life,"[4] override a woman's right to decide "whether or not to terminate her pregnancy."[5] Government may not enforce a particular moral view, however widely held, for "no individual should be compelled to surrender the freedom to make that decision for herself simply because her 'value preferences' are not shared by the majority."[6]

As with religious liberty and freedom of speech, so with privacy, the ideal of neutrality often reflects a voluntarist conception of human agency. Government must be neutral among conceptions of the good life in order to respect the capacity of persons to choose their values and relationships for themselves. So close is the connection between privacy rights and the voluntarist conception of the self that commentators frequently assimilate the values of privacy and autonomy: Privacy rights are said to be "grounded in notions of individual autonomy," because "[t]he human dignity protected by constitutional guarantees would be seriously diminished if people were not free to choose and adopt a lifestyle which allows expression of their uniqueness and individuality."[7] In "recognizing a constitutional right to privacy," the Court has given effect to the view "that persons have the capacity to live autonomously and the right to exercise that capacity."[8] Supreme Court decisions voiding laws against contraceptives "not only protect the individual who chooses not to procreate, but also the autonomy of a couple's association."[9] They protect men and women "against an unchosen commitment" to unwanted children, and "against a compelled identification with the social role of parent."[10]

In Supreme Court decisions and dissents alike, the justices have often tied privacy rights to voluntarist assumptions. The Court has thus characterized laws banning the use of contraceptives as violating "the constitutional protection of individual autonomy in matters of childbearing."[11] It has defended the right to an abortion on the grounds that few decision are "more properly private, or more basic to individual dignity and autonomy, than a woman's decision . . . whether to end her pregnancy."[12] Justice Douglas, concurring in an abortion case, emphasized that the right of privacy protects such liberties as "the autonomous control over the development and expression of one's intellect, interests, tastes, and personality," as well as "freedom of choice in the basic decisions of one's life respecting marriage, divorce, procreation, contraception, and the education and upbringing of children."[13] Writing in dissent, Justice Marshall found a regulation limiting the hair length of policemen "inconsistent with the values of privacy, self-identity, autonomy, and personal integrity" he believed the Constitution was designed to protect.[14] And four justices would have extended privacy protection to consensual homosexual activity on the grounds that "much of the richness of a relationship will come from the freedom an individual has to *choose* the form and nature of these intensely personal bonds."[15]

Although the link between privacy and autonomy is now so familiar as to seem natural, even necessary, the right of privacy need not presuppose a voluntarist conception of the person. In fact, through most of its history in American law, the right of privacy has implied neither the ideal of the neutral state nor the ideal of a self freely choosing its aims and attachments.

Where the contemporary right of privacy is the right to engage in certain conduct without government restraint, the traditional version is the right to keep certain personal facts from public view. The new privacy protects a person's "independence in making certain kinds of important decisions," whereas the old privacy protects a person's interest "in avoiding disclosure of personal matters."[16]

The tendency to identify privacy with autonomy not only obscures these shifting understandings of privacy; it also restricts the range of reasons for protecting it. Although the new privacy typically relies on voluntarist justifications, it can also be justified in other ways. A right to be free of governmental interference in matters of marriage, for example, can be defended not only in the name of individual choice, but also in the name of the intrinsic value or social importance of the practice it protects. As the Court has acknowledged, "certain kinds of personal bonds have played a critical role in the culture and traditions of the Nation by cultivating and transmitting shared ideals and beliefs; they thereby foster diversity and act as critical buffers between the individual and the power of the State."[17] The Court's greater tendency, however, has been to view privacy in voluntarist terms, as protecting "the ability independently to define one's identity."[18]

II
From the Old Privacy to the New

The right to privacy first gained legal recognition in the United States as a doctrine of tort law, not constitutional law. In an influential article in 1890, Louis Brandeis, then a Boston lawyer, and his one-time law partner Samuel Warren argued that the civil law should protect "the right to privacy."[19] Far from later-day concerns with sexual freedoms, Brandeis and Warren's privacy was quaint by comparison, concerned with the publication of high society gossip by the sensationalist press, or the unauthorized use of people's portraits in advertising.[20] Gradually at first, then more frequently in the 1930s, this right to privacy gained recognition in the civil law of most states.[21] Prior to the 1960s, however, privacy received scant attention in constitutional law.

Two members of the Supreme Court first addressed the right of privacy as such in 1961 when a Connecticut pharmacist challenged the state's ban on contraceptives in *Poe v. Ullman*.[22] Although the majority dismissed the case on technical grounds,[23] Justices Douglas and Harlan dissented, arguing that the law violated the right of privacy. The privacy they defended was privacy in the traditional sense. The right at stake was not the right to use contraceptives but the right to be free of the surveillance that enforcement would require. "If we imagine a regime of full enforcement of the law," wrote Douglas, "we would reach the point where search warrants issued and officers appeared in bedrooms to find out what went on. . . . If [the State] can make this law, it can enforce it. And proof of its violation necessarily involves an inquiry into the relation between man and wife."[24] Banning the sale would be different from banning their use, Douglas observed. Banning the sale would restrict access to contraceptives but would not expose intimate relations to public inspection. Enforcement would take police to the drugstore, not the bedroom, and so would not offend privacy in the traditional sense.[25]

Justice Harlan also objected to the law on grounds that distinguish the old privacy from the new. He did not object that the law against contraceptives failed to be neutral among competing moral conceptions. Although Harlan acknowledged that the law was based on the belief that contraception is immoral in itself, and encourages such "dissolute action" as fornication and adultery by minimizing their "disastrous consequence,"[26] he did not find this failure of neutrality contrary to the Constitution. In a statement clearly opposed to the strictures of neutrality, Harlan argued that morality is a legitimate concern of government.

> The very inclusion of the category of morality among state concerns indicates that society is not limited to its objects only to the physical well-being of the community, but has traditionally concerned itself with the moral soundness of its people as well. Indeed to attempt a line between public behavior and that which is purely consensual or solitary would be to withdraw from community concern a range of subjects with which every society in civilized times has found it necessary to deal.[27]

Though he rejected the ideal of the neutral state, Harlan did not conclude that Connecticut could prohibit married couples from using contraceptives. Like Douglas, he reasoned that enforcing the law would intrude on the privacy essential to the prized institution of marriage. He objected to the violation of privacy in the traditional sense, to the "intrusion of the whole machinery of the criminal law into the very heart of marital privacy, requiring husband and wife to render account before a criminal tribunal of their uses of that intimacy."[28] According to Harlan, the state was entitled to embody in law the belief that contraception is immoral, but not to implement "the obnoxiously intrusive means it ha[d] chosen to effectuate that policy."[29]

Four years later, in *Griswold v. Connecticut*,[30] the dissenters prevailed. The Supreme Court invalidated Connecticut's law against contraceptives and for the first time explicitly recognized a constitutional right of privacy. Although the right was located in the Constitution rather than tort law, it remained tied to the traditional notion of privacy as the interest in keeping intimate affairs from public view. The violation of privacy consisted in the intrusion required to enforce the law, not the restriction on the freedom to use contraceptives. "Would we allow the police to search the sacred precincts of marital bedrooms for telltale signs of the use of contraceptives?," wrote Justice Douglas for the Court. "The very idea is repulsive to the notions of privacy surrounding the marriage relationship."[31]

The justification for the right was not voluntarist but unabashedly teleological; the privacy the Court vindicated was not for the sake of letting people lead their sexual lives as they choose, but rather for the sake of affirming and protecting the social institution of marriage.

> Marriage is a coming together for better or for worse, hopefully enduring, and intimate to the degree of being sacred. It is an association that promotes a way of life, . . . a harmony in living, . . . a bilateral loyalty. . . . [I]t is an association for as noble a purpose as any involved in our prior decisions.[32]

Although commentators and judges often view *Griswold* as a dramatic constitutional departure, the privacy right it proclaimed was consistent with traditional notions of privacy going back to the turn of the century. From the standpoint of shifting privacy conceptions, the more decisive turn came seven years later in *Eisenstadt v. Baird*,[33] a seemingly similar case. Like *Griswold*, it involved a state law restricting contraceptives. In *Eisenstadt*, however, the challenged law restricted the distribution of contraceptives, not their use. While it therefore limited access to contraceptives, its enforcement could not be said to require governmental surveillance of intimate activities. It did not violate privacy in the traditional sense.[34] Furthermore, the law prohibited distributing contraceptives only to unmarried persons, and so did not burden the institution of marriage as the Connecticut law did.

Despite these differences, the Supreme Court struck down the law with only a single dissent. Its decision involved two innovations, one explicit, the other unacknowledged. The explicit innovation redescribed the bearers of privacy rights from persons *qua* participants in the social institution of marriage to persons *qua* individuals, independent of their roles or attachments. As the Court explained, "It is true that in *Griswold* the right of privacy in question inhered in the marital relationship. Yet the marital couple is not an independent entity with a mind and heart of its own, but an association of two individuals each with a separate intellectual and emotional makeup."[35]

The subtler, though no less fateful change in *Eisenstadt* was in the shift from the old privacy to the new. Rather than conceiving privacy as freedom from surveillance or disclosure of intimate affairs, the Court found that the right to privacy now protected the freedom to engage in certain activities without governmental restriction. Although privacy in *Griswold* prevented intrusion into "the sacred precincts of marital bedrooms,"[36] privacy in *Eisenstadt* prevented intrusion into *decisions* of certain kinds. Moreover, as the meaning of privacy changed, so did its justification. The Court protected privacy in *Eisenstadt* not for the social practices it promoted but for the individual choice it secured. "If the right of privacy means anything, it is the right of the *individual,* married or single, to be free from unwarranted governmental intrusion into matters so fundamentally affecting a person as the decision whether to bear or beget a child."[37]

One year later, in *Roe v. Wade,*[38] the Supreme Court gave the new privacy its most controversial application by striking down a Texas law against abortion and extending privacy to "encompass a woman's decision whether or not to terminate her pregnancy."[39] First with contraception, then with abortion, the right of privacy had become the right to make certain sorts of choices, free of interference by the state. The choice had also to be free of interference by husbands or parents. In *Planned Parenthood of Missouri v. Danforth,*[40] the Court struck down a law requiring a husband's consent, or parental consent in the case of unmarried minors, as a condition for an abortion. Since the state may not prevent even minors from having abortions in the first trimester, it cannot delegate to a "third party" such as a husband or parent the authority to do so.[41]

The voluntarist grounds of the new privacy found explicit statement in a 1977 case invalidating a New York law prohibiting the sale of contraceptives to minors under age sixteen.[42] For the first time, the Court used the language of autonomy to describe the interest privacy protects, and argued openly for the shift from the old privacy to the new. Writing for the Court in *Carey v. Population Services International,* Justice Brennan admitted that *Griswold* focused on the fact that a law forbidding the *use* of contraceptives can bring the police into marital bedrooms.[43] "But subsequent decisions have made clear that the constitutional protection of individual autonomy in matters of childbearing is not dependent on that element."[44] Surveying the previous cases, he emphasized that *Eisenstadt* protected the "*decision* whether to bear or beget a child,"[45] and *Roe* protected "a woman's *decision* whether or not to terminate her pregnancy."[46] He concluded that "the teaching of *Griswold* is that the Constitution protects individual decisions in matters of childbearing from unjustified intrusion by the State."[47]

Given the voluntarist interpretation of privacy, restricting the *sale* of contraceptives violates privacy as harshly as banning their *use;* the one limits choice as surely as the other. "Indeed, in practice," Brennan observed, "a prohibition against all sales, since more easily and less offensively enforced, might have an even more devastating effect upon the freedom to choose contraception."[48] Ironically, the very fact that a ban on sales does *not* threaten the old privacy makes it a greater threat to the new.

Later decisions upholding abortion rights also used the language of autonomy to describe the privacy interest at stake. The Court held in a recent opinion that "[f]ew decisions are ... more properly private, or more basic to individual dignity and autonomy than a woman's decision ... whether to end her pregnancy. A woman's right to make that choice freely is fundamental."[49]

Despite its increasing tendency to identify privacy with autonomy, the Court refused, in a 5–4 decision, to extend privacy protection to consensual homosexual activity. Writing for the majority, Justice White emphasized that the Court's previous privacy cases protected choice only with respect to child rearing and education, family relationships, procreation, marriage, contraception, and abortion. "[W]e think it evident," he held, "that none of the rights announced in those cases bears any resemblance to the claimed constitutional right of homosexuals to engage in acts of sodomy. . . ."[50] He also rejected the claim that Georgia's citizens could not embody in law their belief "that homosexual sodomy is immoral and unacceptable."[51] Neutrality to the contrary, "[t]he law ... is constantly based on notions of morality, and if all laws representing essentially moral choices are to be invalidated under the Due Process Clause, the court will be very busy indeed."[52]

Writing for the four dissenters, Justice Blackmun argued that the Court's previous privacy decisions did not depend on the virtue of the practices they protected but on the principle of free individual choice in intimate matters. "We protect those rights not because they contribute ... to the general public welfare, but because they form so central a part of an individual's life. '[T]he concept of privacy embodies the "moral fact that a person belongs to himself and not others nor to society as a whole."'"[53]

Blackmun argued for the application of earlier privacy rulings in the considerations of homosexual practices by casting the Court's concern for conventional family ties in individualist terms: "We protect the decision whether to have a child because parenthood alters so dramatically an individual's self-definition. ... And we protect the family because it contributes so powerfully to the happiness of individuals, not because of a preference for stereotypical households."[54] Because the right of privacy in sexual relationships protects "the freedom an individual has to *choose* the form and nature of these intensely personal bonds,"[55] it protects homosexual activity no less than other intimate choices.

Defending the ideal of the neutral state, Blackmun added that traditional religious condemnations of homosexuality "give[ ] the State no license to impose their judgments on the entire citizenry."[56] To the contrary, the State's appeal to religious teachings against homosexuality undermines its claim that the law "represents a legitimate use of secular coercive power."[57]

Despite the Court's reluctance to extend privacy rights to homosexuals, the privacy cases of the last twenty-five years offer ample evidence of assumptions drawn from the liberal conception of the person. They also raise two questions about the liberalism they reflect: First whether bracketing controversial moral issues is even possible; and second whether the voluntarist conception of privacy limits the range of reasons for protecting privacy. . . .

*   *   *

III
The Voluntarist Case for Toleration: Homosexuality

The dissenters' argument for toleration in *Bowers v. Hardwick*[58] illustrates the difficulties with the version of liberalism that ties toleration to autonomy rights alone. In refusing to extend the rights of privacy to homosexuals, the majority in *Bowers* declared that none of the rights announced in earlier privacy cases resembled the rights homosexuals were seeking: "No connection between family, marriage, or procreation on the one hand and homosexual activity on the other has been demonstrated. . . ."[59] Any reply to the Court's position would have to show some connection between the practices already subject to privacy protection and the homosexual practices not yet protected. What then is the resemblance between heterosexual intimacies on the one hand, and homosexual intimacies on the other, such that both are entitled to a constitutional right of privacy?

This question might be answered in at least two different ways — one voluntarist, the other substantive. The first argues from the autonomy the practices reflect, whereas the second appeals to the human goods the practices realize. The voluntarist answer holds that people should be free to choose their intimate associations for themselves, regardless of the virtue or popularity of the practices they choose so long as they do not harm others. In this view, homosexual relationships resemble the heterosexual relationships the Court has already protected in that all reflect the choices of autonomous selves.

By contrast, the substantive answer claims that much that is valuable in conventional marriage is also present in homosexual unions. In this view, the connection between heterosexual and homosexual relations is not that both result from individual choice but that both realize important human goods. Rather than rely on autonomy alone, this second line of reply articulates the virtues homosexual intimacy may share with heterosexual intimacy, along with any distinctive virtues of its own. It defends homosexual privacy the way *Griswold* defended marital privacy, by arguing that, like marriage, homosexual union may also be "intimate to the degree of being sacred . . . a harmony in living . . . a bilateral loyalty," an association for a "noble . . . purpose."[60]

Of these two possible replies, the dissenters in *Bowers* relied wholly on the first. Rather than protect homosexual intimacies for the human goods they share with intimacies the Court already protects, Justice Blackmun cast the Court's earlier cases in individualist terms, and found their reading applied equally to homosexuality because "much of the richness of a relationship will come from the freedom an individual has to *choose* the form and nature of these intensely personal bonds."[61] At issue was not homosexuality as such but respect for the fact that "different individuals will make different choices" in deciding how to conduct their lives.[62]

Justice Stevens, in a separate dissent, also avoided referring to the values homosexual intimacy may share with heterosexual love. Instead, he wrote broadly of "'the individual's right to make certain unusually important decisions'" and "'respect for the dignity of individual choice,'"[63] rejecting the notion that such liberty belongs to heterosexuals alone. "From the standpoint of the individual, the homosexual and the heterosexual have the same interest in deciding how he will live his own life, and, more narrowly, how he will conduct himself in his personal voluntary associations with his companions."[64]

The voluntarist argument so dominates the *Bowers* dissents that it seems difficult to imagine a judicial rendering of the substantive view. But a glimmer of this view can be found in the appeals court opinion in the same case.[65] The United States Court of Appeals had ruled in Hardwick's favor and had struck down the law under which he was convicted. Like Blackmun and Stevens, the appeals court constructed an analogy between privacy in marriage and privacy in homosexual relations. But unlike the Supreme Court dissenters, it did not rest the analogy on voluntarist grounds alone. It argued instead that both practices may realize important human goods.

The marital relationship is significant, wrote the court of appeals, not only because of its procreative purpose but also "because of the unsurpassed opportunity for mutual support and self-expression that it provides."[66] It recalled the Supreme Court's observation in *Griswold* that "[m]arriage is a coming together for better or for worse, hopefully enduring, and intimate to the degree of being sacred."[67] And it went on to suggest that the qualities the Court so prized in *Griswold* could be present in homosexual unions as well: "For some, the sexual activity in question here serves the same purpose as the intimacy of marriage."[68]

Ironically, this way of extending privacy rights to homosexuals depends on an "old-fashioned" reading of *Griswold* as protecting the human goods realized in marriage, a reading the Court has long since renounced in favor of an individualist reading.[69] By drawing on the teleological dimension of *Griswold,* the substantive case for homosexual privacy offends the liberalism that insists on neutrality. It grounds the right of privacy on the good of the practice it would protect, and so fails to be neutral among conceptions of the good.

The more frequently employed precedent for homosexual rights is not *Griswold* but *Stanley v. Georgia*,[70] which upheld the right to possess obscene materials in the privacy of one's home. *Stanley* did not hold that the obscene films found in the defendant's bedroom served a "noble purpose," only that he had a right to view them in private. The toleration *Stanley* defended was wholly independent of the value or importance of the thing being tolerated.[71]

In the 1980 case of *People v. Onofre*,[72] the New York Court of Appeals vindicated privacy rights for homosexuals on precisely these grounds. The court reasoned that if, following *Stanley*, there is a right to the "satisfaction of sexual desires by resort to material condemned as obscene," there should also be a right "to seek sexual gratification from what at least once was commonly regarded as 'deviant' conduct," so long as it is private and consensual.[73] The court emphasized its neutrality toward the conduct it protected: "We express no view as to any theological, moral or psychological evaluation of consensual sodomy. These are aspects of the issue on which informed, competent authorities and individuals may and do differ."[74] The court's role was simply to ensure that the State bracketed these competing moral views, rather than embodying any one of them in law.[75]

The case for toleration that brackets the morality of homosexuality has a powerful appeal. In the face of deep disagreement about values, it seems to ask the least of the contending parties. It offers social peace and respect for rights without the need for moral conversion. Those who view sodomy as sin need not be persuaded to change their minds, only to tolerate those who practice it in private. By insisting only that each respect the freedom of others to live the lives they choose, this toleration promises a basis for political agreement that does not await shared conceptions of morality.

Despite its promise, however, the neutral case for toleration is subject to two related difficulties. First, as a practical matter, it is by no means clear that social cooperation can be secured on the strength of autonomy rights alone, absent some measure of agreement on the moral permissibility of the practices at issue. It may not be accidental that the first practices subject to the right of privacy were accorded constitutional protection in cases that spoke of the sanctity of marriage and procreation. Only later did the Court abstract privacy right from these practices and protect them without reference to the human goods they were once thought to make possible. This suggests that the voluntarist justification of privacy rights is dependent—politically as well as philosophically—on some measure of agreement that the practices protected are morally permissible.

A second difficulty with the voluntarist case for toleration concerns the quality of respect it secures. As the New York case suggests, the analogy with *Stanley* tolerates homosexuality at the price of demeaning it; it puts homosexual intimacy on a par with obscenity—a base thing that should nonetheless be tolerated so long as it takes place in private. If *Stanley* rather than *Griswold* is the relevant analogy, the interest at stake is bound to be reduced, as the New York court reduced it, to "sexual gratification." (The only intimate relationship at stake in *Stanley* was between a man and his pornography.)

The majority in *Bowers* exploited this assumption by ridiculing the notion of a "fundamental right to engage in homosexual sodomy."[76] The obvious reply is that *Bowers* is no more about a right to homosexual sodomy than *Griswold* was about a right to heterosexual intercourse. But by refusing to articulate the human goods that homosexual intimacy may share with heterosexual unions, the voluntarist case for toleration forfeits the analogy with *Griswold* and makes the ridicule difficult to refute.

The problem with the neutral case for toleration is the opposite side of its appeal; it leaves wholly unchallenged the adverse views of homosexuality itself. Unless those views can be plausibly addressed, even a Court ruling in their favor is unlikely to win for homosexuals more than a thin and fragile toleration. A fuller respect would require, if not admiration, at least some appreciation of the lives homosexuals live. Such appreciation, however, is unlikely to be cultivated by a legal and political discourse conducted in terms of autonomy rights alone.

The liberal may reply that autonomy arguments in court need not foreclose more substantive, affirmative arguments elsewhere; bracketing moral argument for constitutional purposes does not mean bracketing moral argument altogether. Once their freedom of choice in sexual practice is secured, homosexuals can seek, by argument and example, to win from their fellow citizens a deeper respect than autonomy can supply.

The liberal reply, however, underestimates the extent to which constitutional discourse has come to constitute the terms of political discourse in American public life. While most at home in constitutional law, the main motifs of contemporary liberalism—rights as trumps, the neutral state, and the unencumbered self—figure with increasing prominence in our moral and political debate in general.

Conclusion

Admittedly, the tendency to bracket substantive moral questions makes it difficult to argue for toleration in the language of the good. Defining privacy rights by defending the practices privacy protects seems either reckless or quaint; reckless because it rests so much on moral argument, quaint because it recalls the traditional view that ties the case for privacy to the merits of the conduct privacy protects. But as the abortion and sodomy cases illustrate, the attempt to bracket moral questions faces difficulties of its own. They suggest the truth in the "naive" view, that the justice or injustice of laws against abortion and homosexual sodomy may have something to do with the morality or immorality of these practices after all.

Notes

1. I do not defend the stronger claim that the morality (or immorality) of a practice is the only relevant reason in deciding whether there should be a law against it.

2. 410 U.S. 113 (1973).

3. 478 U.S. 186 (1986).

4. Roe v. Wade, 410 U.S. 113, 162 (1973).

5. *Id.* at 153.

6. Thornburgh v. American College of Obstetricians & Gynecologists, 476 U.S. 747, 777 (1986) (Stevens, J., concurring).

7. Eichbaum, *Towards an Autonomy-Based Theory of Constitutional Privacy: Beyond the Ideology of Familial Privacy.* 14 HARV. C.R.-C.L. L. REV. 361, 362, 365 (1979).

8. Richards, *The Individual, the Family, and the Constitution: A Jurisprudential Perspective,* 55 N.Y.U. L. REV. 1, 31 (1980).

9. Karst, *The Freedom of Intimate Association,* 89 YALE L.J. 624, 641 (1980). For articles discussing the connection between privacy and autonomy rights, see also Henkin, *Privacy and Autonomy,* 74 COLUM. L. REV. 1410 (1974); Smith, *The Constitution and Autonomy,* 60 TEX. L. REV. 175 (1982); Wilkinson III & White, *Constitutional Protection for Personal Lifestyles,* 62 CORNELL L. REV. 563 (1977).

10. Karst, *supra* note 9, at 641.

11. Carey v. Population Services Int'l, 431 U.S. 678, 687 (1977).

12. Thornburgh v. American College of Obstetricians & Gynecologists, 476 U.S. 747, 772 (1986).

13. Doe v. Bolton, 410 U.S. 238, 251 (1973) (Douglas, J. concurring) (emphasis omitted).

14. Kelley v. Johnson, 425 U.S. 238, 251 (1976) (Marshall, J., dissenting).

15. Bowers v. Hardwick, 478 U.S. 186, 205 (1986) (Blackmun, J., dissenting).

16. Whalen v. Roe, 429 U.S. 589, 599–600 (1977).

17. Roberts v. United States Jaycees, 468 U.S. 609, 618–19 (1984).

18. *Id.* at 619.

19. Warren & Brandeis, *The Right to Privacy,* 4 HARV. L. REV. 193 (1890).

20. *Id.* at 195–96.

21. Prosser, *Privacy,* 48 CALIF. L. REV. 383 (1960) (discussing the ensuing recognition and development of a right to privacy).

22. 367 U.S. 497 (1961).

23. *Id.* at 509.

24. *Id.* at 519–21 (Douglas, J., dissenting).

25. *Id.* at 519.

26. *Id.* at 545 (Harlan, J., dissenting).

27. *Id.* at 545–46.

28. *Id.* at 553.

29. *Id.* at 554.

30. 381 U.S. 479 (1965).

31. *Id.* at 485–86.

32. *Id.* at 486.

33. 405 U.S. 438 (1972).

34. In fact, the case arose when a man was convicted for giving away a contraceptive device at a public lecture. *Id.* at 440.

35. *Id.* at 453.

36. *Griswold,* 381 U.S. at 485.

37. *Eisenstadt,* 405 U.S. at 453. The Court's opinion in *Eisenstadt* camouflages the shift from the old privacy to the new with a false hypothetical premise: "If under *Griswold* the distribution of contraceptives to married persons cannot be prohibited, a ban on distribution to unmarried per-

sons would be equally impermissible." *Id.* But *Griswold* did not hold that distribution to married persons cannot be prohibited.

38. 410 U.S. 113 (1973).

39. *Id.* at 153.

40. 428 U.S. 52 (1976).

41. *Id.* at 69, 75.

42. Carey v. Population Services Int'l, 431 U.S. 678 (1977).

43. *Id.* at 687.

44. *Id.*

45. *Id.* (quoting *Eisenstadt,* 405 U.S. at 453) (emphasis added in *Carey*).

46. *Id.* (quoting *Roe,* 410 U.S. at 153) (emphasis added in *Carey*).

47. *Id.*

48. *Id.* at 688.

49. Thornburgh v. American College of Obstetricians & Gynecologists, 776 U.S. 747, 772 (1986).

50. Bowers v. Hardwick, 478 U.S. 186, 190–91 (1986).

51. *Id.* at 196.

52. *Id.*

53. *Id.* at 204 (Blackmun J., dissenting) (quoting Thornburgh v. American College of Obstetricians & Gynecologists, 476 U.S. at 777 n.5 (Stevens, J., concurring) (quoting Fried, *Correspondence,* 6 PHIL. & PUB. AFF. 288–89 (1977))).

54. *Id.* at 205.

55. *Id.*

56. *Id.* at 211.

57. *Id.* In striking down a similar sodomy law, the New York Court of Appeals clearly expressed the idea that government must be neutral among competing conceptions of the good. "[I]t is not the function of the Penal Law in our governmental policy to provide either a medium for the articulation or the apparatus for the intended enforcement of moral or theological values." People v. Onofre, 51 N.Y.2d 476, 488 n.3, 415 N.E.2d 936, 940 n.3, 434 N.Y.S.2d 947, 951 n.3 (1980), *cert. denied,* 451 U.S. 987 (1981).

58. 478 U.S. 186 (1986).

59. *Id.* at 191.

60. The phrases are from Griswold v. Connecticut 381 U.S. 479 486 (1965).

61. 478 U.S. at 205 (Blackmun, J., dissenting) (emphasis added).

62. *Id.* at 206.

63. *Id.* at 217 (Stevens, J., dissenting) (quoting Fitzgerald v. Porter Memorial Hospital, 523 F.2d 716, 719–20 (7th Cir. 1975), *cert. denied,* 425 U.S. 916 (1976).

64. *Id.* at 218–19.

65. Hardwick v. Bowers, 760 F2d. 1202 (11th Cir. 1985), rev'd 476 U.S. 747 (1986).

66. *Id.* at 1211–12

67. *Id.* at 1212 (quoting Griswold v. Connecticut, 381 U.S. 479, 486 (1965)).

68. *Id.* at 1212.

69. For individualist readings of *Griswold,* see Eisenstadt v. Baird, 405 U.S. 438, 453 (1972) and Carey v. Population Services Int'l, 431 U.S. 678, 687 (1977).

70. 394 U.S. 557 (1969).

71. *Id.* at 564–66, 568 ("This right to receive information and ideas, *regardless of their social worth,* is fundamental to our free society. . . . [T]he States retain broad power to regulate obscenity; that power simply does not extend to mere possession by the individual in the privacy of his own home.") (emphasis added) (citation omitted).

72. 51 N.Y.2d 476, 415 N.E.2d 936, 434 N.Y.S.2d 947 (1980), *cert. denied,* 451 U.S. 987 (1981).

73. *Id.* at 487–88, 415 N.E.2d at 939–41, 434 N.Y.S.2d at 950–51.
74. *Id.* at 488 n.3, 415 N.E.2d at 940 n.3, 434 N.Y.S.2d at 951 n.3.
75. *Id.*
76. Bowers v. Hardwick, 478 U.S. 186, 191 (1986).

JOHN GARVEY

Men Only

Male friendship is a subject that we are uncomfortable dealing with today. There are no modern counterparts to the stories of David and Jonathan, Orestes and Pylades, and Roland and Oliver. Perhaps men don't make friends as they used to when we had a lot of good wars with hand-to-hand combat and when families exerted less centripetal force. Or perhaps the problem lies only in the exposition: Men are just shy about celebrating their relationships. I do not propose to explain the entire phenomenon. But I am interested in it because the topic of love between men has lately assumed legal significance. The issue has been whether the Constitution protects our freedom to form such relationships. And there is a delicious irony in the way it has come up: The claimants have been Rotarians and homosexuals. I want to discuss these cases and to make several points about them. The first is that none of the relationships the U.S. Supreme Court has reviewed have really been about love or friendship. This explains why the claimants have lost. The second is that the legal debate has all been beside the point. The defenders of freedom have misunderstood its value; the partisans of regulation have failed to justify the government's action.

Autonomy

Bowers *and* Clubs

Michael Hardwick was arrested for violating the Georgia sodomy statute, which forbids any person to engage in oral or anal sex. Hardwick had been charged with drinking in public and missed his court appearance. The arresting officer came to his house with a warrant, was admitted by a house guest, and found Hardwick engaged in oral sex in his bedroom with another man. When the district attorney decided not to prosecute, Hardwick sued for a declaration that the Georgia law was unconstitutional. His complaint was dismissed for failure to state a claim but was reinstated by the court of appeals. Hardwick was joined as plaintiff by a married couple who claimed that the law deterred them from engaging in similar activity. They were dismissed for lack of standing and did not pursue their claim beyond the circuit court.

The Supreme Court confined its attention to the law as it applied to Hardwick. In *Bowers v. Hardwick* it held (5–4) that homosexual sodomy was not one of the "fundamental liberties" protected by the due process clause. Such freedoms must be embedded in our traditions, and sodomy has been a criminal offense since 1791, when the Bill of Rights was adopted. All fifty states forbade it in 1961; half do so today. Since there was no fundamental right at stake, Georgia could forbid sodomy simply because a majority of the voters found it immoral.

Justice Blackmun, dissenting, said that sodomy should be considered a fundamental freedom. He argued that the ability to "define one's identity" is central to any concept of liberty and that "individuals define themselves in a significant way through their intimate sexual relationships." We value these relationships precisely because we can "choose [their] form and nature." There is no "right" or "wrong" way to structure them.

This equation of freedoms and self-definition is one the Court has taken for granted in dealing with men's clubs. The issue in these cases has been whether the government can force the clubs to admit women (who would find membership a useful professional asset). The clubs have claimed, and the Court has agreed, that the due process clause protects highly personal relationships. This "safeguards the ability independently to define one's identity that is central to any concept of liberty." The problem has been that the clubs that have gotten to the Court (the Jaycees, the Rotary Club, the members of the New York State Club Association) have been large groups dedicated to holding business lunches and similar affairs. After looking at their "size, purpose, policies, selectivity, congeniality, and other character-istics," the Court has concluded that they are not the kind of relationship that the clause protects.

In this section I want to examine this thesis that freedoms allow for self-definition. This is, in a sense, the reigning ideology about freedom in Amer-ican law. We lump most of the substantive due process cases together under a general right to "autonomy" (or self-legislation). Influential writers on the First Amendment argue that autonomy is the underlying concern behind the protection of free speech. There are even those who contend that the religion clauses are designed to protect our religious autonomy. But you will notice that the thesis does no real work in the cases I am discussing, despite the impassioned talk about it. The majority ignores it in *Bowers v. Hardwick*. It is beside the point in the case of men's clubs. It may be that there is less to the idea than meets the eye.

The Value of Choice

Let us consider what there is to the autonomy thesis. According to Justice Blackmun, sodomy is not an issue of "right" and "wrong." This is not just a peculiar fact about sodomy. No act or form of life is intrinsically "right" or "wrong," "good" or "bad." People used to think otherwise. Aristotle is the standard example. He believed that the good life consists in activity in accordance with moral and intellectual virtue. For him gluttony and other forms of self-indulgence are bad because they are brutish. The glutton lacks the virtue of temperance; he acts more like an animal than a human being. The philosopher, on the other hand, lives the best of lives because he engages in contemplative activity. Some people continue to think this way even today, frequently on the basis of some religious belief. The State of Georgia relied on some such convictions in its defense of the law against sodomy. It pointed out that "traditional Judeo-Christian values proscribe such conduct," noting the condemnations in the Old and New Testaments and in the theology of Aquinas.

The chief difficulty with these views is that they are controversial. There will always be those, like Hardwick, who see nothing wrong with doing a particular act (x). If Aristotle (or the people of Georgia) think otherwise they are simply mistaken. And it is no use pointing to scripture or theology to resolve the disagreement. The authority of those sources depends on private revelation rather than on publicly available standards like science and reason. If a person (X) has not had the requisite revelation, scripture holds no power to convince that person.

The autonomy thesis holds that the only solution for this disagreement is to allow each X to decide what is "good" or "bad." But this is not just something we do *faute de mieux*. It is both justifiable and on some accounts, downright good. Two types of explanations have been offered for it. The first, which I will call metaphysical, holds that: (1) This is how the world really is. No act or form of life is intrinsically good or bad, with this exception: (2) It is good for each X to choose how to act and live.

The metaphysical explanation stresses the idea that each person is an end in himself or herself, sovereign over a kingdom of one. This is the most basic fact about the moral world. It means that we are all (like sovereign nations) free and equal. The standards of good and bad that apply to me must be ones that I choose, since I alone have legislative jurisdiction over my kingdom. If we get together for political purposes we must treat everyone alike and respect everyone's freedom. It would be wrong to give you two votes and me one (that denies my equality); or to insist that I read only approved books (that denies my freedom). All of us are equal and free to shape our own destinies. And it is good for us to do so. If I am an end in myself, if that is my nature, I have to make something of myself. I would cast off my humanity by taking orders from someone else. I would be like one of those satellite countries that used to make up the Eastern bloc, with no mind of my own. It is good for me to choose.

The other explanation, slightly less ambitious, is political. It is agnostic about whether some forms of life are better than others. Although it might actually be better to live as a rabbi than as an aesthete, we cannot form a stable democratic government based on one view or the other. People disagree irreconcilably about the proper answer, and they have strong feelings. To force one opinion upon the minority would be to risk instability. We need to bracket such questions for lawmaking purposes. Freedoms are the device for doing the bracketing: They let people choose the options that appeal to them in matters (like sexual behavior) that count.

Each of the explanations—the metaphysical and the political—provides a persuasive account of why we value freedoms. The first says that we cannot really be human without them. I have no status as a sovereign person if I am constrained by rules that I would not adopt. The second says that we cannot have a society without them. When we conduct politics on a large scale (the nation-state, or even the states of our federal union) it is impossible to legislate morality without alienating a substantial fraction of the population. Political union depends on freedom.

Each explanation also accounts for that remarkable feature of constitutional freedoms—the protection of choice. Freedoms are understood to have a bilateral (or multilateral) character. The same freedoms are used to protect atheism and religion, pornography and Shakespeare, celibacy and sodomy, and so on. How can we value things so contradictory? The autonomy thesis offers two answers. First (the metaphysical), perhaps we really value the choice itself, not any particular selection. It is in choosing that we shape our own destiny. This is what Justice Blackmun said about sodomy in *Bowers*. He claimed that we value our intimate sexual relationships because we can "choose [their] form and nature." Second (the political), perhaps we value the society that permits the choice. And even though most of us find some choices offensive, it's a package deal: The society can't survive without freedom. Justice Blackmun touched on this point, too. He concluded his opinion by saying that suppressing freedom poses a far greater "threat to national cohesion . . . than tolerance of nonconformity could ever do."

Low-Value Choices

The most serious defect of the autonomy thesis is that it explains too much. Neither the metaphysical nor the political version is subtle enough to explain why some choices get more protection than others. Consider this simple fact. If Hardwick had been caught engaging in the practice of optometry rather than sodomy, and if Georgia had had a law against it, there is scarcely a judge in America who would have defended his freedom to act as he did. It would make no difference if Hardwick could honestly claim that optometry was central to his conception of self. This suggests that the value of freedom may be tied in some way to the action in question, rather than to the choosing of it. Here I want to show that this observation applied to the cases I am considering.

One of the funny aspects of *Bowers v. Hardwick* is its abstract quality. Hardwick's sexual partner was a one-night stand—a schoolteacher from North Carolina who pleaded to reduced charges and left town. The courts showed little interest in him. Hardwick's complaint was equally casual. It merely declared that Hardwick was "a practicing homosexual who regularly engages in private homosexual acts and will do so in the future." The "acts" of sodomy were the focus; the identity of the other actor didn't matter. Hardwick's brief in the Supreme Court said that he "of course claims no right whatever to have any homosexual relationship recognized as a marriage." Justice Blackmun's opinion repeatedly talks about the "private," "intimate," "sensitive" nature of Hardwick's sexual relationship, but with an unacknowledged sense of double entendre. The words suggest a kind of closeness, caring, and sharing typical of people who are in love. But all we can be sure they really mean is that Hardwick and his partner were off by themselves ("private"), engaged in sexual activity ("intimate") that felt good ("sensitive"). What Hardwick's suit asked for was the freedom to reach an orgasm in the particular way that he favored.

I don't mean to assert that that pleasure has no value, but I want to be certain that we recognize it for what it is. It is an event that occurs within the body, rather like the pleasure of eating and drinking, though the sensation is different. A friend of mine says that he thinks of sex like a chocolate milkshake. Passion fruit might be more poetic, but the idea is the same. Lucretius calls this pure sexual pleasure Venus and distinguishes it from love. He claims, in fact, that the pleasure is greater if we keep the two separate: "Do not think that by avoiding grand passions you are missing the delights of Venus. Rather, you are reaping such profits as carry with them no penalty. Rest assured that this pleasure is enjoyed in a purer form by the healthy than by the love-sick."[1] I don't want to get too involved in a discussion of the accuracy of this observation, but it does make the rather obvious point that we distinguish Venus from erotic love (if I may use that term to designate the more complex attraction that we associate with love). And the most significant difference is that the identity of one's partner matters a lot in one case and not much in the other. C. S. Lewis makes the point nicely in a discussion of heterosexual love, though I would like to assume for the moment that the gender of the beloved is irrelevant.

[The man pursuing Venus] wants a pleasure for which a woman happens to be the necessary piece of apparatus. How much he cares about the woman as such may be gauged by his attitude to her five minutes after fruition (one does not keep a carton after one has smoked the cigarettes). Now Eros makes a man really want, not a woman, but one particular woman. In some mysterious but quite indisputable fashion the lover desires the Beloved herself, not the pleasure she can give. No lover in the world ever sought the embraces of the woman he loved as a result of a calculation, however unconscious, that they would be more pleasurable than those of any other woman.[2]

The opinions in *Bowers v. Hardwick* spend some time discussing whether Hardwick's action is like adultery or incest, both of which, everyone seems to assume, the state can forbid. But this is a mistake. There is no reason to suppose that adulterous and incestuous relationships, however wrong they may be, are simple pursuits of orgasmic pleasure. There can also be, mixed with the infidelity and oppression, an element of erotic love. A more apt comparison is prostitution. What the customer seeks is the simple delivery of sexual pleasure for which the prostitute is a necessary piece of apparatus, available for a fee. Or a better analogy still (which controls for the element of exploitation in the case of prostitution) is sodomy with animals. That is what Hardwick's claim is like, if it asks for no more than the right to achieve an orgasm in the manner he prefers.

I have tried to bring out the difference between Venus and erotic love, and the similarity of Hardwick's claim to the cases of prostitution and bestiality, for the sake of making what I think is a generally accepted point. It is this: that we do not put a very high value on the simple act of reaching an orgasm, if that is *all* that one is doing. No one would attack laws against bestiality or prostitution by claiming that they interfere with the fundamental freedom to have an orgasm and so must be justified by compelling state interests. On the contrary, we view these as debasing activities. Pornography falls in the same class. A "pornographic item is in a real sense a sexual surrogate." The Constitution permits its suppression when it does nothing more than appeal to the prurient interest. The defenders of pornography seldom talk about the value of masturbation. Their real concern is that suppression will carry over to legitimate publications.

I do not want to overstate my case. The sexual revolution of the 1960s has had at least this effect: Most people do not see Venus, naked and unattached, as evil. Far fewer people today than thirty years ago would condemn masturbation or random couplings (heterosexual or homosexual) as the work of the devil. But at the same time we don't put a high price on them. We do not, for example, raise our children to practice a life of polymorphous sexuality as Marcuse would have had us do.[3] The Supreme Court has held that unmarried people have a right to buy contraceptives, but it has not suggested that they have any right to use them. Its agenda is more like a program of sterile needles for drug abusers: It wants to prevent people from getting hurt if they engage in improvident acts.

I will look at *Bowers* from a different perspective in the next section. Thus far I have tried to defend it by showing that the autonomy (or self-definition) thesis is inconsistent with our intuitions about random sexual conduct. We willingly restrict such activity because it has little value for us. Such restriction is inconsistent with the idea that each person makes his own moral rules and also with the idea that cooperation will founder if we legislate morality.

I now want to make the same defense of the decisions about men's clubs. I frankly do not see much difference among the cases, so I will take *Board of Directors of Rotary International v. Rotary Club of Duarte*[4] as representative. The Board revoked the charter of the Duarte club when it admitted three women in violation of the Rotary constitution. The California courts, at Duarte's request, enjoined the revocation because it violated state law against sex discrimination. The Supreme Court held that this interference with Rotary membership policies did not violate the members' freedom of intimate association.[5]

Rotary had no defenders in the Supreme Court. Indeed, I am surprised that the Court even heard argument. It is difficult for anyone familiar with the phenomenon of "service clubs" to take seriously the claim the Constitution protects their membership policies. Rotary clubs are organizations of "business and professional men" who meet weekly for lunch. There are about twenty thousand such clubs and nearly a million members. Clubs select people according to the work they do, and use a classification system designed to select a leader from each important business, profession, and institution in town. The California court of appeal found that those who belong are motivated by business concerns—companies often pay the dues. The weekly lunches afford a chance for members to get acquainted in the business community. Attendance is mandatory. If a member is traveling and misses a meeting, he is required to make it up at the local club where he happens to be. In addition to holding the luncheons, clubs are supposed to devote themselves to community services (meals for the aged, guidance for high school students, etc.) and raising business and professional standards.

The mandatory lunch meeting, however, is the central activity in this organizational relationship. Having lunch, like having an orgasm, is a rather common activity. *Everybody* eats lunch. It seems weird to argue that the Constitution gives special protection to that activity because it is a way of defining our identity as individual persons. ("I'm the sort of person who eats lunch.") In fact having lunch is almost not a matter of choice. When we get hungry we have to eat.

If there is something that makes lunch constitutionally special, it has to be the people we eat with. This is what the Rotarians claimed—the freedom to associate with only certain people at lunch. But Rotary members are defined in terms of their roles in the business community. "*X* joins me for lunch weekly because he is vice president of the Sharpsville Steel Co. and I am a lawyer." "If *Z* succeeded *X* as vice president, *Z* could also fill *X*'s place at Rotary." This kind of fungibility is typical of market transactions and is quite appropriate in an organization of this kind. But there is nothing special about being an actor playing one of these roles, any more than there is about eating lunch. *X* and *Z* relate to the luncheon crowd in about the same way. Their behavior is not a matter of choice and self-definition. As Sartre suggested in his parody of the waiter, the role defines the actor, not the other way around.[6] Only the most unreconstructed antifeminist would suggest that women can't play those roles as well as men. For all the Rotarians' talk about fellowship, the case was really about playing a role in the business community.

There is nothing at all controversial about this idea. In fact it is the most well settled proposition in the law of substantive due process. For more than half a century we have agreed that doing a particular job is not the kind of activity that the Constitution puts a high value on. The government can, if it wants, forbid *X* to sell filled milk, to practice optometry, to engage in the business of debt adjusting, to sell money orders, or to be a pushcart vendor. It follows that the government can also keep a guild from monopolizing certain places in the business world, even if they are only places around the lunch table.

*   *   *

My discussion of erotic love [omitted—G. D.] shows, I hope, that autonomy doesn't have very much to do with it. In the first place, we don't *choose* whether to love someone. That's almost as natural as eating. There are people who go through life with no experience of erotic love. It is not as necessary for individual life as food is (though it is essential for species survival). But it is interesting to note that religious celibates, who live without it, will often explain their behavior as a kind of self-denial, like fasting.

It is equally weird to say that we *choose* to feel sexual desire for a particular person. Basic sexual impulses are no more voluntary than itches are. Erotic love is a bit more complex if Stendhal is right in saying that it begins with admiration. The trigger of that desire is the appreciation of beauty, wisdom, goodness, and other virtues. But the attraction is no more voluntary for all that. I don't choose to admire Agnes because she is fair-haired and kind. My admiration is an automatic reaction to qualities that I esteem. This is what we mean by "falling in love."

I am not a complete fatalist about erotic love, any more than I am about friendship. Choice plays a very important part when we decide to make a go of it. If Agnes and I get serious we will make promises and commitments: to respect and care for one another, to be faithful in our affections, and so on. People choose whether to take these steps. They also make continuing efforts to carry them out. This kind of deeper love is not possible without choice.

But that is not the same as saying—as the autonomy theory does—that we value erotic love because it involves a choice. That puts the whole thing backward. The person in love will make a choice because love is so important. What he or she values is the person admired, the esteem he or she is held in, the giving and receiving of care and affection—in a word, the relationship itself.

I want now to look at *Bowers v. Hardwick* with these thoughts in mind. It is obvious that the case was not about erotic love, but about a very different kind of relationship. Hardwick and his partner had nothing more in common than an interest in having an orgasm. It is unlikely that their mutual attraction began with the kind of admiration that is the origin of erotic love. Each probably appeared to the other like Stendhal's "fresh, pretty country girl who darts away into a wood"—a person interested in and available for an exchange of sensual pleasure.[7] It is equally difficult to believe that, in the course of a one-night stand, they had developed that sense of benevolence and care for one another that characterizes real love. In fact, after their arrest Hardwick's partner pleaded to a reduced charge and left town. I doubt that either saw their brief encounter as the kind of exclusive and permanent union that lovers envision. Hardwick said in his complaint that he "regularly engages in private homosexual acts and will do so in the future." He gave no indication anywhere in the record that the identity of his partner in those acts mattered. Given all this, I find it hard to understand all the flap the case created. I think the case was easy, and the Court's conclusion incontrovertibly correct.

Bowers is not the last word the Court will utter on erotic love. Let me close this section by mentioning two questions I think it left open. The first is the issue of heterosexual sodomy. The Georgia law on its face made no distinction between homosexual and heterosexual behavior. Most sodomy statutes don't. Hardwick was joined as plaintiff by a married couple, but they were dismissed for lack of standing and did not reach the Supreme Court. The Court therefore considered the law only as it applied to Hardwick.

Other things being equal, if Hardwick's partner had been a woman I think his claim should have been dismissed for the same reasons I have given. I say "other things being equal" because I have in mind the case where the sexual partners seek nothing more than the pleasure of reaching an orgasm in the method they prefer. If there is no love between them their actions are indistinguishable from sex with a prostitute, an animal, or a pornographic surrogate. Love is the foundation of freedom in this area, and there is none here.

The hard question is whether married couples are a different case.[8] I have said that we do not highly prize sex without love. But I think that we *do* prize sex within love. I will not make the classical argument that sex within marriage is different because sex should be procreative. That settles the sodomy question, but its appeal is tightly bound to religious tradition. I also reject the trend to glorify sex as the focus of our emotional life and the motive force behind most of our behavior. I will assume instead that sex is like lunch—something that brings people together, that can be fun and so on, but that is not inherently filled with deep meaning.

This does not mean that the government can regulate the sex life of married couples. Quite the contrary. Consider how it is with lunch. I argued earlier that the government could regulate lunch at the Rotary club. (It could require that women be admitted to the regular Thursday meetings on the same terms as men.) But I doubt that the government could regulate the lunches of married couples. It's the context that matters. We feel differently about married couples because lunch is not just a matter of eating food at noon, with the allied sensations on the palate and in the stomach. And sex is not just a matter of fooling around and producing other pleasant sensations. In each case we also talk about this and that, enjoy one another's company, draw closer together, show a little care and respect for one another (I hold your chair, you light my cigarette), and so on. Neither activity is the Mount Everest of the emotional landscape, but love is often a matter of little things.

Sex within love is different from sex without love, even though the physical sensations may be the same. In fact it is hard to make the comparison because we cannot pick love apart and examine its elements separately. ("Over here is sex. Over there is respect. Over there, benevolence." And so on.) These elements go together. My love and admiration for you can stir up sexual desire and make it something different from desire that originates in anxiety, vanity, or cruelty. In the same way, the sexual experience of those in love fits into their lives in a different way than it does for other people. Sex matters in constitutional law because it is tied up with love, and love is what counts.[9]

I now want to turn to the second question that *Bowers* left open. I have argued that the case is plainly incorrect because our society puts a low value on sexual promiscuity. I have also argued that the Court might protect sodomy within marriage because we put a high value on erotic love, and sex is an inseparable ingredient in such love. My first argument made no reference to the homosexual character of Hardwick's offense. My second made none to the heterosexual character of marriage. Now, suppose that Hardwick and his companion were actually in love. Suppose that they had been living together in a monogamous union for twenty years. For me the hard question that *Bowers* leaves open is whether homosexuals should have a right to marry. (Notice that, if they could, my second argument would authorize them to engage in sodomy.) Hardwick's brief in the Supreme Court said that he "claim[ed] no right . . . to have any homosexual relationship recognized as a marriage." But suppose he had?

There seems to be no reason why the kind of erotic love I have been describing cannot exist between two people of the same sex. I make no pretense of having described the phenomenon completely, but the observations that I made could well be pertinent to homosexual love. The existence of sexual desire I take for granted. But surely gay lovers can satisfy other needs for one another; can admire, appreciate, respect, esteem one another for their good qualities; can care for one another in a benevolent way; and so on.

If that is so, and if I am correct in saying that the right to freedom follows after the good of love, then there is a strong argument for protecting homosexual as well as heterosexual freedom to love. And if sexual activity is limited to married couples, the freedom to love leads inexorably to the freedom to marry.

Notes

1. *On the Nature of the Universe* (Harmondsworth: Penguin Books [R. E. Latham translation], 1951), p. 163.

2. C. S. Lewis, *The Four Loves* (New York: Harcourt, Brace, Jovanovich, 1960), p. 135.

3. Herbert Marcuse, *Eros and Civilization* (Boston: Beacon Press, 1969).

4. 481 U.S. 537 (1987).

5. 481 U.S. 537, 545–547 (1987). The Court also upheld that the California law did not violate the members' First Amendment right to associate for purposes of jointly expressing political (or other) ideas.

6. *Being and Nothingness* (New York: Pocket Books, 1956), p. 101.

7. *On Love 2* (New York: Doubleday, 1983).

8. I speak of married couples for the sake of clarity, but without necessarily wishing to limit my argument to them. Erotic love can certainly exist outside marriage in a great variety of forms.

9. I should add another point, slightly different from what I have been saying but obviously relevant to the question of sodomy. We are well aware in other contexts of the danger of allowing government to micromanage intimate relationships. To take one example there is widespread dissatisfaction with the way courts handle child abuse and neglect cases. The simple explanation is that government agencies lack the requisite information and sensitivity: They are likely to upset the existing equilibrium and leave the participants floundering. Where the cost of nonintervention is physical abuse, this upset is a price worth paying. But where a couple is happily married and the only justification for intruding is to regulate the orthodoxy of their sex life, the price is too high.

7   Good Samaritan Laws

Vermont Good Samaritan Statute

Emergency Medical Care

(a) A person who knows that another is exposed to grave physical harm shall, to the extent that the same can be rendered without danger or peril to himself or without interference with important duties owed to others, give reasonable assistance to the exposed person unless that assistance or care is being provided by others.

(b) A person who provides reasonable assistance in compliance with subsection (a) of this section shall not be liable in civil damages unless his acts constitute gross negligence or unless he will receive or expects to receive remuneration. Nothing contained in this subsection shall alter existing law with respect to tort liability of a practitioner of the healing arts for acts committed in the ordinary course of his practice.

(c) A person who willfully violates subsection (a) of this section shall be fined not more than $100.00.

ERNEST J. WEINRIB

Duty to Rescue

Consideration of the utilitarian approach towards rescue must begin with Jeremy Bentham's thought on the problem. "[I]n cases where the person is in danger," he asked, "why should it not be made the duty of every man to save another from mischief, when it can be done without prejudicing himself . . . ?"[1] Bentham supported the implicit answer to this question with several illustrations: using water at hand to quench a fire in a woman's headdress; moving a sleeping drunk whose face is in a puddle; warning a person about to carry a lighted candle into a room strewn with gunpowder. Bentham clearly had in mind a legal duty that would be triggered by the combination of the victim's emergency and the absence of inconvenience to the rescuer—that is, by the features of most of the proposed reforms requiring rescue. Unfortunately, the rhetorical question was the whole of Bentham's argument for his position. With this question, Bentham appealed directly to his reader's moral intuition; he did not show how his proposed duty can be derived through his distinctive felicific calculus.

Can one supply the Benthamite justification that Bentham himself omitted? Because the avoidance of injury or death obviously contributes to the greatest happiness of the greatest number, the difficulties revolve not around the basic requirement of rescue but around the limitations placed upon that requirement by the notions of emergency and absence of inconvenience. Those limitations have no parallel with respect to participation in putting others at risk; they apply only in cases of nonfeasance. Indeed, Bentham's comments come in a section of his *Introduction to the Principles of Morals and Legislation* that distinguishes beneficence (increasing another's happiness) from probity (forbearing to diminish another's happiness). Yet Bentham had earlier contended that the distinction between acts of omission and acts of commission was of no significance. The utilitarian's only concern is that an individual bring about a situation that results in a higher surplus of pleasure over pain than would any of the alternative situations that his actions could produce. Consequences are important; how they are reached is not. The distinction between nonfeasance and misfeasance has no place in this theory, and neither would the rescue duty's emergency or convenience limitations, which apply only after that distinction is made.

One solution to the apparent inconsistency between the rescue limitations and Benthamite theory's regard only for consequences is to drop the conditions of emergency and convenience as limitations on the duty to rescue. The position could be taken that there is an obligation to rescue whenever rescuing would result in greater net happiness than not rescuing. This principle, it is important to observe, cannot really be a principle about rescuing as that concept is generally understood. As a matter of common usage, a rescue presupposes the existence of an emergency, of a predicament that poses danger of greater magnitude and imminence than one ordinarily encounters. The proposed principle, however, requires no emergency to trigger a duty to act. The principle, in fact, is one of beneficence, not rescue, and should be formulated more generally to require providing aid whenever it will yield greater net happiness than not providing aid.

Eliminating the limitations regarding emergency and convenience might transform a requirement of rescue conceived along utilitarian lines into a requirement of perfect and general altruism. This demand of perfect altruism would be undesirable for several reasons. First, it would encourage the obnoxious character known to the law as the officious intermeddler. Also, its imposition of a duty of continual saintliness and heroism is unrealistic. Moreover, it would overwhelm the relationships founded on friendship and love as well as the distinction between the praiseworthy and the required; it would thereby obscure some efficient ways, in the utilitarian's eyes, of organizing and stimulating beneficence. Finally, and most fundamentally, it would be self-defeating. The requirement of aid assumes that there is some other person who has at least a minimal core of personhood as well as projects of his own that the altruist can further. In a society of perfect and general altruism, however, any potential recipient of aid would himself be an altruist, who must, accordingly, subordinate the pursuit of his own projects to the rendering of aid to others. No one could claim for his own projects the priority that would provide others with a stable object of their altruistic ministrations. Each person would continually find himself obligated to attempt to embrace a phantom.

Although the utilitarian principle that requires the provision of aid whenever it will result in greater net happiness than failure to aid easily slips into the pure-altruism duty, it need not lead to so extreme a position. The obvious alternative interpretation of the principle is that aid is not obligatory whenever the costs to one's own projects outweigh the benefits to the recipient's. This interpretation avoids the embracing-of-phantoms objection to pure altruism, but it is subject to all the other criticisms of the purer theory. Because the cost-benefit calculus is so difficult to perform in particular instances, the duty would remain ill-defined. In many cases, therefore, it would encourage the officious intermeddler, seem unrealistically to require saintliness, overwhelm friendship and love, and obliterate the distinction between the praiseworthy and the required. Moreover, the vagueness of the duty would lead many individuals unhappily and inefficiently to drop their own projects in preference for those of others.

A different formulation of the rescue duty is needed to harness and temper the utilitarian impulses toward altruism and to direct them more precisely toward an intelligible goal. One important weakness of a too-generally beneficent utilitarianism is that it tempts one to consider only the immediate consequences of particular acts, and not the longer term consequences, the most important of which are the expectations generated that such acts will continue. If, as the classical utilitarians believed, the general happiness is advanced when people engage in productive activities that are of value to others, the harm done by a duty of general beneficence, in either version discussed above, would override its specific benefits. The deadening of industry resulting from both reliance on beneficence and devotion to beneficence would in the long run be an evil greater than the countenancing of individual instances of unfulfilled needs or wants. "In all cases of helping," wrote John Stuart Mill, in a passage concerned only with the reliance costs, there are two sets of consequences to be considered: the consequences of the assistance and the consequences of relying on the assistance. The former are generally beneficial, but the latter, for the most part, injurious. . . . There are few things for which it is more mischievous that people should rely on the habitual aid of others than for the means of subsistence, and unhappily there is no lesson which they more easily learn.[2]

Utilitarianism can use the notion of reliance to restrict the requirement of beneficence. If an act of beneficence would tend to induce reliance on similar acts, it should be avoided. If the act of beneficence does not have this tendency, it should be performed as long as the benefit produced is greater than the cost of performance. In the latter case, there are no harmful effects on industry flowing from excessive reliance to outweigh the specific benefits. This rule can account for Bentham's restriction of the duty to rescue to situations of emergency. People do not regularly expose themselves to extraordinary dangers in reliance on the relief that may be available if the emergency materializes, and only a fool would deliberately court a peril because he or others had previously been rescued from a similar one. As Sidgwick put it, an emergency rescue "will have no bad effect on the receiver, from the exceptional nature of the emergency." Furthermore, an emergency is not only a desperate situation; it is also a situation that deviates from society's usual pattern. The relief of an emergency is therefore unlikely to induce reliance on the assistance of others in normal conditions. The abnormality of emergencies also means that rescuers can confidently pursue their own projects under normal circumstances. The motive for industry that Bentham located in each person's needs is not undermined by extraordinary and isolated events.

The role of emergency in the utilitarian obligation to rescue corresponds to, and illuminates, the definition of a legal duty to rescue by reference to the absence of contract values, as set out in the previous section. Utilitarian philosophy and the concept of the market are closely related. Both regard individuals as maximizers of their own happiness, and both see the use of contracts to acquire and to exchange property as conducive to the public good. Contract law's refusal to enforce certain transactions sets them apart from the usual structure of relationships, in which the satisfaction of the parties' needs and desires can legitimately serve as a stimulus to exchange. The person who sees a member of his own family in difficulty and the police officer who notices a hazard on the highway may not act as ordinary members of the market with respect to those endangered. Those pockets of contractual nonenforcement are sufficiently isolated that they are unlikely to be generalized: they will not generate a widespread reliance on assistance or sense of obligation to assist in settings where market exchanges are permitted and common.

An emergency is similar. Contract values are absent in such a situation because the assistance required is of such a kind that it cannot be purchased on ordinary commercial terms. Suspension of contract values in an emergency will not result in a general deadening of individual industry; the utilitarian can therefore confine his calculus to the specific consequences of the rescue. The denial of relief to the Southwark squatters is a case in point. The desperate situation there was a consequence of poverty and not an extraordinary condition that deviated from the ordinary pattern of contemporary existence. The utilitarian must be concerned in that situation that judicially coercing individual assistance to the poor will generate a reliance whose harmful effects will, in the long run and across society as a whole, outweigh the benefits of the specific assistance.

Bentham's intuitive restriction of beneficence to situations of emergency can thus be supported on utilitarian grounds. Is the same true of the inconvenience limitation? As with the emergency restriction, finding utilitarian support requires looking behind the specific action to its social and legal context. For the utilitarian, the enforcement of a duty through legal sanctions is always an evil, which can be justified only to avoid a greater evil. If the sanction is applied, the offender suffers the pain of punishment. If the prospect of the sanction is sufficient to deter conduct, those deterred suffer the detriment of frustrated preferences. Moreover, the apparatus of enforcement siphons off social resources from other projects promoting the general happiness.

Accordingly, a utilitarian will be restrained and circumspect in the elaboration of legal duties. In particular, he will not pitch a standard of behavior at too high a level: the higher the standard, the more onerous it will be to the person subjected to it, the greater the pleasure that he must forego in adhering to it, and the greater his resistance to its demands. A high standard entails both more severe punishment and a more elaborate apparatus of detection and enforcement. Applied to the rescue situation, this reasoning implies that some convenience restriction should be adopted as part of the duty. Compelling the rescuer to place himself in physical danger, for instance, would be inefficacious, to use Bentham's terminology, because such coercion cannot influence the will: "the evil, which he sees himself about to undergo . . . is so great that the evil denounced by the penal clause . . . cannot appear greater." Limiting the duty of rescue to emergency situations where the rescue will not inconvenience the rescuer—as judicial decisions would elaborate that limitation and thus give direction to individuals—minimizes both the interference with the rescuer's own preferences and the difficulties of enforcement that would result from recalcitrance. Bentham's second limitation can thus also be supported on a utilitarian basis.

The utilitarian arguments for the duty to rescue and for the limitations on that duty rest primarily on administrative considerations. The arguments focus not so much on the parties and their duties as persons as on the difficulties that might be created throughout the whole range of societal interactions. The elements of the duty are evaluated in terms of their likely consequences, no matter how remote. In the convenience limitation, for instance, whether the rescuer *ought* to feel aggrieved at the requirements of a high standard is of no concern. The likelihood that he *will* feel aggrieved is all that matters: for the Benthamite utilitarian, general happiness is the criterion of evaluation and not itself an object of evaluation. Moreover, recalcitrance necessitates more costly enforcement, and that consequence must also enter the calculus. The same is true for the emergency limitation. The argument for that limitation focused on the possibility that a particular instance of assistance would, by example, induce socially detrimental general reliance or beneficence. This use of example does not explore either the fairness of singling out particular persons for particular treatment or the consistency and scope of certain principles. Rather, the argument examines the cumulative consequences of repetition, and decides whether a particular person should perform a particular act on the basis of the act's implications for the entire society's market arrangements.

At least one philosopher has argued that administrative considerations of this sort are not moral ones at all, or that they are moral only in a derivative sense. In this view, the administrative and enforcement considerations on which the utilitarian account of rescue rests are irrelevant to the individual's obligations as a moral agent. The individual should ask what he ought to do, not how others can compel him to fulfill his duty. The merit of this view is its observation that any utilitarian version of a duty to rescue has nuances that do not ring true to the moral contours of the situation. The person in need of rescue stands in danger of serious physical injury or loss of life, harms not quite comparable by any quantitative measure to other losses of happiness. Health and life are not merely components of the aggregate of goods that an individual enjoys. Rather, they are constitutive of the individual, who partakes of them in a unique and intimate way; they are the preconditions for the enjoyment of other goods. Moreover, there is something false in viewing an act of rescue as a contribution to the greatest happiness of the greatest number. If there is an obligation to rescue, it is owed to particular persons rather than to the greatest number. Any such duty would require the rescuing not only of the eminent heart surgeon but also of the hermit bachelor; and even the duty to rescue the heart surgeon would be owed primarily to him, not to his present or prospective patients.

Because the utilitarian account of rescue thus appears to lack an important moral ingredient, and because utilitarianism is not the law's only important philosophical tradition, it is worth attempting to outline a non-utilitarian version of the obligation to rescue. Although the two approaches support the same conclusion, the arguments are different in texture. In particular, the non-utilitarian argument recognizes the distinctive importance of avoiding physical injury or death; it resists the assimilation of health and life to other goods. This attention to the centrality of the person avoids the utilitarian dilemma of either demanding excessive beneficence or having recourse to administrative considerations, which shifts the focus away from the rescuer's obligation to a particular endangered individual. In the non-utilitarian argument, of course, administrative considerations are not ignored; to do so would be impossible in elaborating an argument that attempts to provide an ethical foundation for a judicially enforced duty to rescue. Nonetheless, the non-utilitarian's use of administrative considerations differs from the utilitarian's. The utilitarian weaves the fabric of the duty to rescue out of administrative strands; the cost of administration and enforcement are relevant to the very existence of the duty. The non-utilitarian, by contrast, justifies a legal duty to rescue independently of the administrative costs; the mechanisms of enforcement are invoked only to structure and to coordinate the operation of the duty.

The deontological argument begins with the observation that the idea of an individual's being under a moral duty is intimately related to the notion that health and life are of distinctive importance. The concept of duty applies only to an individual endowed with the capacity to make choices and to set ends for himself. Further, the person, as a purposive and choosing entity, does not merely set physical integrity as one of his ends; he requires it as a precondition to the accomplishment of the purposes that his freedom gives him the power to set. As Kant put it, physical integrity is "the basic *stuff* (the matter) in man without which he could not realize his ends."

A person contemplating the ethical exercise of his freedom of action must impose certain restrictions on that freedom. Because morality is something he shares with all humanity, he cannot claim a preferred moral position for himself. Any moral claim he makes must, by its very nature as a moral claim, be one to which he is subject when others can assert it. Acting on the basis of his own personhood therefore demands recognition of the personhood of others. This recognition, however, cannot be elaborated in the first instance in terms of the enjoyment of ordinary material goods. Because no conception of happiness is shared by everyone and is constant throughout any individual's life, the universal concept of personhood cannot be reflected in a system of moral duties directed at the satisfaction of unstable desires for such goods. Physical integrity, by contrast, is necessary for the accomplishment of any human aim, and so is an appropriate subject for a system of mutually restraining duties.

An individual contemplating his actions from a moral point of view must recognize that all others form their projects on a substratum of physical integrity. If he claims the freedom to pursue his projects as a moral right, he cannot as a rational and moral agent deny to others the same freedom. Because his claim to that freedom implies a right to the physical integrity that is necessary to its exercise, he must concede to others the right to physical integrity that he implicitly and inevitably claims for himself.[3]

This conception of the right to life and health derives from the notion of personhood that is presupposed by the concept of moral action. So too do the right's natural limitations. The duty of beneficence exacted by this right need not collapse into a comprehensive and self-defeating altruism. Respect for another's physical security does not entail foregoing one's own. The right to life and health, seen to give content to the universal concept of personhood, must be ascribed not only to others, but also to oneself. As Kant put it,

> since all *other* men with the exception of myself would not be *all* men, and the maxim would then not have the universality of a law, as it must have in order to be obligatory, the law prescribing the duty of benevolence will include myself, as the object of benevolence, in the command of practical reason.

Moreover, the universalizing process radiates outward from the actor: it is only one's desire to act that makes necessary the exploration of the action's implicit claims and thus of the rights that he must rationally concede to others.[4] The priority of the actor is thus embedded in the structure of the argument and should be reflected in the concrete duties that the argument yields.

This outline of deontological analysis can be applied to examine the standard suggestion that the common law should recognize a duty to effect an easy rescue. Such a duty would be the judicial analogue of the moral obligation to respect the person of another and to safeguard his physical integrity, which is necessary for whatever aims he chooses to pursue. The emergency and convenience limitations also fit quite readily into the analysis. An emergency is a particularly imminent threat to physical security, and the convenience limitation reflects the rescuer's entitlement to the priority of his own physical security over that of the endangered person. Although the proposed legal duty fits comfortably within the deontological moral duty of beneficence, however, the two are not coextensive. Emergencies are not the only circumstances in which life and health are threatened; disease, starvation, and poverty can affect the physical substratum of personhood on a routine basis. If legal duties must reflect moral ones, should not a legal duty to rescue be supplemented by a legal duty to alleviate those less isolated abridgments of physical security?

The convenience limitation on the rescue duty might similarly be loosened in a deontological analysis. One tempting extension would be very far-reaching: if the physical substratum is the "basic *stuff* (the matter) in man without which he could not realize his ends, and if we are under a duty to safeguard that substratum in others as in ourselves, the priority that the rescuer can legitimately grant to himself can be only with respect to his physical integrity. Under this extension, a rescuer could—indeed would be obligated to—abstain from acting only if the act would place him in physical danger; if it would not put him in danger, he would be required to attempt a rescue, no matter what the disruption of his life. In Macaulay's famous example, the surgeon would have to travel from Calcutta to Meerut to perform an operation that only he could perform, because the journey, though inconvenient, would not be dangerous. Indeed, he would have to make the trip even if he were about to leave for Europe or to greet members of his family arriving on an incoming ship. The patient's right to physical security would rank ahead of the satisfaction of the surgeon's contingent desires.

The deontological approach to rescue does not compel such a drastic extension. Although every moral person must value physical integrity, its protection is not an end in itself. Rather, physical security is valued because it allows individuals to realize their own projects and purposes. Whatever the reach of the right to physical integrity, therefore, it must allow the rescuer to satisfy his purposes in a reasonably coherent way. Still, though the extension of the moral duty cannot be so drastic as to require the sacrifice of all of a person's projects, it can be substantial. It can require the rescuer to undergo considerable inconvenience short of fundamental changes in the fabric of his life. The deontological duty relaxes both the emergency and convenience limitations of the duty of easy rescue in emergencies: it applies not only in emergencies but whenever physical integrity is threatened, and it applies even when the rescuer might have to undergo considerable inconveniences. The duty might, after all, obligate Macaulay's surgeon to travel from Calcutta to Meerut. Would it also require the wealthy to use at least some of their resources to alleviate the plight of the starving and the afflicted? For those concerned about the possibility of setting principled limits to a duty of rescue, the question is critical.

The objection to an affirmative answer to the question rests on the premises that even the wealthy are under no obligation to be charitable and that the afflicted have no right to receive charity. Under the deontological theory, those premises are incorrect. The duty of beneficence derives from the concept of personhood; it is therefore not properly called charity, for the benefactor's performance of this duty is no reason for self-congratulation. Although the duty is an imperfect one—"since no determinate limits can be assigned to what should be done, the duty has in it a play-room for doing more or less," as Kant said—it is nonetheless a duty to the performance of which the recipient is entitled.

The extent of the duty of beneficence, of course, can still be troubling. It is the indeterminateness of the duty, the "play-room" that is particularly relevant to this problem. Kant meant by this expression that the form and the amount of the benefaction would vary, depending on the resources of the benefactor, the identity of the recipient, and the recipient's own conception of happiness. The indeterminateness, however, applies not only to the form of the benefaction but also to the linking of particular benefactors to particular beneficiaries. Why should any particular person be singled out of the whole group of potential benefactors, and why should benefit be conferred on one rather than another person in need? If a duty "may be *exacted* from a person, as one exacts a debt," it is a debt that leaves unclear the precise terms of discharge as well as the identities of obligor and obligee.

The proper response to this indeterminacy is not to deny that there is a duty. What is required is to set up social institutions to perform the necessary tasks of coordination and determination. Those institutions would ensure that no person is singled out unfairly either for burdens or for benefits, and that the forms of benefaction correlate both with the resources of those who give and with the needs of those who receive. In fact, all Western democracies undertake to perform this task through programs for social assistance. The institutions they establish, however, are primarily legislative and administrative; precisely because a general duty of beneficence is imperfect, it cannot be judicially enforced. The traditional claim-settling function of courts does not permit the transfer of a resource from one person to another solely because the former has it and the latter needs it. Such judicial action would unfairly prefer one needy person over others and unfairly burden one resourceful person over others. Because the duty of beneficence is general and indeterminate, it does not, in the absence of legislative action that specifies and coordinates, yield judicially enforceable moral claims by individuals against others.

The significant characteristic of the emergency and convenience limitations is that, in combination, they eliminate the "play room" inherent in the duty of beneficence. . . . An emergency marks a particular person as physically endangered in a way that is not general or routine throughout the society. An imminent peril cannot await assistance from the appropriate social institutions. The provision of aid to an emergency victim does not deplete the social resources committed to the alleviation of more routine threats to physical integrity. Moreover, aid in such circumstances presents no unfairness problems in singling out a particular person to receive the aid. Similarly, emergency aid does not unfairly single out one of a class of routinely advantaged persons; the rescuer just happens to find himself for a short period in a position, which few if any others share, to render a service to some specific person. In addition, when a rescue can be accomplished without a significant disruption of his own projects, the rescuer's freedom to realize his own ends is not abridged by the duty to preserve the physical security of another. In sum, when there is an emergency that the rescuer can alleviate with no inconvenience to himself, the general duty of beneficence that is suspended over society like a floating charge is temporarily revealed to identify a particular obligor and obligee, and to define obligations that are specific enough for judicial enforcement.

Notes

1. J. BENTHAM, AN INTRODUCTION TO THE PRINCIPLES OF MORALS AND LEGISLATION (Hafner, 1948), at 293; *see* 1 J. BENTHAM, THE PRINCIPLES OF LEGISLATION 85–86 (R. Hildreth ed. 1840).

2. J.S. MILL, THE PRINCIPLES OF POLITICAL ECONOMY 967 (W. Ashley ed. 1923).

3. The argument leans heavily on the work of Professor Alan Gewirth. *See* A. GEWIRTH, REASON AND MORALITY (University of Chicago, 1978); Gewirth, *The 'Is-Ought' Problem Resolved,* 47 PROC. & ADDRESSES AMER. PHIL. ASS'N 34 (1974); Gewirth, *The Normative Structure of Action,* 25 REV. METAPHYSICS 238 (1971). My purpose is more modest than his in one crucial aspect: it is enough for my purpose that a person who assumes a moral point of view would elaborate a deontological justification of rescue, whereas Gewirth argues that a rational actor must assume the moral point of view. For discussion of this wider claim, see Grunebaum, *Gewirth and a Reluctant Protagonist,* 86 ETHICS 274 (1976); Veatch, *Paying Heed to Gewirth's Principle of Categorial Consistency,* 86 ETHICS 278 (1976); Gewirth, *Action and Rights: A Reply,* 86 ETHICS 288 (1976).

4. Kant wrote: *[R]ational nature exists as an end in itself.* Man necessarily conceives his own existence as being so: so far then this is a *subjective* principle of human actions. But every other rational being regards its existence similarly, just on the same principle, that holds for me; so that it is at the same time an objective principle, from which as a supreme practical law all laws of the will must be capable of being deduced.

I. KANT, FOUNDATIONS OF THE METAPHYSICS OF MORALS WITH CRITICAL ESSAYS 292 (L. Beck trans. R. Wolff ed. 1969). On the priority of the self, see Fried, *The Lawyer as Friend: The Moral Foundations of the Lawyer-Client Relation,* 85 YALE L.J. 1060, 1070 (1976).

8   Commodification

United States Public Health Code

Section 274e. Prohibition of Organ Purchases

(a) Prohibition

It shall be unlawful for any person to knowingly acquire, receive, or otherwise transfer any human organ for valuable consideration for use in human transplantation if the transfer affects interstate commerce.

(b) Penalties

Any person who violates subsection (a) of this section shall be fined not more than $50,000 or imprisoned not more than five years or both.

(c) Definitions

For purposes of subsection (a) of this section:

(1) the term "human organ" means the human (including fetal) kidney, liver, heart, lung, pancreas, bone marrow, cornea, eye, bone and skin or any subpart thereof and any other human organ . . . specified by the Secretary of Health and Human Services by regulation.

(2) The term "valuable consideration" does not include the reasonable payments associated with removal, transportation, implantation, processing, preservation, quality control and storage of a human organ or the expenses of travel, housing, and lost wages incurred by the donor of a human organ in connection with the donation of the organ.

MARGARET JANE RADIN
Market-Inalienability

Like relationships of sexual sharing, parent-child relationships are closely connected with personhood, particularly with personal identity and contextuality. Moreover, poor women caught in the double bind raise the issue of freedom: they may wish to sell a baby on the black market, as they may wish to sell sexual services, perhaps to try to provide adequately for other children or family members. But the double bind is not the only problem of freedom implicated in baby-selling. Under a market regime, prostitutes may be choosing to sell their sexuality, but babies are not choosing for themselves that under current nonideal circumstances they are better off as commodities. If we permit babies to be sold, we commodify not only the mother's (and father's) baby-making capacities—which might be analogous to commodifying sexuality—but we also conceive of the baby itself in market rhetoric. When the baby becomes a commodity, all of its personal attributes—sex, eye color, predicted I.Q., predicted height, and the like—become commodified as well. This is to conceive of potentially all personal attributes in market rhetoric, not merely those of sexuality. Moreover, to conceive of infants in market rhetoric is likewise to conceive of the people they will become in market rhetoric, and to create in those people a commodified self-conception.

Hence, the domino theory has a deep intuitive appeal when we think about the sale of babies. An idealist might suggest, however, that the fact that we do not now value babies in money suggests that we would not do so even if babies were sold. Perhaps babies could be incompletely commodified, valued by the participants to the interaction in a nonmarket way, even though money changed hands. Although this is theoretically possible, it seems too risky in our nonideal world.[1] If a capitalist baby industry were to come into being, with all of its accompanying paraphernalia, how could any of us, even those who did not produce infants for sale, avoid subconsciously measuring the dollar value of our children? How could our children avoid being preoccupied with measuring their own dollar value? This makes our discourse about ourselves (when we are children) and about our children (when we are parents) like our discourse about cars. Seeing commodification of babies as an inevitable and grave injury to personhood appears rather easy. In the worst case, market rhetoric could create a commodified self-conception in everyone, as the result of commodifying every attribute that differentiates us and that other people value in us, and could destroy personhood as we know it.

I suspect that an intuitive grasp of the injury to personhood involved in commodification of human beings is the reason many people lump baby-selling together with slavery. But this intuition can be misleading. Selling a baby, whose personal development requires caretaking, to people who want to act as the caretakers is not the same thing as selling a baby or an adult to people who want to act only as users of her capacities. Moreover, if the reason for our aversion to baby-selling is that we believe it is like slavery, then it is unclear why we do not prohibit baby-giving (release of a child for adoption) on the ground that enslavement is not permitted even without consideration. We might say that respect for persons prohibits slavery but may require adoption in cases in which only adoptive parents will treat the child as a person. But this answer is still somewhat unsatisfactory. It does not tell us whether parents who are financially and psychologically capable of raising a child in a manner we deem proper nevertheless may give up the child for adoption, for what we would consider less than compelling reasons. If parents are morally entitled to give up a child even if the child could have (in some sense) been raised properly by them,[2] our aversion to slavery does not explain why infants are subject only to market-inalienability. There must be another reason why baby-giving is unobjectionable.

The reason, I think, is that we do not fear relinquishment of children unless it is accompanied by market rhetoric.[3] The objection to market rhetoric may be part of a moral prohibition on market treatment of any babies, regardless of whether nonmonetized treatment of other children would remain possible. To the extent that we condemn baby-selling even in the absence of any domino effect, we are saying that this "good" simply should not exist. Conceiving of any child in market rhetoric wrongs personhood. In addition, we fear, based on our assessment of current social norms, that the market value of babies would be decided in ways injurious to their personhood and to the personhood of those who buy and sell on this basis, exacerbating class, race, and gender divisions. To the extent the objection to baby-selling is not (or is not only) to the very idea of this "good" (marketed children), it stems from a fear that the nonmarket version of human beings themselves will become impossible. Conceiving of children in market rhetoric would foster an inferior conception of human flourishing, one that commodifies every personal attribute that might be valued by people in other people. In spite of the double bind, our aversion to commodification of babies has a basis strong enough to recommend that market-inalienability be maintained.

The question of surrogate mothering seems more difficult.[4] I shall consider the surrogacy situation in which a couple desiring a child consists of a fertile male and an infertile female. They find a fertile female to become impregnated with the sperm of the would-be father, to carry the fetus to term, to give birth to the child, and to relinquish it to them for adoption.

This interaction may be paid, in which case surrogacy becomes a good sold on the market, or unpaid, in which case it remains a gift.

Those who view paid surrogacy as tantamount to permitting the sale of babies point out that a surrogate is paid for the same reasons that an ordinary adoption is commissioned: to conceive, carry, and deliver a baby. Moreover, even if an ordinary adoption is not commissioned, there seems to be no substantive difference between paying a woman for carrying a child she then delivers to the employers, who have found her through a brokerage mechanism, and paying her for an already "produced" child whose buyer is found through a brokerage mechanism, (perhaps called an "adoption agency") after she has paid her own costs of "production." Both are adoptions for which consideration is paid. Others view paid surrogacy as better analogized to prostitution (sale of sexual services) than to baby-selling. They would say that the commodity being sold in the surrogacy interaction is not the baby itself, but rather "womb services."

The different conceptions of the good being sold in paid surrogacy can be related to the primary difference between this interaction and (other) baby-selling: the genetic father is more closely involved in the surrogacy than in a standard adoption. The disagreement about how we might conceive of the "good" reflects a deeper ambiguity about the degree of commodification of mothers and children. If we think that ordinarily a mother paid to relinquish a baby for adoption is selling a baby, but that if she is a surrogate, she is merely selling gestational services, it seems we are assuming that the baby cannot be considered the surrogate's property, so as to become alienable by her, but that her gestational services can be considered property and therefore become alienable. If this conception reflects a decision that the baby cannot be property at all—cannot be objectified—then the decision reflects a lesser level of commodification in rhetoric. But this interpretation is implausible because of our willingness to refer to the ordinary paid adoption as baby-selling.[5] A more plausible interpretation of conceiving of the "good" as gestational services is that this conception reflects an understanding that the baby is already someone else's property—the father's. This characterization of the interaction can be understood as both complete commodification in rhetoric and an expression of gender hierarchy. The would-be father is "producing" a baby of his "own," but in order to do so he must purchase these "services" as a necessary input. Surrogacy raises the issue of commodification and gender politics in how we understand even the description of the problem. An oppressive understanding of the interaction is the more plausible one: women—their reproductive capacities, attributes, and genes—are fungible in carrying on the male genetic line.[6]

Whether one analogizes paid surrogacy to sale of sexual services or to baby-selling, the underlying concerns are the same. First, there is the possibility of even further oppression of poor or ignorant women, which must be weighed against a possible step toward their liberation through economic gain from a new alienable entitlement—the double bind. Second, there is the possibility that paid surrogacy should be completely prohibited because it expresses an inferior conception of human flourishing. Third, there is the possibility of a domino effect of commodification in rhetoric that leaves us all inferior human beings.

Paid surrogacy involves a potential double bind. The availability of the surrogacy option could create hard choices for poor women. In the worst case, rich women, even those who are not infertile, might employ poor women to bear children for them. It might be degrading for the surrogate to commodify her gestational services or her baby, but she might find this preferable to her other choices in life. But although surrogates have not tended to be rich women, nor middle-class career women, neither have they (so far) seemed to be the poorest women, the ones most caught in the double bind.[7]

Whether surrogacy is paid or unpaid, there may be a transition problem: an ironic self-deception. Acting in ways that current gender ideology characterizes as empowering might actually be disempowering. Surrogates may feel they are fulfilling their womanhood by producing a baby for someone else, although they may actually be reinforcing oppressive gender roles. It is also possible to view would-be fathers as (perhaps unknowing) oppressors of their own partners. Infertile mothers, believing it to be their duty to raise their partners' genetic children, could be caught in the same kind of false consciousness and relative powerlessness as surrogates who feel called upon to produce children for others. Some women might have conflicts with their partners that they cannot acknowledge, either about raising children under these circumstances instead of adopting unrelated children, or about having children at all. These considerations suggest that to avoid reinforcing gender ideology, both paid and unpaid surrogacy must be prohibited.

Another reason we might choose prohibition of all surrogacy, paid or unpaid, is that allowing surrogacy in our nonideal world would injure the chances of proper personal development for children awaiting adoption. Unlike a mother relinquishing a baby for adoption, the surrogate mother bears a baby only in response to the demand of the would-be parents: their demand is the reason for its being born.[8] There is a danger that unwanted children might remain parentless even if only unpaid surrogacy is allowed, because those seeking children will turn less frequently to adoption. Would-be fathers may strongly prefer adopted children bearing their own genetic codes to adopted children genetically strange to them; perhaps women prefer adopted children bearing their partners' genetic codes. Thus, prohibition of all surrogacy might be grounded on concern for unwanted children and their chances in life.

Perhaps a more visionary reason to consider prohibiting all surrogacy is that the demand for it expresses a limited view of parent-child bonding; in a better view of personal contextuality, bonding should be reconceived. Although allowing surrogacy might be thought to foster ideals of interrelationships between men and their children,[9] it is unclear why we should assume that the ideal of bonding depends especially on genetic connection. Many people who adopt children feel no less bonded to their children than responsible genetic parents; they understand that relational bonds are created in shared life more than in genetic codes.[10] We might make better progress toward ideals of interpersonal sharing—toward a better view of contextual personhood—by breaking down the notion that children are fathers'—or parents'—genetic property.[11]

In spite of these concerns, attempting to prohibit surrogacy now seems too utopian, because it ignores a transition problem. At present, people seem to believe that they need genetic offspring in order to fulfill themselves; at present, some surrogates believe their actions to be altruistic. To try to create an ideal world all at once would do violence to things people make central to themselves. This problem suggests that surrogacy should not be altogether prohibited.

Concerns about commodification of women and children, however, might counsel permitting only unpaid surrogacy (market-inalienability). Market-inalienability might be grounded in a judgment that commodification of women's reproductive capacity is harmful for the identity aspect of their personhood and in a judgment that the closeness of paid surrogacy to baby-selling harms our self-conception too deeply. There is certainly the danger that women's attributes, such as height, eye color, race, intelligence, and athletic ability, will be monetized. Surrogates with "better" qualities will command higher prices in virtue of those qualities. This monetization commodifies women more broadly than merely with respect to their sexual services or reproductive capacity. Hence, if we wish to avoid the dangers of commodification and, at the same time, recognize that there are some situations in which a surrogate can be understood to be proceeding out of love or altruism and not out of economic necessity or desire for monetary gain, we could prohibit sales but allow surrogates to give their services.[12] We might allow them to accept payment of their reasonable out-of-pocket expenses—a form of market-inalienability similar to that governing ordinary adoption.[13]

Fear of a domino effect might also counsel market-inalienability. At the moment, it does not seem that women's reproductive capabilities are as commodified as their sexuality. Of course, we cannot tell whether this means that reproductive capabilities are more resistant to commodification or whether the trend toward commodification is still at an early stage. Reproductive capacity, however, is not the only thing in danger of commodification of children. The risk is serious indeed, because, if there is a significant domino effect, commodification of some children means commodification of everyone. Yet, as long as fathers do have an unmonetized attachment to their genes (and as long as their partners tend to share it), even though the attachment may be nonideal, we need not see children born in a paid surrogacy arrangement—and they need not see themselves—as fully commodified. Hence, there may be less reason to fear the domino effect with paid surrogacy than with baby-selling. The most credible fear of a domino effect—one that paid surrogacy does share with commissioned adoption—is that all women's personal attributes will be commodified. The pricing of surrogates' services will not immediately transform the rhetoric in which women conceive of themselves and in which they are conceived, but that is its tendency. This fear, even though remote, seems grave enough to take steps to ensure that paid surrogacy does not become the kind of institution that could permeate our discourse.

Thus, for several reasons market-inalienability seems an attractive solution. But, in choosing this regime, we would have to recognize the danger that the double bind might force simulations of altruism by those who would find living on an expense allowance preferable to their current circumstances. Furthermore, the fact that they are not being paid "full" price exacerbates the double bind and is not really helpful in preventing a domino effect. We would also have to recognize that there would probably not be enough altruistic surrogates available to alleviate the frustration and suffering of those who desire children genetically related to fathers,[14] if this desire is widespread.

The other possible choice is to create an incomplete commodification similar to the one suggested for sale of sexual services. The problem of surrogacy is more difficult, however, primarily because the interaction produces a new person whose interests must be respected. In such an incomplete commodification. performance of surrogacy agreements by willing parties should be permitted, but women who change their minds should not be forced to perform.[15] The surrogate who changes her mind before birth can choose abortion; at birth, she can decide to keep the baby.[16] Neither should those who hire a surrogate and then change their minds be forced to keep and raise a child they do not want. But if a baby is brought into the world and nobody wants it, the surrogate who intended to relinquish the child should not be forced to keep and raise it.[17] Instead, those who, out of a desire for genetically related offspring, initiated the interaction should bear the responsibility for providing for the child's future in a manner that can respect the child's personhood and not create the impression that children are commodities that can be abandoned as well as alienated.

We should be aware that the case for incomplete commodification is much more uneasy for surrogacy than for prostitution. The potential for commodification of women is deeper, because, as with commissioned adoption, we risk conceiving of all women's personal attributes in market rhetoric, and because paid surrogacy within the current gender structure may symbolize that women are fungible baby-makers for men whose seed must be carried on. Moreover, as with commissioned adoption, the interaction brings forth a new person who did not choose commodification and whose potential personal identity and contextuality must be respected even if the parties to the interaction fail to do so.

Because the double bind has similar force whether a woman wishes to be a paid surrogate or simply to create a baby for sale on demand, the magnitude of the difference between paid surrogacy and commissioned adoption is largely dependent on the weight we give to the father's genetic link to the baby. If we place enough weight on this distinction, then incomplete commodification for surrogacy, but not for baby-selling, will be justified. But we should be aware, if we choose incomplete commodification for surrogacy, that this choice might seriously weaken the general market-inalienability of babies, which prohibits commissioned adoptions. If, on balance, incomplete commodification rather than market-inalienability comes to seem right for now, it will appear so for these reasons: because we judge the double bind to suggest that we should not completely foreclose women's choice of paid surrogacy, even though we foreclose commissioned adoptions; because we judge that people's (including women's) strong commitment to maintaining men's genetic lineage will ward off commodification and the domino effect, distinguishing paid surrogacy adequately from commissioned adoptions; and because we judge that commitment cannot be overridden without harm to central aspects of people's self-conception. If we choose market-inalienability, it will be because we judge the double bind to suggest that poor women will be further disempowered if paid surrogacy becomes a middle-class option, and because we judge that people's commitment to men's genetic lineage is an artifact of gender ideology that can neither save us from commodification nor result in less harm to personhood than its reinforcement would now create. In my view, a form of market-inalienability similar to our regime for ordinary adoption will probably be the better nonideal solution.

Notes

1. Perhaps we should separately evaluate the risk in the cases of selling "unwanted" babies and selling babies commissioned for adoption or otherwise "produced" for sale. The risk of complete commodification may be greater if we officially sanction bringing babies into the world for purposes of sale than if we sanction accepting money once they are already born. It seems such a distinction would be quite difficult to enforce, however, because nothing prevents the would-be seller from declaring any child to be "unwanted." Thus, permitting the sale of any babies is perhaps tantamount to permitting the production of them for sale.

2. But perhaps we should prophylactically decline to trust any parents who wished to give a child away for "frivolous" reasons adequately to raise a child if forced to keep her.

3. Relinquishing a child may be seen as admirable altruism. Some people who give up children for adoption do so with pain, but with the belief that the child will have a better life with someone else who needs and wants her, and that they are contributing immeasurably to the adoptive parents' lives as well as to the child's. Baby-selling might undermine this belief, because if wealth determined who gets a child, we would know that the adoptive parents valued the child as much as a Volvo but not a Mercedes; if an explicit sum of money entered into the decision to give the child up, then we would not as readily place the altruistic interpretation on our own motives. If babies could be seen as incompletely commodified, however, the altruism might coexist with sales.

4. Surrogacy is often popularly viewed as baby-selling, and the thirteenth amendment is invoked. The slavery analogy is inadequate for the reasons detailed above.

Surrogacy has engendered a number of different viewpoints. *See, e.g.,* Hollinger, *From Coitus to Commerce: Legal and Social Consequences of Noncoital Reproduction,* 18 U. MICH. J.L. RES. 865, 870 (1985) (arguing that "any legal efforts to prohibit this [baby-making] market from operating would be unwise"); Katz, *Surrogate Motherhood and the Baby-Selling Laws,* 20 COLUM. J.L & SOC. PROBS. I, 52–53 (1986) (arguing that surrogate motherhood is "fundamentally different from baby-selling" and could provide "a new solution for infertility"); Krimmel, "The Case Against Surrogate Parenting," 13 *Hastings Center Report* (Oct. 1983), at 35 (maintaining that it is ethically impermissible to bring a child into the world for purposes other than the desire to act as her parents); Mellown, *An Incomplete Picture: The Debate About Surrogate Motherhood,* 8 HARV.WOMEN'S L.J. 23 (1985) (pointing out shortcomings of viewing surrogacy either from the perspective of the liberal ideology of free contract or from the conservative perspective of preserving the traditional family); Note, *Developing a Concept of the Modern "Family": A Proposed Uniform Surrogate Parenthood Act,* 73 GEO. L.J. 1283 (1985) (presenting, with extensive commentary, a statute legalizing surrogacy and regulating the interaction by requiring the participation of doctors, psychologists, and lawyers, limiting compensation of the surrogate to $25,000, prohibiting reduction in compensation if the child is stillborn or impaired, and making specific performance available to both parties); Note, *Reproductive Technology and the Procreative Rights of the Unmarried,* 98 HARV. L. REV. 669, 684–85 (1985) (arguing that the Supreme Court has implicitly recognized a right to procreate and that individuals should not be "arbitrarily deprived of the ability to exercise [that right] through the use of reproductive technology"); Note, *Rumpelstiltskin Revisited: The Inalienable Rights of Surrogate Mothers,* 99 HARV. L. REV. 1936, 1954–55 (1986) (defending the inalienability of abortion rights for surrogate mothers and the alienability of their rights to rear the children once born); *see also* Magisterium of the Catholic Church, Instruction on Respect for Human Life in Its Origin and on the Dignity of Procreation: Replies to Certain Questions of the Day 25 (Feb. 22, 1987) (stating that surrogacy, like artificial insemination by a donor, is "contrary to the unity of marriage and to the dignity of the procreation of the human person").

5. If we were assuming that babies cannot be property, we would more readily envision an ordinary adoption for a price not as baby-selling, but rather as sale of gestational services, or fetal growth support services, followed by the gift of an unmonetized child.

6. Biblical "surrogate " interactions may be seen in this way. *See Genesis* 16 (Abraham, Sarah, and Hagar); *Genesis* 30 (Jacob, Rachel, and Bilhah). Perhaps some would see artificial insemination as analogously oppressive to men, but the situations are asymmetrical because of the present gender structure.

7. *See, e.g., Surrogate Motherhood: A Practice That's Still Undergoing Birth Pangs,* L.A. Times, Mar. 22, 1987, § 6, at 12. col. 2 (citing research finding that "[t]he average surrogate mother is white, attended two years of college, married young and has all the children she and her husband want"). Perhaps allowing surrogacy but not permitting adoption for a price would worsen the double bind for poor women, who are less likely to be chosen as surrogates by the

couples who seek this arrangement. To underscore the irony of the double bind, consider the testimony of an adopting mother who fears that surrogacy "can exploit the lower classes and the women of the Third World," and thus finds it "unconscionable" to choose as surrogates women who are poverty-stricken and need the money. *Id.* § 6, at 12, col. I.

8. This is true whether the surrogate gives or sells the baby or her services (however we wish to characterize the thing transferred). If an adoption is commissioned, the baby would not have been born but for the would-be parents' demand, but probably even if these transactions were permitted there would still be a substantial number of unwanted children also available for adoption.

9. People who are sensitive to what men lose by not having the bonds with children traditionally thought characteristic of motherhood might argue that if we hope for "new" men that are more bound up with their children, we should foster progress toward this ideal by assuming a deep and personal bond between men and their genetic offspring. Hence, we might think we should respect and encourage men's desires for surrogacy.

10. True, there is usually a deep bond between a baby and the woman who carries it, but it seems to me that this bond too is created by shared life, the physical and emotional interdependence of mother and child, more than by the identity of the genetic material. It will be difficult to study this question unless childbearing by embryo transfer, in which a woman can carry a fetus that is not genetically related to her, becomes widespread.

11. *See* Smith, *Parenting and Property,* in MOTHERING: ESSAYS IN FEMINIST THEORY 199 (J. Trebilcot ed. 1983). Artificial insemination—and for that matter traditional procreation— poses a similar issue of genetic property. It is just as inappropriate to conceive of parent-child bonding in terms of women's genetic "property" as in terms of men's. But in the context of the present gender structure, the desire to carry on the woman's genetic line is less likely to make men fungible. Moreover, the interests of women and men are asymmetrical because the carrying of the child in the woman's body (whether or not it is hers genetically) is a stronger factor in interrelationships with a child than an abstract genetic relationship.

12. One such example occurs when a woman bears a child for her childless sister.

13. To prevent women from benefiting financially from reproductive services, some states have passed criminal statutes prohibiting women who relinquish children for adoption from receiving expenses. Others require a full accounting of fees received.

14. In light of the apparent strength of people's desires for fathers' genetic offspring, the ban on profit would also be difficult to enforce. As with adoption, we would see a black market develop in surrogacy.

 15. The issue of whether surrogacy agreements should be specifically performed—whether the mother who changes her mind should nonetheless be forced to hand over the baby—has received the most popular attention recently. *See, e.g., Father of Baby M Granted Custody; Contract Upheld,* N.Y. Times, Apr. 1, 1987, § A, at I, col. 5. We should not think however, that we are faced with merely a binary choice: either banning paid surrogacy arrangements or granting specific performance of them. To conceive of surrogacy as a special situation requiring specific performance seems to place undue weight on the supposed genetic interests of would-be fathers in their unique "property" and to undervalue both the personal development of unwanted children they might otherwise adopt (and become bonded to) and the personal identity of women torn between economic need and deep attachment to a baby.

16. Of course, we should decide upon a reasonable time limit during which she must make up her mind, for it would be injurious to the child if her life were in limbo for very long. This could be done analogously with statutory waiting periods for adoption to become final after birth. *See, e.g.,* Surrogate Parenting Assocs. v. Kentucky *ex rel* Armstrong, 707 S.W. 2d 209, 213 (Ky. 1986) (holding that the five-day waiting period in Kentucky's termination of parental rights statute and consent to adoption statute "take[s] precedence over the parties' contractual commitments, meaning that the surrogate mother is free to change her mind"). We might wish to make the birth mother's decision to keep the child not an absolute right but only a very strong presumption, such as would be used in a custody dispute over a newborn baby in a divorce. In my view, however,

adoption is the better analogy: except in very special cases, both surrogates and others who are considering relinquishing children for adoption should be able to decide after birth to keep the child. *See. e.g., id.* (stating that if a surrogate decides to keep her child, "[s]he would be in the same position vis-a-vis the child and the biological father as any other mother with a child born out of wedlock" and that the "parental rights and obligations between the biological father and mother, and the obligations they owe the child," would be those imposed by the statutes applicable to this situation).

17. Because a pregnancy and a child's life are involved in the surrogacy interaction, rather than just one sexual encounter as with prostitution, "official" recognition of the interaction, with its contribution to commodification, will have to be tolerated, regardless of whether we choose market-inalienability or incomplete commodification. Decisions will have to be made about restitution in case of breach, about payment of the surrogate's expenses, and above all, about care for the child if all parties fail to take responsibility. Even if we choose incomplete commodification, contract remedies should be avoided. Specific performance should be avoided because of the analogy to personal service agreements, and also because we should not conceive of children as unique goods, *see supra* note [15]: damage remedies should be avoided because of the obvious "official" commodification involved in setting a dollar value on the loss. It is not my purpose here, however, to try to draft an appropriate statute or guidelines for courts.

GERALD DWORKIN

Markets and Morals: The Case for Organ Sales

Arthur Caplan has said that "perhaps the most pressing policy issue facing those within and outside of the field [of organ transplantation] concerns the shortage of organs available for transplantation to those with end-stage organ failure" (1). The options available to increase the supply of scarce goods are basically three—donation, conscription, or sale. A good deal of attention has been focused on the first two methods (I take presumed consent to be basically conscription with an option to opt out before death), but the sale of organs has been little discussed.

I focus on the issue of whether there are good arguments of an ethical nature which rule out a market in organs. I leave to one side discussion of whether such markets would in fact increase the supply of organs, whether there are practical difficulties in the implementation of such a scheme, whether political considerations (in the broad sense) would make it difficult to gain support for such a system. My only task today is to assess the moral arguments.

The first distinction we must make is between a futures market and a current market—that is, between the decision of an individual to sell the right to his organs after his death, and the decision to sell organs while he is alive.

I assume, for the sake of this discussion, that if there are moral objections to the sale of organs they will take their strongest form against the sale of organs from living donors. Hence if one can show that there are no conclusive arguments against such sales, one will have shown, ipso facto, that there are no conclusive objections against the sale of cadaver organs.

I first briefly consider the arguments in favor of a market in organs and claim that in the absence of moral objections, there is no reason for not having such markets. I then want to consider all the plausible arguments against the sale of organs and show that they are not legitimate objections. My conclusion will be that, in the absence of further arguments which survive critical scrutiny, there are good reasons for favoring a market in organs.

Arguments for a Market

We currently accept the legitimacy of noncommercial solid-organ donations. We also accept the legitimacy of the sale of blood, semen, ova, hair, and tissue. By doing so we accept the idea that individuals have the right to dispose of their organs and other bodily parts if they so choose. By recognizing such a right we respect the bodily autonomy of individuals, that is, their capacity to make choices about how their body is to be treated by others. By recognizing such a right we also produce good consequences for others, that is, save lives, allow infertile couples to have children, further medical research, and so on. But the primary good achieved by such a right is the recognition of the individual as sovereign over his own body. A market transaction is one species of the larger class of voluntary transactions. Allowing people to sell things is one way of recognizing their sphere of control.

Finally, by allowing individuals to either barter or sell something, we increase their level of well-being. Since such transactions are voluntary, they are presumably only engaged in when the individual believes himself or herself better off without the good and with the cash (or an alternative good in the case of barter) than without the cash and with the good.

So markets can increase both autonomy and well-being.

Arguments Against a Market

There are often compelling reasons why we should not allow individuals to sell what they could give. We do not allow markets in votes, in babies, in judicial decisions, in college grades. In these cases we recognize countervailing considerations which are sufficient to overrule the considerations in favor of markets. So the question before us is whether there are such counterarguments in the case of markets for human organs. I propose to consider the arguments that have been adduced and show that they are not compelling.

Exploitation of the Poor

One of the most powerful arguments against a market in organs is the element of exploitation of the poor. Clearly, those who are most likely to wish to sell their organs are those whose financial situation is most desperate. Those who have alternative sources of income are not likely to choose an option which entails some health risk, some disfigurement, some pain and discomfort. The risks of such sales will certainly fall disproportionately by income class.

But what exactly is supposed to follow from these facts? Is it that, because of this, the choices of the poor are not, in fact, fully voluntary? This seems to me false. Or if it is true, it has a much wider implication than that organs should not be sold. It suggests that poor people should not be allowed to enter the army, to engage in hazardous occupations such as high-steel construction, to become paid subjects for medical experimentation. There are certainly objections of justice to the current highly unequal income distribution. But it seems to me paternalistic in the extreme, given that injustice, to deny poor people choices which they perceive as increasing their well-being.

Here it is important to have some idea of the size of the risk we are talking about. One study has estimated that the increased risk of death to a 35-year-old from giving up one kidney is roughly the same as that associated with driving a car to work 16 miles a day (2). Imagine saying to a poor person either that her choice to commute such a distance is not voluntary, or that if it is, she still ought not to be allowed to commute such a distance, although we will allow middle-class persons to do so.

To make this point more vivid, what would your reaction be to the following proposal made by one author in response to this objection? Prohibit purchases from individuals whose average income is less than 80% of median family income. This has the effect of removing persons in the lower 40% of the income distribution from the market (3). Would you now be more, or less, inclined to favor organ sales?

Note also in the context of arguments about justice that the poor are disproportionately represented among those who need transplants. Thus, assuming—as is currently the case—that the government subsidizes most organ transplants, they stand to gain as a class more than the rich.

Another objection based on the fact of income inequality is that because of unequal bargaining power the price paid to the poor will not be a fair one. They will not get the full market value of their organs. If there were evidence that this was true, the solution would be to regulate the market, not forbid the sale. One could establish minimum prices analogous to minimum wage laws.

Distributional Consequences

If organs are for sale to the highest bidder, the rich will get them and the poor will not.

First, this seems an objection not to the sale of organs but to the general system of medical care based on ability to pay. There are currently at least 50 different types of artificial body parts which are distributed according to ability to pay. Why is it better for the rich to have better access to artificial than to human kidneys?

Second, currently, few individuals pay for transplants out of their own funds. Most transplants are paid for by public and private insurance. So the issue again is access to health insurance, not access to organs.

Note also that the main costs associated with transplants are likely to remain the fees of doctors and hospitals and the costs of drugs, all determined by markets. Why is it legitimate for these to be the results of markets and not the organs themselves?

But if one finds that the distributional implications are unsatisfactory, regulations or restriction on sales are called for. We could adopt a scheme, for example, in which it would be illegal for private individuals to sell organs to other private individuals. They could only sell them to the state. The state then could adopt whatever scheme of distribution would ensure justice in transfer—perhaps a lottery among the equally medically needy, or a first-come, first-served principle.

Irreversibility

One objection to the sale of organs, as opposed to renewable tissues such as blood or semen, is that the decision is irreversible. Individuals may come to regret the fact that they have sold a kidney—particularly if they develop kidney problems with the remaining organ. But we currently allow individuals to make many permanent changes in their body, including breast diminishment and sterilization. If we feel the problem is more severe we can establish waiting periods, counselling, and so forth.

More Choices Not Always Better

The argument that more choices are not always better says that allowing new options does not leave the old options unaltered. Applied to the sale of organs, the claim is that once a market price is established for organs, individuals who choose not to sell do so in the knowledge that they have made a choice which leaves their family worse off economically than they might have been. Individuals are choosing to decline an option which they formerly did not have. They may be psychically worse off than if they never had such a choice. I agree that this is a cost. I do not see, however, that it is anywhere near the psychic costs that are incurred by individuals and their families who face blindness and death as a result of an inadequate supply of organs.

Another psychic cost is more significant, as Hansman argues (3). If one assumes that because of tissue matches, the most efficient donations are from family members, it is likely that introducing markets is liable to strain family relations. Family members are likely to be resentful of being asked to contribute without compensation when a stranger would receive substantial payment. It seems, however, that the rapid development of immunosuppressive drugs may considerably weaken the first premise of this argument.

Commodification

Finally we come to a large class of arguments which object to the commodification of organs. These arguments are rather diverse in character—many are discussed by Radin (4)—and one has to examine them carefully to see how they differ and whether any of them have sufficient force to overcome the presumption in favor of allowing sales of organs.

Altered Nature of the Transaction

Peter Singer, in a well-known argument against the sale of blood which would carry over to the sale of organs, claims that the nature of giving changes when blood is allowed to be sold as well as donated:

> If blood is a commodity with a price, to give blood means merely to save someone money. Blood has a cash value of a certain number of dollars, and the importance of the gift will vary with the wealth of the recipient. If blood cannot be bought, however, the gift's value depends upon the need of the recipient (5).

There are actually two arguments here. The first is that the sale of blood means that the significance of the transfer will vary with the wealth rather than the need of the recipient. Unfortunately this argument is much too powerful, since it is an argument against the sale of anything. Why distinguish blood from food?

The second argument has more weight. It is that if one adds to the existing practice of donation the use of a market, the situation for donors is altered. Whereas before they were able to give something that could not also be purchased, now they can only give something that has a price as well. The nature of their gift is changed. Although I concede that this is true, I do not see it as a compelling objection to allowing such sales. Donors do not have the right to have their gift retain its special character, and if the price of so doing is that potential recipients of life-saving resources are excluded from receiving them (because the supply of donations is limited), the consequences alone would argue for not forbidding such sales.

Alienation

Charles Fried argues that:

> When a man sells his body he does not sell what is his, he sells himself. What is disturbing, therefore, about selling human tissue is that the seller treats his

body as a foreign object ... the shame of selling one's body is just that one splits apart an entity one knows should not be so split (6).

Notice first that this argument (similar to one given by Kant) applies to the sale of blood and semen as well as organs. So if this argument is good, it shows that our current policies are illegitimate. (Although Fried seems to take it back in a footnote [6, p. 143] saying that the selling of blood is "personally bad ... though not in any sense wrong.")

But the main objection to this argument is that it implies not only that the sale of blood or hair is bad, but also that the donation of such bodily parts is bad as well. For if selling organs splits apart an entity one knows should not be so split, so does donating it. One treats one's body just as much as a foreign object if one gives away a kidney as if one sells it.

The danger we want to avoid at almost all cost is that people start to be treated as property by others. But this is avoided by leaving all decisions about their organs, tissues, and so on to the persons themselves, and insuring that their decisions are voluntary.

Driving Out Altruism

The argument about driving out altruism is that allowing a market in some item will make it less likely that those who were inclined to give on altruistic grounds will continue to do so. The data on blood are ambiguous on this point—some tending to show such an effect, some not. It is clear, however, that the presence of markets does not generally drive out altruistic motives. Most hospital workers are paid, but there are still volunteer workers. There are markets for used clothing, but many people give their used clothing to the needy. Lawyers are paid for their services, but many contribute a portion of their time pro bono. Finally, even if it were true that a market in organs would somewhat reduce the number of people who donate organs, if the total supply is increased, one has to weigh the loss of altruism against the gain in human lives. I see no reason to suppose that the balance will be negative. After all, we allow a commercial market for caregivers for our elderly parents—surely an arena in which not only generalized altruism but debts of gratitude play an important role.

Conclusions

It seems to me that if we take into account all the welfare losses that will accrue because of the introduction of markets for organs, it will still be the case that if the supply of such organs is significantly increased, the two major gains in welfare (improved health and decreased mortality, and increased income for sellers) will significantly outweigh the losses. If there are no non-consequentialist considerations (such as denials of rights or considerations of justice) which might trump such consequentialist considerations, the consequences ought to be determining.

My conclusion is that, absent other and stronger arguments than those considered, given that both rights and welfare argue in favor of a market for living organ donations, there is no reason not to allow them. In addition, whatever the force of these objections, most of them are considerably weaker when applied to the sale of future rights in cadaver organs. So such a scheme is, I believe, certainly warranted.

References

1. Caplan A. Beg, borrow, or steal: the ethics of solid organ procurement. In: Mathieu D, ed. Organ substitution technology. Boulder: Westview Press, 1989, 60.
2. Hamburger J, Crosnier J. Moral and ethical problems in transplantation. In: Johnson D, ed. Blood policy: issues and alternatives. Washington: American Enterprise Institute, 1968.
3. Hansmann H. The economics and ethics of markets for human organs. J Health Politics Policy Law 1989; 14(1):74.
4. Radin M. Market-inalienability. Harvard Law Rev 1987; 100.
5. Singer P. Altruism and commerce: a defense of titmuss against arrow. Phil Publ Affairs 1973; 2:314.
6. Fried C. Right and wrong. Cambridge: Harvard University Press, 1978, 142.

9 Blackmail

People v. Fichtner

[*New York Supreme Court, Appellate Division, Second Department 281 A.D. 159, 118 N.Y.S.2d 392 (1952). Affirmed without opinion,* 305 N.Y. 864, 114 N.E.2d 212 (1952).]

Johnston, J. Section 850 of the Penal Law provides: "Extortion is the obtaining of property from another . . ., with his consent, induced by a wrongful use of . . . fear. . . ."

Section 851 of the Penal Law provides:

> Fear, such as will constitute extortion, may be induced by an oral or written threat: . . . 2. To accuse him or any relative of his or any member of his family, of any crime; or 3. To expose, or impute to him, or any of them, any . . . disgrace. . . .

Defendant Fichtner is the manager, and defendant McGuinness the assistant manager, of the Hill Supermarket in Freeport, Nassau County. On January 30, 1951, an indictment was filed against both defendants, charging them in two counts with the crime of extortion in that on January 18, 1951, defendants, aiding and abetting each other, obtained $25 from one Smith, with his consent, which consent defendants induced by a wrongful use of fear by threatening to accuse Smith of the crime of petit larceny, and to expose and impute to him a disgrace unless Smith paid them $25.

Smith testified that on January 18, 1951, he purchased a number of articles in the Hill store for a total of about $12, but left the store without paying for a fifty-three-cent jar of coffee, which he had concealed in his pocket. After Smith left the store he returned at defendant Fichtner's request. Defendants then threatened to call a policeman, to arrest Smith for petit larceny, with resulting publicity in the newspapers and over the radio, unless he paid $75 and signed a paper admitting that during the course of several months he had unlawfully taken merchandise from the store in that amount. Although Smith admitted he had shopped in Hill's Freeport store about sixteen times and in Hill's Merrick store for about two years, he insisted that the only merchandise he had ever stolen was the fifty-three-cent jar of coffee on the evening in question, and a sixty-five-cent roll of bologna one week previously. However, he finally signed the paper admitting that he had unlawfully taken $50 worth of merchandise from the store during a period of four months. That evening Smith paid $25 in cash and promised to pay the balance in weekly installments of $5. He testified he was induced to sign the paper and make the payment because defendants threatened to accuse him of petit larceny and to expose him to the disgrace of the criminal charge and the resulting publicity. It is not disputed that the $25 taken from Smith was "rung up" on the store register; that the money went into the company funds and that defendants received no part of the money. During the following week Smith reported the incident to the police, and defendants were arrested on January 25, 1951, when Smith, accompanied by a detective, returned to the store and paid the first $5 installment.

Defendants testified that over the course of several weeks they saw Smith steal merchandise amounting to $5.61, and they honestly believed that during the several months that Smith had been shopping, he had stolen merchandise of the value of $75; that on January 18, 1951, Smith freely admitted that during the four-month period he stole merchandise of the value of $50, and that he voluntarily signed the paper admitting thefts in that amount; that on that date he paid $25 on account and promised to pay the balance in weekly installments.

That the Smith incident was not an isolated one, but rather part of a course of conduct pursued by defendants, even after warning by the police to discontinue the practice, was not only clearly established but admitted by defendant Fichtner.

The court charged, without exception, that (1) in order to convict, there must be a finding of intent on the part of defendants wrongfully to obtain money from Smith by means of unlawful threats; (2) it is immaterial that the person who obtains the money retains no part of the proceeds; the gist of the crime is the loss of money by Smith by reason of a criminal act on the part of defendants; (3) threats to do a lawful act may become unlawful if made with an unlawful motive for an unlawful purpose; (4) to accuse one of the crime of petit larceny or to impute disgrace to him may be lawful under certain circumstances; that where one steals a small amount of money and is threatened with prosecution if he does not return the money, that is a lawful threat because in such a case the intent would be to have the wrongdoer return the amount he owes; on the other hand, if one threatens to prosecute a person unless he pays an amount over and above what is rightfully due, and by such threat it is intended thereby to induce fear in that person, [*163] such a threat would be an unlawful threat to do an unlawful injury, and would constitute extortion; (5) the fact that Smith was guilty of larceny does not preclude the jury from finding defendants guilty of extortion. As heretofore stated, defendants were found guilty on both counts.

In my opinion, the verdict is amply supported by the evidence. . . .

*   *   *

The law does not authorize the collection of just debts by threatening to accuse the debtor of crime, even though the complainant is in fact guilty of the crime. In my opinion, it makes no difference whether the indebtedness for which a defendant demands repayment is one arising out of the crime for the prosecution of which he threatens the complainant, or is entirely independent and having no connection with the crime which forms the basis of the accusation. The result in both cases is the concealment and compounding of a felony to the injury of the State. It is that result which the extortion statutes were intended to prevent.

Note

New York's statutes have since been changed. N.Y. Penal Law § 155.15(2) provides:

> In any prosecution for larceny by extortion committed by instilling in the victim a fear that he or another would be charged with a crime, it is an affirmative defense that the defendant reasonably believed the threatened charge to be true and that his sole purpose was to compel or induce the victim to take reasonable action to make good the wrong which was the subject of such threatened charge.

Section 215.45 provides:

> 1. A person is guilty of compounding a crime when: (a) He solicits, accepts or agrees to accept any benefit upon an agreement or understanding that he will refrain from initiating a prosecution for a crime; or (b) He confers, or offers or agrees to confer, any benefit upon another person upon an agreement or understanding that such other person will refrain from initiating a prosecution for a crime.
> 2. In any prosecution under this section, it is an affirmative defense that the benefit did not exceed an amount which the defendant reasonably believed to be due as restitution or indemnification for harm caused by the crime.

KATHLEEN SULLIVAN
Unconstitutional Conditions

. . . Consider two examples from criminal law: the crimes of blackmail and extortion by color of public office. Blackmail is treated as a species of coercion—specifically, as theft[1]—rather than as a legitimate commercial exchange, even though blackmail involves no force or threat of force—only the threat to publicize true information the victim would rather suppress. Blackmail thus forbids a threat to perform an act that the blackmailer would ordinarily have a right to perform when that threat is used to extract a payment of money—hence, "the paradox of blackmail."[2] The crime of extortion under color of public office likewise prohibits offers of exchange in the absence of force or threat of force, even where the extorting official has absolute discretion over the official action he offers to perform in exchange for the victim's payment.

Labor law furnishes a third example of how a threat to do what one has a right to do can be treated as coercive. Under federal law, it is an unfair labor practice for an employer "to interfere with, restrain, or *coerce* employees in the exercise of [their] rights." Cases interpreting this provision have found employer speech to employees coercive not only when the employer threatens wrongful retaliation for unionization, but also when the employer engages in "conscious overstatements" about the possible economic consequences of unionization that employees might hear "as coercive threats rather than honest forecasts." The former threatens to do what the employer has no right to do; the latter is much more difficult to characterize.

Fourth, in corporate takeover law, offers of exchange are frequently viewed as coercive when designed to induce shareholders to tender shares at a price they view as too low, lest they suffer worse consequences. Partial tender offers without any commitment to pay a fixed price for shares if control is established, for example, are deemed coercive because they induce shareholders to tender even if they think the stock is worth more than the offer. Likewise, "two-tier" tender offers, which offer a premium to those who tender before control is acquired over the price to be paid for remaining shares if control is acquired, are commonly deemed coercive. Various regulatory measures have been proposed or enacted to reduce such coercion, on the theory that coercive offers give shareholders less than they would have received in "free and fair negotiation."

2. Coercion as a Normative Concept.—In each of the settings just described, "coercion" constituted more than a lack of choice ("reasonable alternatives") on the part of the offeree. In each, a finding of coercion depended on some moral condemnation of the offer itself. In other words, the concept of coercion is inescapably normative.[3] This observation has prompted some to abandon any attempt to distinguish coercive from non-coercive offers in the first place, and others to attempt to specify the norms that would make such a distinction meaningful.

The first response is exemplified by the polar positions that all exchange is consensual or that all exchange is coercive. The first position, universal con-sensualism, would view all transactions in the absence of literal bodily com-pulsion as uncoerced. Arms-length transactions based on full information in a competitive market are obviously voluntary on this view, but so is the sur-render of money to a highwayman who says, "your money or your life." Richard Posner, for example, has written that both sides in the latter ex-change exercise "free will," for the victim at knifepoint is "eager to exchange the note for [the knifewielder's] forbearance to kill him."[4] Here, as in a mar-ket transaction, the offeree willingly trades what he values less for what he values more. Intermediate cases, such as market transactions under condi-tions of imperfect competition, are similarly voluntary; trading partners do not *coerce* one another into exchange.[5]

The opposite position, universal coercionism, was most starkly expressed by Robert Hale, the legal realist who, among other things, wrote the classic early study of unconstitutional conditions. Hale argued elsewhere that every exchange, even in a competitive market, is coerced:

> Exaction of a price for any article restricts freedom to consume it. Every price, like every tax, is in some measure regulatory. . . . He who refrains from con-suming as much as he wishes in order to avoid payment of the price "yields to compulsion precisely the same as though he did so to avoid a term in jail."[6]

Trades between private parties are coercive, according to Hale, because be-hind such trades stands the power of the state to enforce property rights; "the bargaining power to exact a price for the use of property stems from the state's restriction of the liberty of nonowners to make unauthorized use of the property."[7] However extreme this claim may sound, it merely extends the more general and less controversial realist view that public power is inev-itably implicated in private transactions.[8]

Universal consensualism and universal coercionism, although in one sense opposites, have one crucial feature in common: both would reject the effort to distinguish coercive from noncoercive offers of exchange as futile or mis-guided, and would substitute an alternative, consequentialist ground by which to judge the legitimacy or desirability of various kinds of exchange. An alternative approach would instead retain the distinction between coer-cion and consent and specify the normative theory underlying it.

The first possible theory would seek to define the minimal preconditions for human autonomy. Robert Nozick's justly famous article on coercion[9] reads as if it were presenting a purely descriptive or empirical account. It is better understood, however, as importing a necessarily normative account of human freedom. Nozick argues that coercion is limited to "threats," and that a "threat" is an offer the "rational man" would rather not receive:

> If the alternatives among which Q must choose are intentionally changed by P, and P made this change in order to get Q to do A, and before the change Q would not have chosen (and would have been unwilling to choose) to have the change made (and after it's made, Q would prefer that it hadn't been made), and before the change was made Q wouldn't have chosen to do A, and after the change is made Q does A, then Q's choice to do A is not fully his own.[10]

The first hidden assumption is that human autonomy depends on freedom from captivity to another person's will. The core of coercion, accordingly, is intentionality by human agents. This view recognizes neither social or structural coercion,[11] nor the possibility that coercion might be the unconscious byproduct of human action primarily directed at other ends, nor the possibility that one might "coerce" by exploiting limitations on the freedom of others not of one's own making. On this view, the background circumstances that may make us unfree do not "coerce" us.[12] The second hidden assumption is that coercion is determined by the *preferences* of a rational Q. Whether autonomy can be defined by reference to preferences alone, however, is a matter of deep philosophical debate.

A second normative account would collapse coercion into conceptions not of freedom but of desert. For example, Anthony Kronman has argued that in contract law, the line between consent and coercion, or more accurately, permissible and impermissible "advantage-taking," cannot be drawn, except arbitrarily, by reference solely to the value of liberty itself. Rather, it can be drawn only by reference to conceptions of distributive justice. He advocates a "paretian" criterion that evaluates the permissibility of advantage-taking by reference to whether a practice makes the class it disadvantages in the near term better off in the long run.[13] Although Kronman disavows utility as his evaluative principle,[14] he acknowledges that utility offers an alternative criterion by which to free the concept of coercion from some quantitative definition of liberty from another party's will.[15]

A third normative account would define coercion as a departure from appropriate conditions of equality. Such an approach deems "coercive" the threat not to treat one the same as other similarly situated persons, with the intent of inducing one to perform or refrain from some action. This analysis depends on a prior determination that one deserves to be treated the same as everyone else. Such a determination, however, would seem to recast the problem as one of inappropriately unequal treatment, whether "coercive" or not.

While unconstitutional conditions doctrine thus is hardly unique in deeming some offers of benefit coercive, the concept of coercion will depend just as inescapably on independent conceptions of utility, autonomy, fairness, or desert in the unconstitutional conditions context as in other contexts. Coercion is a judgment, not a state of being. . . .

Notes

1. *See* MODEL PENAL CODE § 223.4 (1985); 2 W. LaFave & A. Scott, Substantive Criminal Law § 8.12, at 458–63 (1986).

2. *See* Lindgren, *Unraveling the Paradox of Blackmail,* 84 Colum. L. Rev. 670 (1984). For other important contributions to the debate over the criminalization of blackmail, see Block & Gordon, *Blackmail, Extortion and Free Speech: A Reply to Posner, Epstein, Nozick and Lindgren,* 19 Loy. L.A.L. Rev. 37 (1985); Coase, *The 1987 McCorkle Lecture—Blackmail,* 74 Va. L. Rev. 655 (1988); Epstein, *Blackmail, Inc.,* 50 U. Chi. L. Rev. 553 (1983); and Lindgren, *Blackmail: On Waste, Morals, and Ronald Coase,* 36 UCLA L. Rev. 597 (1989).

3. Philosophical commentators have often stressed this point. *See* J. Elster, Making Sense of Marx 212–16 (1985); J. Raz, The Morality of Freedom 148–57 (1986); A. Wertheimer, Coercion (Princeton University Press, 1987), at 211–17 (1987) (advocating a moralized conception of coercive proposals); Murphy, *Consent, Coercion, and Hard Choices,* 67 Va. L. Rev. (1981). For a particularly succinct statement of the point in the context of contractual duress, see C. Fried, Contract as Promise 97 (1981): "we cannot escape using some normative criterion to distinguish offers from threats [i.e., coercion]. And that is a pity since the purpose of the [contractual duress] inquiry is itself normative. . . ."

4. R. Posner Economic Analysis of Law 101 (3rd ed. 1986).

5. A less extreme position, modified consensualism, might view action taken under force or threat of force, but not offers of benefit, as inherently coercive. Adherents of this position would argue that people are weaker in the face of pain than gain. Fear of force, on this view, moves us to act by something akin to mere instinct or reflex, but offers of benefit permit detached reflection. The prospect of gain is something that, however tempting, we have the capacity to resist. On this view, offers of benefits might be ranked as more or less attractive, but none could be said to coerce.

6. R. Hale, Freedom Through Law: Public Control of Private Governing Power 294 (1952) (quoting Carter v. Carter Coal Co., 298 U.S. 238, 289 (1936) (describing compulsion of "[o]ne who does a thing in order to avoid a monetary penalty").

7. R. Hale, *op. cit.,* at 295.

8. *See* Singer, *Legal Realism Now* (Book Review), 76 Cal. L. Rev. 465, 477–95 (1988).

9. *See* Nozick, *Coercion,* in Philosophy, Science, and Method 440 (S. Morgenbesser, P. Suppes & M. White eds. 1969). Commentary on Nozick's article is a cottage industry in moral philosophy. Virtually all philosophical commentators writing in Nozick's wake agree with the basic premise of his article: that coercive proposals ("threats," in Nozick's terminology), unlike noncoercive proposals ("offers," in Nozick's terminology), involve a departure from some baseline of "the normal or natural or expected course of events" that makes the recipient worse off. *See id.* at 447. They disagree, however, about how to define the appropriate baseline. *See* Westen, *"Freedom" and "Coercion"—Virtue Words and Vice Words,* 1985 Duke L.J. 541, 572, 588.

The debated baselines fall roughly into two categories: descriptive and moral. Some descriptive accounts focus on the recipient's own preferences and expectations. Nozick himself defines threats as proposals that put recipients to an objectively undesirable choice: the rational person would not choose to move from the pre-proposal to the post-proposal situation. *See* Nozick, *supra,* at 464. Others focus on the recipient's subjective desire to avoid a coercive proposal. *See, e.g.,*

A. WERTHEIMER, COERCION (Princeton University Press, 1987), at 207 (describing a "phenomenological" nonmoral baseline tracking what the recipient expects or believes is morally required to happen in the normal course of events); Frankfurt, *Coercion and Moral Responsibility,* in ESSAYS ON FREEDOM OF ACTION 66, 80 (T. Honderich ed. 1973) ("An offer is coercive . . . when the person who receives it is moved into compliance by a desire which is not only irresistible but which he would overcome if he could. In that case the desire which drives the person is a desire by which he does not want to be driven." (citation omitted)); Zimmerman, *Coercive Wage Offers,* 10 PHIL. & PUB. AFF. 121, 132–34 (1981) (defining a coercive offer as one that prevents the proposal situation that the offeree would strongly prefer). Still others recommend descriptive baselines that turn not on what the recipient wants or expects, but rather on what interaction is statistically likely to occur between offeror and offeree in the normal course of events. *See, e.g.,* J. FEINBERG, HARM TO SELF 219 (1986) (describing coercive offers as departures from a hypothetical "statistically normal set of circumstances"); A. WERTHEIMER, *op. cit.,* at 205–06 (describing "objective" nonmoral baseline). These baselines turn on sociological or anthropological observations about customary social practice rather than on psychological data about the recipient.

Moral baselines track desert rather than expectation. They define as coercive a proposal that departs from what the offeree has a right to expect, or that threatens to put the offeree in a worse position than he ought to be if he declines.

10. Nozick, *supra* note 9, at 463.

11. Contrast the views of Marxian philosophers of coercion summarized in Reiman, *Exploitation, Force, and the Moral Assessment of Capitalism: Thoughts on Roemer and Cohen,* 16 PHIL. & PUB. AFF. 3 (1987), especially with respect to "structural force."

12. *See* Nozick, *supra* note 9, at 440; *see also* R. NOZICK, PHILOSOPHICAL EXPLANATIONS 49 (1981). In this sense, Nozick's view reflects conceptions of negative liberty. Contrast this, for example, with the view of Joseph Raz: "Inasmuch as the liberal concern to limit coercion is a concern for the autonomy of persons, the liberal will also be anxious to secure natural and social conditions which enable individuals to develop an autonomous life."

13. *See* Kronman, *Contract Law and Distributive Justice,* YALE L.J. 472, 489–91 (1980).

14. *See id.* at 487–88.

15. *See id.* at 485.

10　Community Standards

Paris Adult Theatre I v. Slayton

Mr. Chief Justice BURGER delivered the opinion of the Court.

Petitioners are two Atlanta, Georgia, movie theaters and their owners and managers, operating in the style of "adult" theaters. On December 28, 1970, respondents, the local state district attorney and the solicitor for the local state trial court, filed civil complaints in that court alleging that petitioners were exhibiting to the public for paid admission two allegedly obscene films, contrary to Georgia Code Ann. § 26–2101.[1] The two films in question, "Magic Mirror" and "It All Comes Out in the End," depict sexual conduct characterized by the Georgia Supreme Court as "hard core pornography" leaving "little to the imagination."

Respondents' complaints, made on behalf of the State of Georgia, demanded that the two films be declared obscene and that petitioners be enjoined from exhibiting the films. The exhibition of the films was not enjoined, but a temporary injunction was granted *ex parte* by the local trial court, restraining petitioners from destroying the films or removing them from the jurisdiction. . . .

On January 13, 1971, 15 days after the proceedings began, the films were produced by petitioners at a jury-waived trial. . . .

The two films were exhibited to the trial court. The only other state evidence was testimony by criminal investigators that they had paid admission to see the films and that nothing on the outside of the theater indicated the true nature of what was shown. In particular, nothing indicated that the films depicted—as they did—scenes of simulated fellatio, cunnilingus, and group sex intercourse. There was no evidence presented that minors had ever entered the theaters. Nor was there evidence presented that petitioners had a systematic policy of barring minors, apart from posting signs at the entrance. On April 12, 1971, the trial judge dismissed respondents' complaints. He assumed "that obscenity is established," but stated:

> "It appears to the Court that the display of these films in a commercial theatre, when surrounded by requisite notice to the public of their nature and by rea-

sonable protection against the exposure of these films to minors, is constitutionally permissible."

On appeal, the Georgia Supreme Court unanimously reversed. . . . Citing the opinion of this Court in United States v. Reidel, the Georgia court stated that "the sale and delivery of obscene material to willing adults is not protected under the first amendment." The Georgia court also held Stanley v. Georgia, to be inapposite since it did not deal with "the commercial distribution of pornography, but with the right of Stanley to possess, in the privacy of his home, pornographic films." . . .

I

[1] It should be clear from the outset that we do not undertake to tell the States what they must do, but rather to define the area in which they may chart their own course in dealing with obscene material. This Court has consistently held that obscene material is not protected by the First Amendment as a limitation on the state police power by virtue of the Fourteenth Amendment.

Georgia case law permits a civil injunction of the exhibition of obscene materials. While this procedure is civil in nature, . . . the Georgia case law permitting civil injunction does adopt the definition of "obscene materials" used by the criminal statute. Today, in Miller v. California, *supra,* we have sought to clarify the constitutional definition of obscene material subject to regulation by the States, and we vacate and remand this case for reconsideration in light of Miller. . . .

II

We categorically disapprove the theory, apparently adopted by the trial judge, that obscene, pornographic films acquire constitutional immunity from state regulation simply because they are exhibited for consenting adults only. This holding was properly rejected by the Georgia Supreme Court. Although we have often pointedly recognized the high importance of the state interest in regulating the exposure of obscene materials to juveniles and unconsenting adults, this Court has never declared these to be the only legitimate state interests permitting regulation of obscene material. The States have a long-recognized legitimate interest in regulating the use of obscene material in local commerce and in all places of public accommodation, as long as these regulations do not run afoul of specific constitutional prohibitions. "In an unbroken series of cases extending over a long stretch of this Court's history it has been accepted as a postulate that 'the primary requirements of decency may be enforced against obscene publications.'"

[8] In particular, we hold that there are legitimate state interests at stake in stemming the tide of commercialized obscenity, even assuming it is feasible to enforce effective safeguards against exposure to juveniles and to passersby.[2] Rights and interests "other than those of the advocates are involved." These include the interest of the public in the quality of life and the total community environment, the tone of commerce in the great city centers, and, possibly, the public safety itself. The Hill-Link Minority Report of the Commission on Obscenity and Pornography indicates that there is at least an arguable correlation between obscene material and crime.[3] Quite apart from sex crimes, however, there remains one problem of large proportions aptly described by Professor Bickel:

> "It concerns the tone of the society, the mode, or to use terms that have perhaps greater currency, the style and quality of life, now and in the future. A man may be entitled to read an obscene book in his room, or expose himself indecently there. . . . We should protect his privacy. But if he demands a right to obtain the books and pictures he wants in the market, and to foregather in public places—discreet, if you will, but accessible to all—with others who share his tastes, *then to grant him his right is to affect the world about the rest of us, and to impinge on other privacies.* Even supposing that each of us can, if he wishes, effectively avert the eye and stop the ear (which, in truth, we cannot), what is commonly read and seen and heard and done intrudes upon us all, want it or not." 22 The Public Interest 25–26 (Winter 1971). (Emphasis added.)

But, it is argued, there are no scientific data which conclusively demonstrate that exposure to obscene material adversely affects men and women or their society. It is urged on behalf of the petitioners that, absent such demonstration, any kind of state regulation is "impermissible." We reject this argument. It is not for us to resolve empirical uncertainties underlying such legislation, save in the exceptional case where that legislation plainly impinges upon rights protected by the Constitution itself. Although there is no conclusive proof of a connection between antisocial behavior and obscene material, the legislature of Georgia could quite reasonably determine that such a connection does or might exist. In deciding *Roth,* this Court implicitly accepted that a legislature could legitimately act on such a conclusion to protect *"the social interest in order and morality."* . . .

Finally, petitioners argue that conduct which directly involves "consenting adults" only has, for that sole reason, a special claim to constitutional protection. Our Constitution establishes a broad range of conditions on the exercise of power by the States, but for us to say that our Constitution incorporates the proposition that conduct involving consenting adults only is always beyond state regulation, is a step we are unable to take.[4] Commercial exploitation of depictions, descriptions, or exhibitions of obscene conduct on commercial premises open to the adult public falls within a state's broad power to regulate commerce and protect the public environment. The issue in this context goes beyond whether someone, or even the majority, considers the conduct depicted as "wrong" or "sinful." The States have the power to make a morally neutral judgment that public exhibition of obscene material, or commerce in such material, has a tendency to injure the community as a whole, to endanger the public safety, or to jeopardize in Mr. Chief Justice Warren's words, the States' "right . . . to maintain a decent society." . . .

Vacated and remanded.

Mr. Justice BRENNAN, with whom Mr. Justice STEWART and Mr. Justice MARSHALL join, dissenting.

This case requires the Court to confront once again the vexing problem of reconciling state efforts to suppress sexually oriented expression with the protections of the First Amendment, as applied to the States through the Fourteenth Amendment. . . . I am convinced that the approach initiated 16 years ago in Roth v. United States (1957), and culminating in the Court's decision today, cannot bring stability to this area of the law without jeopardizing fundamental First Amendment values, and I have concluded that the time has come to make a significant departure from that approach. . . .

The opinions in *Redrup* and *Stanley* reflected our emerging view that the state interests in protecting children and in protecting unconsenting adults may stand on a different footing from the other asserted state interests. It may well be, as one commentator has argued, that "exposure to [erotic material] is for some persons an intense emotional experience. A communication of this nature, imposed upon a person contrary to his wishes, has all the characteristics of a physical assault. . . . [And it] constitutes an invasion of his privacy. . . ."[5] Similarly, if children are "not possessed of that full capacity for individual choice which is the presupposition of the First Amendment guarantees," then the State may have a substantial interest in precluding the flow of obscene materials even to consenting juveniles.

But, whatever the strength of the state interests in protecting juveniles and unconsenting adults from exposure to sexually oriented materials, those interests cannot be asserted in defense of the holding of the Georgia Supreme Court in this case. That court assumed for the purposes of its decision that the films in issue were exhibited only to persons over the age of 21 who viewed them willingly and with prior knowledge of the nature of their contents. And on that assumption the state court held that the films could still be suppressed. The justification for the suppression must be found, therefore, in some independent interest in regulating the reading and viewing habits of consenting adults. . . .

In *Stanley* we pointed out that "[t]here appears to be little empirical basis for" the assertion that "exposure to obscene materials may lead to deviant sexual behavior or crimes of sexual violence."[6] In any event, we added that "if the State is only concerned about printed or filmed materials inducing antisocial conduct, we believe that in the context of private consumption of ideas and information we should adhere to the view that '[a]mong free men, the deterrents ordinarily to be applied to prevent crime are education and punishment for violations of the law. . . .'"

Moreover, in *Stanley* we rejected as "wholly inconsistent with the philosophy of the First Amendment," the notion that there is a legitimate state concern in the "control [of] the moral content of a person's thoughts," and we held that a State "cannot constitutionally premise legislation on the desirability of controlling a person's private thoughts." That is not to say, of course, that a State must remain utterly indifferent to—and take no action bearing on—the morality of the community. The traditional description of state police power does embrace the regulation of morals as well as the health, safety, and general welfare of the citizenry. And much legislation—compulsory public education laws, civil rights laws, even the abolition of capital punishment—is grounded, at least in part, on a concern with the morality of the community. But the State's interest in regulating morality by suppressing obscenity, while often asserted, remains essentially unfocused and ill defined. And, since the attempt to curtail unprotected speech necessarily spills over into the area of protected speech, the effort to serve this speculative interest through the suppression of obscene material must tread heavily on rights protected by the First Amendment.

In Roe v. Wade, we held constitutionally invalid a state abortion law, even though we were aware of

> "the sensitive and emotional nature of the abortion controversy, of the vigorous opposing views, even among physicians, and of the deep and seemingly absolute convictions that the subject inspires. One's philosophy, one's experiences, one's exposure to the raw edges of human existence, one's religious training, one's attitudes toward life and family and their values, and the moral standards one establishes and seeks to observe, are all likely to influence and to color one's thinking and conclusions about abortion."

Like the proscription of abortions, the effort to suppress obscenity is predicated on unprovable, although strongly held, assumptions about human behavior, morality, sex, and religion. The existence of these assumptions cannot validate a statute that substantially undermines the guarantees of the First Amendment, any more than the existence of similar assumptions on the issue of abortion can validate a statute that infringes the constitutionally protected privacy interests of a pregnant woman.

If, as the Court today assumes, "a state legislature may . . . act on the . . . assumption that commerce in obscene books, or public exhibitions focused on obscene conduct, have a tendency to exert a corrupting and debasing impact leading to antisocial behavior," then it is hard to see how state-ordered regimentation of our minds can ever be forestalled. For if a State, in an effort to maintain or create a particular moral tone, may prescribe what its citizens cannot read or cannot see, then it would seem to follow that in pursuit of that same objective a State could decree that its citizens must read certain books or must view certain films. However laudable its goal—and that is obviously a question on which reasonable minds may differ—the State cannot proceed by means that violate the Constitution. The precise point was established a half century ago in Meyer v. Nebraska.

"That the State may do much, go very far, indeed, in order to improve the quality of its citizens, physically, mentally and morally, is clear; but the individual has certain fundamental rights which must be respected. The protection of the Constitution extends to all, to those who speak other languages as well as to those born with English on the tongue. Perhaps it would be highly advantageous if all had ready understanding of our ordinary speech, but this cannot be coerced by methods which conflict with the Constitution—a desirable end cannot be promoted by prohibited means." . . .

Notes

1. Georgia Code Ann. § 26–2101 reads in relevant part: "Distributing obscene materials. (a) A person commits the offense of distributing obscene materials when he sells, lends, rents, leases, gives, advertises, publishes, exhibits or otherwise disseminates to any person any obscene material of any description, knowing the obscene nature thereof, or who offers to do so, or who possesses such material with the intent so to do. . . . (b) Material is obscene if considered as a whole, applying community standards, its predominant appeal is to prurient interest, that is, a shameful or morbid interest in nudity, sex or excretion, and utterly without redeeming social value and if, in addition, it goes substantially beyond customary limits of candor in describing or representing such matters. . . ."

* * *

"(d) A person convicted of distributing obscene material shall for the first offense be punished as for a misdemeanor, and for any subsequent offense shall be punished by imprisonment for not less than one nor more than five years, or by a fine not to exceed $5,000, or both."

2. It is conceivable that an "adult" theater can—if it really insists—prevent the exposure of its obscene wares to juveniles. An "adult" bookstore, dealing in obscene books, magazines, and pictures, cannot realistically make this claim. The Hill-Link Minority Report of the Commission on Obscenity and Pornography emphasizes evidence (the Abelson National Survey of Youth and Adults) that, although most pornography may be bought by elders, "the heavy users and most highly exposed people to pornography are adolescent females (among women) and adolescent and young adult males (among men)." The Report of the Commission on Obscenity and Pornography 401 (1970). The legitimate interest in preventing exposure of juveniles to obscene materials cannot be fully served by simply barring juveniles from the immediate physical premises of "adult" book stores, when there is a flourishing "outside business" in these materials.

3. The Report of the Commission on Obscenity and Pornography 390–412 (1970). For a discussion of earlier studies indicating "a division of thought [among behavioral scientists] on the correlation between obscenity and socially deleterious behavior", Memoirs v. Massachusetts, *supra*, 383 U.S., at 451, 86 S.Ct., at 993, and references to expert opinions that obscene material may induce crime and antisocial conduct, see *id.*, at 451–453, 86 S.Ct., at 993–995 (Clark, J.,

dissenting). As Mr. Justice Clark emphasized: "While erotic stimulation caused by pornography may be legally insignificant in itself, there are medical experts who believe that such stimulation frequently manifests itself in criminal sexual behavior or other antisocial conduct. For example, Dr. George W. Henry of Cornell University has expressed the opinion that obscenity, with its exaggerated and morbid emphasis on sex, particularly abnormal and perverted practices, and its unrealistic presentation of sexual behavior and attitudes, may induce antisocial conduct by the average person. A number of sociologists think that this material may have adverse effects upon individual mental health, with potentially disruptive consequences for the community."

*   *   *

"Congress and the legislatures of every State have enacted measures to restrict the distribution of erotic and pornographic material, justify these controls by reference to evidence that antisocial behavior may result in part from reading obscenity." *Id.,* at 452–453, 86 S.Ct., at 994–995 (footnotes omitted).

4. The state statute books are replete with constitutionally unchallenged laws against prostitution, suicide, voluntary self-mutilation, brutalizing "bare fist" prize fights, and duels, although these crimes may only directly involve "consenting adults." Statutes making bigamy a crime surely cut into an individual's freedom to associate, but few today seriously claim such statutes violate the First Amendment or any other constitutional provision. See also the summary of state statutes prohibiting bearbaiting, cock-fighting, and other brutalizing animal "sports," in Stevens, Fighting and Baiting, in Animals and Their Legal Rights 112–127 (Leavitt ed. 1970). As Professor Irving Kristol has observed: "Bearbaiting and cockfighting are prohibited only in part out of compassion for the suffering animals; the main reason they were abolished was because it was felt that they debased and brutalized the citizenry who flocked to witness such spectacles." On the Democratic Idea in America 33 (1972).

5. T. Emerson, The System of Freedom of Expression 496 (1970).

6. Indeed, since *Stanley* was decided, the President's Commission on Obscenity and Pornography has concluded: "In sum, empirical research designed to clarify the question has found no evidence to date that exposure to explicit sexual materials plays a significant role in the causation of delinquent or criminal behavior among youth or adults. The Commission cannot conclude that exposure to erotic materials is a factor in the causation of sex crime or sex delinquency." Report of the Commission on Obscenity and Pornography 27 (1970) (footnote omitted). To the contrary, the Commission found that "[o]n the positive side, explicit sexual materials are sought as a source of entertainment and information by substantial numbers of American adults. At times, these materials also appear to serve to increase and facilitate constructive communication about sexual matters within marriage." *Id.,* at 53.

Barnes v. Glen Theatre

Chief Justice REHNQUIST delivered the opinion of the Court.

Respondents are two establishments in South Bend, Indiana, that wish to provide totally nude dancing as entertainment, and individual dancers who are employed at these establishments. They claim that the First Amendment's guarantee of freedom of expression prevents the State of Indiana from enforcing its public indecency law to prevent this form of dancing. We reject their claim.

The Kitty Kat Lounge, Inc. (Kitty Kat) is located in the city of South Bend. It sells alcoholic beverages and presents "go-go dancing." Its proprietor desires to present "totally nude dancing," but an applicable Indiana statute regulating public nudity requires that the dancers wear "pasties" and a "G-string" when they dance. The dancers are not paid an hourly wage, but work on commissions. They receive a 100 percent commission on the first $60 in drink sales during their performances. Darlene Miller, one of the respondents in the action, had worked at the Kitty Kat for about two years at the time this action was brought. Miller wishes to dance nude because she believes she would make more money doing so.

Respondent Glen Theatre, Inc., is an Indiana corporation with a place of business in South Bend. Its primary business is supplying so-called adult entertainment through written and printed materials, movie showings, and live entertainment at an enclosed "bookstore." The live entertainment at the "bookstore" consists of nude and seminude performances and showings of the female body through glass panels. Customers sit in a booth and insert coins into a timing mechanism that permits them to observe the live nude and seminude dancers for a period of time. . . .

Respondents sued in the United States District Court for the Northern District of Indiana to enjoin the enforcement of the Indiana public indecency statute, Ind.Code § 35 45 4 1 (1988), asserting that its prohibition against complete nudity in public places violated the First Amendment. The District Court originally granted respondents' prayer for an injunction. . . . The Court of Appeals for the Seventh Circuit reversed, . . . and remanded to the District Court in order for the plaintiffs to pursue their claim that the statute violated the First Amendment as applied to their dancing. On remand, the District Court concluded that "the type of dancing these plaintiffs wish to perform is not expressive activity protected by the Constitution of the United States," and rendered judgment in favor of the defendants. The case was again appealed to the Seventh Circuit, and a panel of that court reversed the District Court, holding that the nude dancing involved here was expressive conduct protected by the First Amendment. The Court of Appeals then heard the case *en banc,* and the court rendered a series of comprehensive and thoughtful opinions. The majority concluded that nonobscene nude dancing performed for entertainment is expression protected by the First Amendment, and that the public indecency statute was an improper infringement of that expressive activity because its purpose was to prevent the message of eroticism and sexuality conveyed by the dancers. We granted certiorari, and now hold that the Indiana statutory requirement that the dancers in the establishments involved in this case must wear pasties and a G-string does not violate the First Amendment.

[1] Several of our cases contain language suggesting that nude dancing of the kind involved here is expressive conduct protected by the First Amendment. . . .

* * *

We must determine the level of protection to be afforded to the expressive conduct at issue, and must determine whether the Indiana statute is an impermissible infringement of that protected activity.

Indiana, of course, has not banned nude dancing as such, but has proscribed public nudity across the board. The Supreme Court of Indiana has construed the Indiana statute to preclude nudity in what are essentially places of public accommodation such as the Glen Theatre and the Kitty Kat Lounge. In such places, respondents point out, minors are excluded and there are no non-consenting viewers. Respondents contend that while the state may license establishments such as the ones involved here, and limit the geographical area in which they do business, it may not in any way limit the performance of the dances within them without violating the First Amendment. The petitioner contends, on the other hand, that Indiana's restriction on nude dancing is a valid "time, place or manner" restriction under cases such as *Clark v. Community for Creative Non-Violence*.

The "time, place, or manner" test was developed for evaluating restrictions on expression taking place on public property which had been dedicated as a "public forum," although we have on at least one occasion applied it to conduct occurring on private property. In *Clark* we observed that this test has been interpreted to embody much the same standards as those set forth in *United States v. O'Brien*, and we turn, therefore, to the rule enunciated in *O'Brien*.

[2] O'Brien burned his draft card on the steps of the South Boston courthouse in the presence of a sizable crowd, and was convicted of violating a statute that prohibited the knowing destruction or mutilation of such a card. He claimed that his conviction was contrary to the First Amendment because his act was "symbolic speech"—expressive conduct. The court rejected his contention that symbolic speech is entitled to full First Amendment protection. . . .

[3] Applying the four-part *O'Brien* test, we find that Indiana's public indecency statute is justified despite its incidental limitations on some expressive activity. The public indecency statute is clearly within the constitutional power of the State and furthers substantial governmental interests. . . . The statutes's purpose of protecting societal order and morality is clear from its text and history. Public indecency statutes of this sort are of ancient origin, and presently exist in at least 47 States. Public indecency, including nudity, was a criminal offense at common law, and this Court recognized the com-

mon-law roots of the offense of "gross and open indecency" in *Winters v. New York*. Public nudity was considered an act *malum en se*. Public indecency statutes such as the one before us reflect moral disapproval of people appearing in the nude among strangers in public places.

This public indecency statute follows a long line of earlier Indiana statutes banning all public nudity. The history of Indiana's public indecency statute shows that it predates barroom nude dancing and was enacted as a general prohibition. At least as early as 1831, Indiana had a statute punishing "open and notorious lewdness, or . . . any grossly scandalous and public indecency." A gap during which no statute was in effect was filled by the Indiana Supreme Court in *Ardery v. State,* which held that the court could sustain a conviction for exhibition of "privates" in the presence of others. The court traced the offense to the Bible story of Adam and Eve. In 1881, a statute was enacted that would remain essentially unchanged for nearly a century:

> "Whoever, being over fourteen years of age, makes an indecent exposure of his person in a public place, or in any place where there are other persons to be offended or annoyed thereby, . . . is guilty of public indecency. . . ." 1881 Ind. Acts, ch. 37, § 90.

The language quoted above remained unchanged until it was simultaneously repealed and replaced with the present statute in 1976.

This and other public indecency statutes were designed to protect morals and public order. The traditional police power of the States is defined as the authority to provide for the public health, safety, and morals, and we have upheld such a basis for legislation. In *Paris Adult Theatre I v. Slaton,* we said:

> "In deciding *Roth,* this Court implicitly accepted that a legislature could legitimately act on such a conclusion to protect 'the social interest in order and morality.'" (Emphasis omitted.)

And in *Bowers v. Hardwick* we said:

> "The law, however, is constantly based on notions of morality, and if all laws representing essentially moral choices are to be invalidated under the Due Process Clause, the courts will be very busy indeed."

Thus, the public indecency statute furthers a substantial government interest in protecting order and morality.

This interest is unrelated to the suppression of free expression. Some may view restricting nudity on moral grounds as necessarily related to expression. We disagree. . . . But the court rejected this expansive notion of "expressive conduct" in *O'Brien,* saying:

"We cannot accept the view that an apparently limitless variety of conduct can be labelled 'speech' whenever the person engaging in the conduct intends thereby to express an idea."

Respondents contend that even though prohibiting nudity in public generally may not be related to suppressing expression, prohibiting the performance of nude dancing is related to expression because the state seeks to prevent its erotic message. Therefore, they reason that the application of the Indiana statute to the nude dancing in this case violates the First Amendment, because it fails the third part of the O'Brien test, viz: the governmental interest must be unrelated to the suppression of free expression.

But we do not think that when Indiana applies its statute to the nude dancing in these nightclubs it is proscribing nudity because of the erotic message conveyed by the dancers. Presumably numerous other erotic performances are presented at these establishments and similar clubs without any interference from the state, so long as the performers wear a scant amount of clothing. Likewise, the requirement that the dancers don pasties and a G-string does not deprive the dance of whatever erotic message it conveys; it simply makes the message slightly less graphic. The perceived evil that Indiana seeks to address is not erotic dancing, but public nudity. The appearance of people of all shapes, sizes and ages in the nude at a beach, for example, would convey little if any erotic message, yet the state still seeks to prevent it. Public nudity is the evil the state seeks to prevent, whether or not it is combined with expressive activity. . . .

The fourth part of the *O'Brien* test requires that the incidental restriction on First Amendment freedom be no greater than is essential to the furtherance of the governmental interest. As indicated in the discussion above, the governmental interest served by the text of the prohibition is societal disapproval of nudity in public places and among strangers. The statutory prohibition is not a means to some greater end, but an end in itself. It is without cavil that the public indecency statute is "narrowly tailored;" Indiana's requirement that the dancers wear at least pasties and a G-string is modest, and the bare minimum necessary to achieve the state's purpose.

The judgment of the Court of Appeals accordingly is

Reversed.

Justice SCALIA, concurring in the judgment.

I agree that the judgment of the Court of Appeals must be reversed. In my view, however, the challenged regulation must be upheld, not because it survives some lower level of First-Amendment scrutiny, but because, as a general law regulating conduct and not specifically directed at expression, it is not subject to First-Amendment scrutiny at all.

I

Indiana's public indecency statute provides:

"(a) A person who knowingly or intentionally, in a public place:
  "(1) engages in sexual intercourse;
  "(2) engages in deviate sexual conduct;
  "(3) appears in a state of nudity; or
  "(4) fondles the genitals of himself or another person;
  commits public indecency, a Class A misdemeanor.

"(b) 'Nudity' means the showing of the human male or female genitals, pubic area, or buttocks with less than a fully opaque covering, the showing of the female breast with less than a fully opaque covering of any part of the nipple, or the showing of covered male genitals in a discernibly turgid state." Ind.Code § 35–45–4–1 (1988).

On its face, this law is not directed at expression in particular. As Judge Easterbrook put it in his dissent below: "Indiana does not regulate dancing. It regulates public nudity. . . . Almost the entire domain of Indiana's statute is unrelated to expression, unless we view nude beaches and topless hot dog vendors as speech." . . .

Indiana's statute is in the line of a long tradition of laws against public nudity, which have never been thought to run afoul of traditional understanding of "the freedom of speech." Public indecency—including public nudity—has long been an offense at common law. Indiana's first public nudity statue, Rev. Laws of Indiana, ch. 26, § 60 (1831), predated by many years the appearance of nude barroom dancing. It was general in scope, directed at all public nudity, and not just at public nude expression; and all succeeding statutes, down to the present one, have been the same. Were it the case that Indiana *in practice* targeted only expressive nudity, while turning a blind eye to nude beaches and unclothed purveyors of hot dogs and machine tools, it might be said that what posed as a regulation of conduct in general was in reality a regulation of only communicative conduct. Respondents have adduced no evidence of that. Indiana officials have brought many public indecency prosecutions for activities having no communicative element.

The dissent confidently asserts, that the purpose of restricting nudity in public places in general is to protect nonconsenting parties from offense; and argues that since only consenting, admission-paying patrons see respondents dance, that purpose cannot apply and the only remaining purpose must relate to the communicative elements of the performance. Perhaps the dissenters believe that "offense to others" *ought* to be the only reason for restricting nudity in public places generally, but there is no basis for thinking that our society has ever shared that Thoreauvian "you-may-do-what-you-like-so-long-as-it-does-not-injure-someone-else" beau ideal—much less for thinking that it was written into the Constitution. The purpose of Indiana's nudity law would be violated, I think, if 60,000 fully consenting adults crowded into the Hoosierdome to display their genitals to one another, even if there were not an offended innocent in the crowd. Our society prohibits, and all human societies have prohibited, certain activities not because they harm others but because they are considered, in the traditional phrase, "contra bonos mores," i.e., immoral. In American society, such prohibitions have included, for example, sadomasochism, cockfighting, bestiality, suicide, drug use, prostitution, and sodomy. While there may be great diversity of view on whether various of these prohibitions should exist (though I have found few ready to abandon, in principle, all of them) there is no doubt that, absent specific constitutional protection for the conduct involved, the Constitution does not prohibit them simply because they regulate "morality." The purpose of the Indiana statute, as both its text and the manner of its enforcement demonstrate, is to enforce the traditional moral belief that people should not expose their private parts indiscriminately, regardless of whether those who see them are disedified. Since that is so, the dissent has no basis for positing that, where only thoroughly edified adults are present, the purpose must be repression of communication.

II

Since the Indiana regulation is a general law not specifically targeted at expressive conduct, its application to such conduct does not in my view implicate the First Amendment. . . .

III

While I do not think the plurality's conclusions differ greatly from my own, I cannot entirely endorse its reasoning. The plurality purports to apply to this general law, insofar as it regulates this allegedly expressive conduct, an intermediate level of First Amendment scrutiny: the government interest in the regulation must be "'important or substantial,'" As I have indicated, I do not believe such a heightened standard exists. I think we should avoid wherever possible, moreover, a method of analysis that requires judicial assessment of the "importance" of government interests—and especially of government interests in various aspects of morality. . . .

In *Bowers*, we held that since homosexual behavior is not a fundamental right, a Georgia law prohibiting private homosexual intercourse needed only a rational basis in order to comply with the Due Process Clause. Moral opposition to homosexuality, we said, provided that rational basis. I would uphold the Indiana statute on precisely the same ground: moral opposition to nudity supplies a rational basis for its prohibition, and since the First Amendment has no application to this case no more than that is needed.

* * *

Indiana may constitutionally enforce its prohibition of public nudity even against those who choose to use public nudity as a means of communication. The State is regulating conduct, not expression, and those who choose to employ conduct as a means of expression must make sure that the conduct they select is not generally forbidden. For these reasons, I agree that the judgment should be reversed. . . .

Justice WHITE, with whom Justice MARSHALL, Justice BLACKMUN, and Justice STEVENS join, dissenting.

The first question presented to us in this case is whether nonobscene nude dancing performed as entertainment is expressive conduct protected by the First Amendment. The Court of Appeals held that it is, observing that our prior decisions permit no other conclusion. Not surprisingly, then, the Court now concedes that "nude dancing of the kind sought to be performed here is expressive conduct within the outer perimeters of the First Amendment. . . ."

Having arrived at the conclusion that nude dancing performed as entertainment enjoys First Amendment protection, the Court states that it must "determine the level of protection to be afforded to the expressive conduct at issue, and must determine whether the Indiana statute is an impermissible infringement of that protected activity." For guidance, the Court turns to *United States v. O'Brien,* (1968), which held that expressive conduct could be narrowly regulated or forbidden in pursuit of an important or substantial governmental interest that is unrelated to the content of the expression. The Court finds that the Indiana statute satisfies the *O'Brien* test in all respects.

The Court acknowledges that it is impossible to discern the exact state interests which the Indiana legislature had in mind when it enacted the Indiana statute, but the Court nonetheless concludes that it is clear from the statute's text and history that the law's purpose is to protect "societal order and morality." The Court goes on to conclude that Indiana's statute "was enacted as *a general prohibition,* (emphasis added), on people appearing in the nude among strangers in public places. The Court then points to cases in which we upheld legislation based on the State's police power, and ultimately concludes that the Indiana statute "furthers a substantial government interest in protecting order and morality." The Court also holds that the basis for banning nude dancing is unrelated to free expression and that it is narrowly drawn to serve the State's interest.

The Court's analysis is erroneous in several respects. Both the Court and Justice SCALIA in his concurring opinion overlook a fundamental and critical aspect of our cases upholding the States' exercise of their police powers. None of the cases they rely upon, including *O'Brien* and *Bowers v. Hardwick,* involved anything less than truly *general* proscriptions on individual conduct. In *O'Brien,* for example, individuals were prohibited from destroying their draft cards at any time and in any place, even in completely private places such as the home. Likewise, in *Bowers,* the State prohibited sodomy, regardless of where the conduct might occur, including the home as was true in that case. . . . By contrast, in this case Indiana does not suggest that its statute applies to, or could be applied to, nudity wherever it occurs, including the home. We do not understand the Court or Justice SCALIA to be suggesting that Indiana could constitutionally enact such an intrusive prohibition, nor do we think such a suggestion would be tenable in light of our decision in *Stanley v. Georgia,* (1969), in which we held that States could not punish the mere possession of obscenity in the privacy of one's own home. . . .

The Indiana statute is not a *general* prohibition of the type we have upheld in prior cases. As a result, the Court's and Justice SCALIA's simple references to the States's general interest in promoting societal order and morality is not sufficient justification for a statute which concededly reaches a significant amount of protected expressive activity. Instead, in applying the *O'Brien* test, we are obligated to carefully examine the reasons the State has chosen to regulate this expressive conduct in a less than general statute. In other words, when the State enacts a law which draws a line between expressive conduct which is regulated and nonexpressive conduct of the same type which is not regulated, *O'Brien* places the burden on the State to justify the distinctions it has made. Closer inquiry as to the purpose of the statute is surely appropriate.

Legislators do not just randomly select certain conduct for proscription; they have reasons for doing so and those reasons illuminate the purpose of the law that is passed. Indeed, a law may have multiple purposes. The purpose of forbidding people from appearing nude in parks, beaches, hot dog stands, and like public places is to protect others from offense. But that could not possibly be the purpose of preventing nude dancing in theaters and barrooms since the viewers are exclusively consenting adults who pay money to see these dances. The purpose of the proscription in these contexts is to protect the viewers from what the State believes is the harmful message that nude dancing communicates. This is why *Clark v. Community for Creative Non-Violence* (1984), is of no help to the State: "In *Clark* . . . the damage to the parks was the same whether the sleepers were camping out for fun, were in fact homeless, or wished by sleeping in the park to make a symbolic statement on behalf of the homeless." 904 F.2d, at 1103 (Posner, J., concurring). That cannot be said in this case: the perceived damage to the public interest caused by appearing nude on the streets or in the parks, as I have said, is not what the State seeks to avoid in preventing nude dancing in theaters and taverns. There the perceived harm is the communicative aspect of the erotic dance. As the State now tells us, and as Justice SOUTER agrees, the State's goal in applying what it describes as its "content neutral" statute to the nude dancing in this case is "deterrence of prostitution, sexual assaults, criminal activity, degradation of women, and other activities which break down family structure." The attainment of these goals, however, depends on preventing an expressive activity. . . .

Texas v. Johnson

JUSTICE BRENNAN delivered the opinion of the Court [in which MARSHALL, BLACKMUN, SCALIA, and KENNEDY, JJ., joined].

After publicly burning an American flag as a means of political protest, Gregory Lee Johnson was convicted of desecrating a flag in violation of Texas law. This case presents the question whether his conviction is consistent with the First Amendment. We hold that it is not.

CHIEF JUSTICE REHNQUIST, with whom JUSTICE WHITE and JUSTICE O'CONNOR join, dissenting.

In holding this Texas statute unconstitutional, the Court ignores Justice Holmes' familiar aphorism that "a page of history is worth a volume of logic." For more than 200 years, the American flag has occupied a unique position as the symbol of our Nation, a uniqueness that justifies a governmental prohibition against flag burning in the way respondent Johnson did here.

[Chief Justice Rehnquist details a lengthy history of the flag, including its celebration in songs and poems, its use in war, and the negative impact on troop morale in Vietnam resulting from flag burnings in the United States, which led to the enactment of the Federal Flag Desecration Statute in 1967.]

No other American symbol has been as universally honored as the flag. In 1931, Congress declared "The Star-Spangled Banner" to be our national anthem. In 1949, Congress declared June 14th to be Flag Day. In 1987, John Philip Sousa's "The Stars and Stripes Forever" was designated as the national march. Congress has also established "The Pledge of Allegiance to the Flag" and the manner of its deliverance. The flag has appeared as the principal symbol on approximately 33 United States postal stamps and in the design of at least 43 more, more times than any other symbol.

Both Congress and the States have enacted numerous laws regulating misuse of the American flag. Until 1967, Congress left the regulation of misuse of the flag to the States. Now, however, Title 18 U.S.C. @ 700(a) provides that:

> "Whoever knowingly casts contempt upon any flag of the United States by publicly mutilating, defacing, defiling, burning, or trampling upon it shall be fined not more than $1,000 or imprisoned for not more than one year, or both."

Congress has also prescribed, inter alia, detailed rules for the design of the flag, the time and occasion of the flag's display, the position and manner of its display, respect for the flag, and conduct during hoisting, lowering, and passing of the flag. With the exception of Alaska and Wyoming, all of the States now have statutes prohibiting the burning of the flag. Most of the state statutes are patterned after the Uniform Flag Act of 1917, which in § 3 provides: "No person shall publicly mutilate, deface, defile, defy, trample upon, or by word or act cast contempt upon any such flag, standard, color, ensign or shield." Most were passed by the States at about the time of World War I. Rosenblatt, Flag Desecration Statutes: History and Analysis, 1972 Wash. U. L. Q. 193, 197.

The American flag, then, throughout more than 200 years of our history, has come to be the visible symbol embodying our Nation. It does not represent the views of any particular political party, and it does not represent any particular political philosophy. The flag is not simply another "idea" or "point of view" competing for recognition in the marketplace of ideas. Millions and millions of Americans regard it with an almost mystical reverence regardless of what sort of social, political, or philosophical beliefs they may have. I cannot agree that the First Amendment invalidates the Act of Congress, and the laws of 48 of the 50 States, which make criminal the public burning of the flag.

More than 80 years ago in *Halter v. Nebraska,* 205 U.S. 34 (1907), this Court upheld the constitutionality of a Nebraska statute that forbade the use of representations of the American flag for advertising purposes upon articles of merchandise. The Court there said:

> "For that flag every true American has not simply an appreciation but a deep affection. . . . Hence, it has often occurred that insults to a flag have been the cause of war, and indignities put upon it, in the presence of those who revere it, have often been resented and sometimes punished on the spot."

Only two Terms ago, in *San Francisco Arts & Athletics, Inc. v. United States Olympic Committee,* 483 U.S. 522 (1987), the Court held that Congress could grant exclusive use of the word "Olympic" to the United States Olympic Committee. The Court thought that this "restriction on expressive speech properly [was] characterized as incidental to the primary congressional purpose of encouraging and rewarding the USOC's activities." As the Court stated, "when a work [or symbol] acquires value 'as the result of organization and the expenditure of labor, skill, and money' by an entity, that entity constitutionally may obtain a limited property right in the word [or symbol]." Surely Congress or the States may recognize a similar interest in the flag.

But the Court insists that the Texas statute prohibiting the public burning of the American flag infringes on respondent Johnson's freedom of expression. Such freedom, of course, is not absolute. See *Schenck v. United States,* 249 U.S. 47 (1919). In *Chaplinsky v. New Hampshire,* 315 U.S. 568 (1942), a unanimous Court said:

> "Allowing the broadest scope to the language and purpose of the Fourteenth Amendment, it is well understood that the right of free speech is not absolute at all times and under all circumstances. There are certain well-defined and narrowly limited classes of speech, the prevention and punishment of which have never been thought to raise any Constitutional problem. These include the lewd and obscene, the profane, the libelous, and the insulting or 'fighting' words—those which by their very utterance inflict injury or tend to incite an immediate breach of the peace. It has been well observed that such utterances are no essential part of any exposition of ideas, and are of such slight social value as a step to truth that any benefit that may be derived from them is clearly outweighed by the social interest in order and morality."

* * *

The result of the Texas statute is obviously to deny one in Johnson's frame of mind one of many means of "symbolic speech." Far from being a case of "one picture being worth a thousand words," flag burning is the equivalent of an inarticulate grunt or roar that, it seems fair to say, is most likely to be indulged in not to express any particular idea, but to antagonize others. Only five years ago we said in *City Council of Los Angeles v. Taxpayers for Vincent,* 466 U.S. 789, 812 (1948), that "the First Amendment does not guarantee the right to employ every conceivable method of communication at all times and in all places." The Texas statute deprived Johnson of only one rather inarticulate symbolic form of protest—a form of protest that was profoundly offensive to many—and left him with a full panoply of other symbols and every conceivable form of verbal expression to express his deep disapproval of national policy. Thus, in no way can it be said that Texas is punishing him because his hearers—or any other group of people—were profoundly opposed to the message that he sought to convey. Such opposition is no proper basis for restricting speech or expression under the First Amendment. It was Johnson's use of this particular symbol, and not the idea that he sought to convey by it or by his many other expressions, for which he was punished.

Our prior cases dealing with flag desecration statutes have left open the question that the Court resolves today. In *Street v. New York*, 394 U.S. 576, 579 (1969), the defendant burned a flag in the street, shouting "We don't need no damned flag" and, "if they let that happen to Meredith we don't need an American flag." The Court ruled that since the defendant might have been convicted solely on the basis of his words, the conviction could not stand, but it expressly reserved the question whether a defendant could constitutionally be convicted for burning the flag.

Chief Justice Warren, in dissent, stated: "I believe that the States and Federal Government do have the power to protect the flag from acts of desecration and disgrace. . . . It is difficult for me to imagine that, had the Court faced this issue, it would have concluded otherwise." *Id.*, at 605. Justices Black and Fortas also expressed their personal view that a prohibition on flag burning did not violate the Constitution. See *id.*, at 610 (Black, J., dissenting) ("It passes my belief that anything in the Federal Constitution bars a State from making the deliberate burning of the American Flag an offense"); *id.*, at 615–617 (Fortas, J., dissenting) ("The States and the Federal Government have the power to protect the flag from acts of desecration committed in public. . . . The flag is a special kind of personality. Its use is traditionally and universally subject to special rules and regulation. . . . A person may 'own' a flag, but ownership is subject to special burdens and responsibilities. A flag may be property, in a sense; but it is property burdened with peculiar obligations and restrictions. Certainly . . . these special conditions are not per se arbitrary or beyond governmental power under our Constitution").

In *Spence v. Washington*, 418 U.S. 405 (1974), the Court reversed the conviction of a college student who displayed the flag with a peace symbol affixed to it by means of removable black tape from the window of his apartment. Unlike the instant case, there was no risk of a breach of the peace, no one other than the arresting officers saw the flag, and the defendant owned the flag in question. The Court concluded that the student's conduct was protected under the First Amendment, because "no interest the State may have in preserving the physical integrity of a privately owned flag was significantly impaired on these facts." The Court was careful to note, however, that the defendant "was not charged under the desecration statute, nor did he permanently disfigure the flag or destroy it."

In another related case, *Smith v. Goguen*, 415 U.S.566 (1974), the appellee, who wore a small flag on the seat of his trousers, was convicted under a Massachusetts flag-misuse statute that subjected to criminal liability anyone who "publicly . . . treats contemptuously the flag of the United States." The Court affirmed the lower court's reversal of appellee's conviction, because the phrase "treats contemptuously" was unconstitutionally broad and vague. The Court was again careful to point out that "certainly nothing prevents a legislature from defining with substantial specificity what constitutes forbidden treatment of United States flags." See also *id.*, at 587 (WHITE, J., concurring in judgment) ("The flag is a national property, and the Nation may regulate those who would make, imitate, sell, possess, or use it. I would not question those statutes which proscribe mutilation, defacement, or burning of the flag or which otherwise protect its physical integrity, without regard to whether such conduct might provoke violence. . . . There would seem to be little question about the power of Congress to forbid the mutilation of the Lincoln Memorial. . . . The flag is itself a monument, subject to similar protection"); *id.*, at 591 (BLACKMUN, J., dissenting) ("Goguen's punishment was constitutionally permissible for harming the physical integrity of the flag by wearing it affixed to the seat of his pants").

But the Court today will have none of this. The uniquely deep awe and respect for our flag felt by virtually all of us are bundled off under the rubric of "designated symbols" that the First Amendment prohibits the government from "establishing." But the government has not "established" this feeling; 200 years of history have done that. The government is simply recognizing as a fact the profound regard for the American flag created by that history when it enacts statutes prohibiting the disrespectful public burning of the flag.

The Court concludes its opinion with a regrettably patronizing civics lecture, presumably addressed to the Members of both Houses of Congress, the members of the 48 state legislatures that enacted prohibitions against flag burning, and the troops fighting under that flag in Vietnam who objected to its being burned: "The way to preserve the flag's special role is not to punish those who feel differently about these matters. It is to persuade them that they are wrong." The Court's role as the final expositor of the Constitution is well established, but its role as a platonic guardian admonishing those responsible to public opinion as if they were truant school children has no similar place in our system of government. The cry of "no taxation without representation" animated those who revolted against the English Crown to found our Nation—the idea that those who submitted to government should have some say as to what kind of laws would be passed. Surely one of the high purposes of a democratic society is to legislate against conduct that is regarded as evil and profoundly offensive to the majority of people—whether it be murder, embezzlement, pollution, or flag burning.

Our Constitution wisely places limits on powers of legislative majorities to act, but the declaration of such limits by this Court "is, at all times, a question of much delicacy, which ought seldom, if ever, to be decided in the affirmative, in a doubtful case." *Fletcher v. Peck,* 6 Cranch 87, 128 (1810) (Marshall, C. J.). Uncritical extension of constitutional protection to the burning of the flag risks the frustration of the very purpose for which organized governments are instituted. The Court decides that the American flag is just another symbol, about which not only must opinions pros and con be tolerated, but for which the most minimal public respect may not be enjoined. The government may conscript men into the Armed Forces where they must fight and perhaps die for the flag, but the government may not prohibit the public burning of the banner under which they fight. I would uphold the Texas statute as applied in this case.

JUSTICE STEVENS, dissenting.

As the Court analyzes this case, it presents the question whether the State of Texas, or indeed the Federal Government, has the power to prohibit the public desecration of the American flag. The question is unique. In my judgment rules that apply to a host of other symbols, such as state flags, armbands, or various privately promoted emblems of political or commercial identity, are not necessarily controlling. Even if flag burning could be considered just another species of symbolic speech under the logical application of the rules that the Court has developed in its interpretation of the First Amendment in other contexts, this case has an intangible dimension that makes those rules inapplicable.

A country's flag is a symbol of more than "nationhood and national unity." It also signifies the ideas that characterize the society that has chosen that emblem as well as the special history that has animated the growth and power of those ideas. The fleurs-de-lis and the tricolor both symbolized "nationhood and national unity," but they had vastly different meanings. The message conveyed by some flags—the swastika, for example—may survive long after it has outlived its usefulness as a symbol of regimented unity in a particular nation.

So it is with the American flag. It is more than a proud symbol of the courage, the determination, and the gifts of nature that transformed 13 fledgling Colonies into a world power. It is a symbol of freedom, of equal opportunity, of religious tolerance, and of good will for other peoples who share our aspirations. The symbol carries its message to dissidents both at home and abroad who may have no interest at all in our national unity or survival.

The value of the flag as a symbol cannot be measured. Even so, I have no doubt that the interest in preserving that value for the future is both significant and legitimate. Conceivably that value will be enhanced by the Court's conclusion that our national commitment to free expression is so strong that even the United States as ultimate guarantor of that freedom is without power to prohibit the desecration of its unique symbol. But I am unpersuaded. The creation of a federal right to post bulletin boards and graffiti on the Washington Monument might enlarge the market for free expression, but at a cost I would not pay. Similarly, in my considered judgment, sanctioning the public desecration of the flag will tarnish its value—both for those who cherish the ideas for which it waves and for those who desire to don the robes of martyrdom by burning it. That tarnish is not justified by the trivial burden on free expression occasioned by requiring that an available, alternative mode of expression—including uttering words critical of the flag, see *Street v. New York*, 394 U.S. 576 (1969)—be employed.

It is appropriate to emphasize certain propositions that are not implicated by this case. The statutory prohibition of flag desecration does not "prescribe what shall be orthodox in politics, nationalism, religion, or other matters of opinion or force citizens to confess by word or act their faith therein." *West Virginia Board of Education v. Barnette*, 319 U.S. 624, 642 (1943). The statute does not compel any conduct or any profession of respect for any idea or any symbol.

Nor does the statute violate "the government's paramount obligation of neutrality in its regulation of protected communication." *Young v. American Mini Theatres, Inc.*, 427 U.S. 50, 70 (1976) (plurality opinion).The content of respondent's message has no relevance whatsoever to the case. The concept of "desecration" does not turn on the substance of the message the actor intends to convey, but rather on whether those who view the act will take serious offense. Accordingly, one intending to convey a message of respect for the flag by burning it in a public square might nonetheless be guilty of desecration if he knows that others—perhaps simply because they misperceive the intended message—will be seriously offended. Indeed, even if the actor knows that all possible witnesses will understand that he intends to send a message of respect, he might still be guilty of desecration if he also knows that this understanding does not lessen the offense taken by some of those witnesses. Thus, this is not a case in which the fact that "it is the speaker's opinion that gives offense" provides a special "reason for according it constitutional protection," *FCC v. Pacifica Foundation*, 438 U.S. 726, 745 (1978) (plurality opinion). The case has nothing to do with "disagreeable ideas," see ante. It involves disagreeable conduct that, in my opinion, diminishes the value of an important national asset.

The Court is therefore quite wrong in blandly asserting that respondent "was prosecuted for his expression of dissatisfaction with the policies of this country, expression situated at the core of our First Amendment values." Respondent was prosecuted because of the method he chose to express his dissatisfaction with those policies. Had he chosen to spray-paint—or perhaps convey with a motion picture projector—his message of dissatisfaction on the facade of the Lincoln Memorial, there would be no question about the power of the Government to prohibit his means of expression. The prohibition would be supported by the legitimate interest in preserving the quality of an important national asset. Though the asset at stake in this case is intangible, given its unique value, the same interest supports a prohibition on the desecration of the American flag.

The ideas of liberty and equality have been an irresistible force in motivating leaders like Patrick Henry, Susan B. Anthony, and Abraham Lincoln, schoolteachers like Nathan Hale and Booker T. Washington, the Philippine Scouts who fought at Bataan, and the soldiers who scaled the bluff at Omaha Beach. If those ideas are worth fighting for—and our history demonstrates that they are—it cannot be true that the flag that uniquely symbolizes their power is not itself worthy of protection from unnecessary desecration.

I respectfully dissent.

Ordinance No. 87-71, City of Hialeah (Adopted September 8, 1987)

WHEREAS, the City Council of the City of Hialeah, Florida, has determined that the sacrificing of animals within the city limits is contrary to the public health, safety, welfare and morals of the community;

Now, therefore, be it ordained by the Mayor and City Council of the City of Hialeah, Florida, that:

Section 1. For the purpose of this ordinance, the word sacrifice shall mean: to unnecessarily kill, torment, torture, or mutilate an animal in a public or private ritual or ceremony not for the purpose of food consumption.

Section 2. For the purpose of this ordinance, the word animal shall mean: any living dumb creature.

Section 3. It shall be unlawful for any person, persons, corporations or associations to sacrifice any animal within the corporate limits of the City of Hialeah, Florida.

New York State Alcoholic Beverage Control Law

6-b. No retail licensee for on-premises consumption shall suffer or permit any contest or promotion which endangers the health, safety, and welfare of any person with dwarfism. Any retail license in violation of this section shall be subject to the suspension or revocation of said licensee's license to sell alcoholic beverages for on-premises consumption. For the purposes of this section, the term "dwarfism" means a condition of being abnormally small which is caused by heredity, endocrine dysfunction, renal insufficiency or deficiency or skeletal diseases that result in disproportionate short stature and adult height of less than four feet ten inches.

Note: This statute was intended to stop "dwarf tossing," that is, contests held in bars to see who could throw dwarfs, dressed in protective clothing, the farthest.

ROBERT C. POST

Democratic Community

It is on one level relatively easy to imagine an unproblematic account of the concept of "democratic community." If democracy is defined in terms of majoritarian decisionmaking procedures, we can envision a government in which such procedures are used to enact community values into law. We could call such a government a democratic community, and we could accurately ascribe this status to most contemporary democracies. Even our own government would qualify, for in America laws enacted through majoritarian procedures commonly function to place the force of the state behind the norms of the national community. A good example would be the many antidiscrimination laws that resulted from the civil rights movement, which serve graphically to express our communal commitment to egalitarian ideals.

But this account of "democratic community" is unsatisfactory if what we mean by democracy is not the external mechanics of a decisionmaking procedure, but rather the internal purposes of responsive democracy. For these purposes appear in important respects to contradict those that define the concept of community. Thus if we put ourselves in the position of a lawmaker who must fashion law to create forms of social order, we will face a constant choice whether to design legal doctrine to sustain the common, socially embedded identities of citizens, or instead to protect the space for autonomous citizens independently to create their own social arrangements. To put the matter concretely, we must, if we are judges, decide whether to permit or to constitutionally prohibit the prosecution of flag burners.[1] To opt for the former is to enable law to be used to maintain popular identification with a particular conception of our community; to opt for the latter is instead to clear a public space in which hurtful and offensive (and therefore profoundly different) conceptions of our community can be displayed with impunity. Or, to offer another example, we must decide whether to allow persons to sue for compensation for emotional harms caused by unconscionably outrageous speech within public discourse.[2] If the function of law is to uphold norms that reciprocally define personal and communal identity, such suits ought to be permitted. They ought to be prohibited, however, if the function of law is instead to enable independent persons to advocate and exemplify new forms of life.

Such examples can be multiplied indefinitely; they are the stuff of everyday constitutional adjudication. They suggest a vision of responsive democracy and community as deeply antagonistic forms of social order. That vision, it is fair to say, is uniquely characteristic of the legal order of the United States, due no doubt to the reciprocally reinforcing influences of our immense cultural diversity and the centrality of individualism to what Samuel Huntington has aptly termed our "American Creed." The sharp polarity of that vision runs like a rift throughout our constitutional tradition, dividing in contemporary times "liberal" from "conservative" justices.

But this polarity is misleading, for while it signifies the real tension between community and responsive democracy at the level of particular cases, it obscures the fact that at a more general systemic level, responsive democracy actually requires the maintenance of healthy and vigorous forms of community life. This is true for (at least) three reasons. First, as I have discussed previously, responsive democracy is predicated upon a commitment to the value of self-determination, which presupposes community institutions designed to inculcate this value. Hence the importance to democracy of establishing, as a matter of sheer "conscious social reproduction," a "nonneutral" educational system aimed at "cultivating the kind of character conducive to democratic sovereignty."

Second, responsive democracy attempts to reconcile individuals with the general will by establishing processes of deliberation that will instantiate a sense of self-determination. The formal opportunity to speak and to hear constitutes a necessary but not sufficient condition for the creation of this sense of self-determination.[3] Necessary also is the feeling of participation that at root must rest upon an identification with the aspirations of a culture that attempts to reconcile differences through deliberative interaction. This identification is essential for the functioning, as well as for the reproduction, of responsive democracy, and it too must ultimately depend upon the inculcation of particular forms of identity through community institutions.

Third, responsive democracy aspires to conditions of deliberation, to some form of "reconciliation through public reason." Such deliberation, in turn, presupposes civility and respect, for speech lacking these qualities is likely to be experienced as coercive and irrational, as an instrument "of aggression and personal assault."[4] The exercise of public reason is thus always inseparable from and made possible by historically particular community norms that give content to the values of respect and civility. In this sense also responsive democracy requires the continued maintenance of healthy forms of community life.

The concept of democratic community, therefore, cuts a complex figure in our constitutional tradition. At the level of specific cases, responsive democracy and community appear oppositional, dictating conflicting perspectives and conclusions. But at the systemic level they appear reconcilable, perhaps even interdependent. This strange disjunction renders the concept of democratic community intrinsically unstable and contestable. In any particular circumstance it can always be argued either that legal enforcement of community norms is necessary for the survival of community, and hence for the ultimate health of responsive democracy, or that such enforcement is not necessary for the maintenance of community and therefore merely a betrayal of the principles of self-determination required by responsive democracy.

Notes

1. See, e.g., *United States v. Eichman,* 110 S.Ct. 2404 (1990); *Texas v. Johnson,* 491 U.S. 397 (1989).

2. See, e.g., *Hustler Magazine v. Falwell,* 485 U.S. 46 (1988).

3. Recent proposals for the regulation of racist speech, for example, might most profitably be conceptualized as setting forth the claim that formal opportunities for communication have not translated for victimized minorities into the experience of participation necessary for responsive democracy, and that such regulation is necessary, as a matter of contingent historical circumstances, to realize the value of self-determination. See Post, Racist Speech, Democracy, and the First Amendment, 32 *William & Mary Law Review,* 32 (1991), 302–17.

4. *Time, Inc. v. Hill,* 385 U.S. 374, 412 (1967) (Fortas, J., dissenting).

About the Book and Editor

Some of the most difficult and wrenching social and political issues in U.S. society today are about the relationship between strongly held moral values and the laws of the land. There is no consensus about whether the law should deal with morality at all, and if it is to do so, there is no agreement over *whose* morality is to be reflected in the law.

In this compact and carefully edited anthology, Gerald Dworkin presents the readings necessary for an understanding of these issues. The volume contains classical and contemporary philosophical statements as well as a generous sampling of legal cases and opinions, including such topics of current interest as flag-burning, nude dancing, the sale of human organs, and sexual behavior. The volume represents the best in applied legal and moral philosophy.

Gerald Dworkin is professor of philosophy at the University of Illinois at Chicago. He is the author of *The Theory and Practice of Autonomy,* the editor of several influential anthologies, and the author of dozens of articles and reviews on political, legal, and moral philosophy.